Rich Dad's
Conspiracy
of
The Rich

Rich Dad's
CONSPIRACY
OF
THE RICH

The 8 New Rules of Money

Robert T. Kiyosaki

**BUSINESS
PLUS**

NEW YORK   BOSTON

Copyright © 2009 by Robert T. Kiyosaki
All rights reserved. Except as permitted under the U.S. Copyright Act of 1976, no part of this publication may be reproduced, distributed, or transmitted in any form or by any means, or stored in a database or retrieval system, without the prior written permission of the publisher.

"Precious Metals Bullion Stocks" graph appears with permission from the CPM Group. CPM Group is a leading commodities research firm. Visit www.cpmgroup.com for more information.

"Return Performance Comparison" chart and "Gold-DJI" charts are reproduced with permission of Yahoo! Inc. ©2009 Yahoo! Inc. YAHOO! and the YAHOO! logo are registered trademarks of Yahoo! Inc.

"Cone of Learning" is from Dale. *Audio-Visual Methods in Teaching,* 1E. © 1969 Wadsworth, a part of Cengage Learning, Inc. Reproduced by permission. www.cengage.com/permissions

Published by Business Plus in association with CASHFLOW Technologies, Inc.

CASHFLOW is a trademark of CASHFLOW Technologies, Inc.

 are trademarks of
CASHFLOW Technologies, Inc.

Business Plus
Hachette Book Group
237 Park Avenue
New York, NY 10017

Visit our website at www.HachetteBookGroup.com.

Business Plus is an imprint of Grand Central Publishing.
The Business Plus name and logo are trademarks of Hachette Book Group, Inc.

Printed in the United States of America

First Edition: September 2009

10   9   8   7   6

Library of Congress Control Number: 2009932483

ISBN: 978-0-446-55980-5

Contents

Acknowledgments

My rich dad always said, "Business and investing are team sports." The same can be said when writing a book—especially a book like the one you have in your hand. We have made history with *Rich Dad's Conspiracy of the Rich*. As the first truly interactive online book in the Rich Dad series, it took me into uncharted waters. Thankfully, I have a great team, and I relied on them often. Each one of them stepped up to the plate and delivered even beyond my expectations.

Above all, thank you to my beautiful bride, Kim, for her encouragement and support. You've been with me along every step of our financial journey, both the good and not so good. You are my partner and my reason for success.

Thank you to Jake Johnson of Elevate Consulting Company (elevatecompany.net) for his help in shaping the book and my thoughts, and for helping take this book from an idea to a reality. Also, thanks to my editors Rick Wolff and Leah Tracosas at Hachette for their tireless efforts to make this project a success—and for taking a chance.

Special thanks to Rhonda Shenkiryk of the Rich Dad Company and Rachael Pierson of Metaphour (metaphour.com) for their tireless efforts on the promotion of the book, and for the top-notch website that was home to this book for so long.

Much thanks to the Rich Dad Team Members who are in the trenches every day, and who have persevered and stuck with Kim and me through thick and thin. You are the heartbeat of our organization.

A Note from Robert Kiyosaki: Why I Wrote This Book for You

In 1971, President Richard Nixon, without the approval of Congress, took the U.S. dollar off the gold standard and changed the rules of money—not just for the United States, but also for the world. This change was one in a series of changes leading to our current financial crisis that began in 2007. In effect, this change allowed the United States to print almost unlimited amounts of money and create as much debt as it wanted.

Is our current economic crisis just an accident, a one-off event? Some say yes. I say no.

Can those in power solve our current economic crisis? Many hope so, but again I say no. How can the crisis be solved when the very people and organizations that created the crisis—and profit from it—are still in charge? The problem is that the crisis is getting bigger, not diminishing as some would hope. In the 1980s, government bailouts were in the millions. By the 1990s they were in the billions. And today, they are in the trillions.

One definition of *crisis* I like to use is "change screaming to occur." I personally do not think our leaders will change. That means you and I must change instead.

While this book is about a conspiracy, it is not meant to be a witch hunt, to place blame, or to call for resignations. As we all know, the world is filled with conspiracies, some benign, some more sinister. Every time a sports team goes into the locker room at halftime, that act is technically a conspiracy against the opposing team. Wherever there is self-interest, there is a conspiracy.

The reason this book is titled *Rich Dad's Conspiracy of the Rich* is because it is about how the rich control the world economy via the banks, governments, and financial markets. As you may know, this has been going on for centuries and will continue to go on as long as humans walk the earth.

This book is divided into two parts. Part One of this book is about the history of the conspiracy and how the ultra-rich took control of the world's financial and political systems via the money supply. Much of modern financial history revolves around the relationship between the Federal Reserve (which is not federal, has no reserves, and is not really a bank) and the U.S. Treasury. Some of the subjects covered in Part One are why big banks can never go broke, why we do not have financial education in our school system, why saving money is foolish, how money evolved over time, and why today our money is no longer money but rather currency. Part One will also explain why Congress changed the rules for employees in 1974 and influenced workers to invest in the stock market via their retirement plans in vehicles such as the 401(k) plan, in spite of the fact that workers had little-to-no financial education, as a way to get to our money via our retirement plans. That is one reason why I personally do not have a retirement plan. I prefer to give my money to *me* rather than the super-rich who run this government-sponsored conspiracy.

Simply said, Part One is about history, because by understanding history we can better prepare for and see a brighter future.

Part Two of this book is about what you and I can do with our money— about beating the conspirators at their own game. You will learn why the rich are getting richer while at the same time they ask us to live below our means. Simply put, the rich are getting richer because they live by a different set of rules. The old rules—work hard, save money, buy a house, get out of debt, and invest for the long term in a diversified portfolio of stocks, bonds, and mutual funds—are rules that keep people struggling financially. These old rules of money have led millions of people into financial trouble, causing them to lose tremendous wealth in their homes and retirement savings.

Ultimately, this book is about the four things that keep people poor:

- Taxes
- Debt

- Inflation
- Retirement

These forces are what the conspirators use to take your money. Because the conspirators play by a different set of rules, they know how to use these forces to increase their riches—while the very same forces make others poor. If you want to financially change your life, you will need to change your financial rules. This can only be accomplished by increasing your financial IQ through financial education. Financial education is the unfair advantage of the rich. Having a rich dad who taught me about money and how it works gave me an unfair advantage. My rich dad taught me about taxes, debt, inflation, and retirement, and how to use them to my advantage. I learned at a young age how the rich played the game of money.

By the end of this book you will know why today, when so many people are worried about their financial futures, the rich are getting richer. But more important, you will know what you can do to prepare and protect your financial future. By increasing your financial education and changing your rules of money, you can learn how to use and profit from the forces of taxes, debt, inflation, and retirement—not be a victim of them.

Many people are waiting for the political and financial systems of the world to change. To me, that is a waste of time. In my opinion, it is easier to change myself rather than to wait for our leaders and systems to change.

Is it time for you to take control of your money and your financial future? Is it time to find out what those who control the financial world don't want you to know? Do you want complex and confusing financial concepts to be made simple? If you answered yes to these questions, then this book is for you.

In 1971, after President Nixon took the U.S. dollar off the gold standard, the rules of money changed, and today, money is no longer money. That is why the first new rule of money is *Money is knowledge*.

I wrote this book for those who want to increase their financial knowledge, because the time is now to take control of your money and your financial future.

**Bonus download offered
from The Rich Dad Company.**

**See exclusive videos from Robert Kiyosaki
at www.richdad.com/conspiracy-of-the-rich.**

PART ONE

THE CONSPIRACY

The Root of All Evil

Is *the love of money* the root of all evil? Or is *the ignorance of money* the root of all evil?

What did you learn about money in school? Have you ever wondered why our school systems do not teach us much—if anything—about money? Is the lack of financial education in our schools simply an oversight by our educational leaders? Or is it part of a larger conspiracy?

Regardless, whether we are rich or poor, educated or uneducated, child or adult, retired or working, we all use money. Like it or not, money has a tremendous impact on our lives in today's world. To omit the subject of money from our educational system is cruel and unconscionable.

Reader Comments

If we don't wake up as a country, and start taking responsibility for our own education in money matters, and teach that to our children, we are in for a train wreck of catastrophic portions.

—Kathryn Morgan

> *I went to high school and junior high school in Florida and Oklahoma. I received no financial education. I was however forced to take wood shop and metal shop.*
>
>   —Wayne Porter

Changing the Rules of Money

In 1971, President Richard Nixon changed the rules of money: Without the approval of Congress, he severed the U.S. dollar's relationship with gold. He made this unilateral decision during a quietly held two-day meeting on Minot Island in Maine, without consulting his State Department or the international monetary system.

President Nixon changed the rules because foreign countries being paid in U.S. dollars grew skeptical when the U.S. Treasury was printing more and more money to cover our debts, and they began exchanging their dollars directly for gold in earnest, depleting most of the U.S. gold reserves. The vault was being emptied because the government was importing more than it was exporting and because of the costly Vietnam War. As our economy grew, we were also importing more and more oil.

In everyday terms, America was going bankrupt. We were spending more than we earned. The United States could not pay its bills—as long as our bills were to be paid in gold. By freeing the dollar from gold, and making it illegal to directly exchange dollars for gold, Nixon created a way for the United States to print its way out of debt.

In 1971, the world's rules of money were changed and the biggest economic boom in the history of the world began. The boom continued as long as the world accepted our funny money, money backed by nothing but a promise by U.S. taxpayers to pay the bills of the United States.

Thanks to Nixon's change in the rules of money, inflation took off. The party was on. As more and more money was printed each decade, the value of the dollar decreased and the prices of goods and assets went up. Even middle-class Americans became millionaires as home prices kept climbing. They received credit cards in the mail. Money was flowing freely. To pay off their credit cards, people used their homes as ATMs. After all, houses always went up in value, right?

Blinded by greed and easy credit, however, many people either didn't see or ignored the dire warning signs such a system created.

In 2007, a new term crept into our vocabulary: *subprime borrower*—a person who borrowed money to buy a house he could not afford. At first, people thought the problem of subprime borrowers was limited to poor, financially foolish individuals who dreamed of owning their own home. Or they thought it was limited to speculators trying to make a quick buck—flippers. Even Republican presidential candidate John McCain did not take the crisis seriously in late 2008, trying to reassure everyone by saying, "The fundamentals of our economy are strong."

Around the same time, another word crept into our daily conversation: *bailout*—saving our biggest banks from the same problems that faced subprime borrowers: too much debt and not enough cash. As the financial crisis spread, millions of people lost their jobs, their homes, their savings, their college funds, and their retirement funds. Those who so far have not lost anything are afraid they might be next. Even states felt the pinch: California Governor Arnold Schwarzenegger began talking about issuing IOUs instead of paychecks for government lawmakers because California, one of the biggest economies in the world, was going broke.

As 2009 began, the world looked to a newly elected president, Barack Obama, for salvation.

A Cash Heist

In 1983, I read a book by R. Buckminster Fuller entitled *Grunch of Giants*. The word *grunch* is an acronym standing for G̲ross U̲niverse C̲ash H̲eist. It is a book about the super-rich and über-powerful and how they have been stealing from and exploiting people for centuries. It is a book about a conspiracy of the rich.

Grunch of Giants moves from kings and queens of thousands of years ago to modern times. It explains how the rich and powerful have always dominated the masses. It also explains that modern-day bank robbers do not wear masks. Rather, they wear suits and ties, sport college degrees, and rob banks from the inside, not the outside. After reading *Grunch of Giants* so many years ago, I could see our current financial crisis coming—I just did not know exactly when it would arrive. One reason why my investments and business ventures do well, in spite of this economic crisis, is because I read *Grunch of Giants*. The book gave me time to prepare for this crisis.

Books about conspiracies are often written by someone from the fringe. Dr. R. Buckminster Fuller, although ahead of his time in terms of his thinking, was hardly a fringe person. He attended Harvard University, and although he didn't graduate from there, he did quite well (like another famous Harvard dropout, Bill Gates). The American Institute of Architects honors Fuller as one of the country's greatest architects and designers. He is considered to be among the most accomplished Americans in history, having a substantial number of patents to his name. He was a respected futurist and inspiration for John Denver's lyric "grandfather of the future" in his song "What One Man Can Do." Fuller was an environmentalist before most people knew what the word meant. But most of all, he is respected because he used his genius to work for a world that benefited everyone . . . not just himself or the rich and powerful.

I read a number of Dr. Fuller's books before reading *Grunch of Giants*. The problem for me was that most of his earlier books were on math and science. Those books went right over my head. But *Grunch of Giants* I understood.

Reading *Grunch of Giants* confirmed many of my unspoken suspicions regarding the way the world worked. I began to understand why we do not teach kids about money in school. I also knew why I was sent to Vietnam to fight a war we should never have fought. Simply put, war is profitable. War is often about greed, not patriotism. After nine years in the military, four attending a federal military academy, and five as a Marine Corps pilot who served in Vietnam twice, I could only agree with Dr. Fuller. I understood from firsthand experience why he refers to the CIA as Capitalism's Invisible Army.

The best thing about *Grunch of Giants* was that it awakened the student in me. For the first time in my life, I wanted to study a subject, the subject of how the rich and powerful exploit the rest of us—legally. Since 1983, I have studied and read over fifty books on this subject. In each book, I found one or two pieces of the puzzle. The book you are reading now will put those many puzzle pieces together.

Is There a Conspiracy?

Conspiracy theories are a dime a dozen. We have all heard them. There are conspiracy theories about who killed Presidents Lincoln and Kennedy, and about who killed Dr. Martin Luther King, Jr. There are also conspiracy theories about September 11, 2001. Those theories will never die. Theories are theories. They are based on suspicions and unanswered questions.

I am not writing this book to sell you another conspiracy theory. My research has convinced me that there have been many conspiracies of the rich, both in the past and the present, and there will be more conspiracies in the future. When money and power are at stake, there will always be conspiracies. Money and power will always cause people to commit corrupt acts. In 2008, for instance, Bernard Madoff was accused of running a $50 billion Ponzi scheme to defraud not only wealthy clients, but also schools, charities, and pension funds. He once held the highly respected position of head of NASDAQ; he did not need more money, yet he allegedly stole it for years from very smart people and worthy organizations dependent upon his competence in financial markets.

Another example of the corruption of money and power is spending over half a billion dollars to be elected the president of the United States, a job that pays only $400,000. Spending money like that on an election is not healthy for our country.

So has there been a conspiracy? I believe so, in a way. But the question is, So what? What are you and I going to do about it? Most of the people who caused this latest financial crisis are dead, yet their work lives on. Arguing with dead people would be rather futile.

Regardless of whether there is a conspiracy, there are certain circumstances and events that impact your life in profound and unseen ways. Let's look at financial education, for instance. I've often marveled at the lack of financial education in our modern school system. At best, our children are taught how to balance a checkbook, speculate in the stock market, save money in banks, and invest in a retirement plan for the long term. In other words, they are taught to turn their money over to the rich, who supposedly have their best interest at heart.

Every time an educator brings a banker or a financial planner into their classroom, supposedly in the name of financial education, they are actually allowing the fox to enter the henhouse. I am not saying bankers and financial planners are bad people. All I am saying is that they are agents of the rich and powerful. Their job is not to educate but to recruit future customers. That is why they preach the doctrine of saving your money and investing in mutual funds. It helps the bank, not you. Again, I reiterate this is not bad. It's good business for the bank. It is no different than Army and Marine recruiters coming on campus when I was in high school and selling students on the glory of serving our country.

One of the causes of this financial crisis is that most people do not know good financial advice from bad financial advice. Most people cannot tell a good financial advisor from a con man. Most people cannot tell a good investment from a bad one. Most people go to school so they can get a good job, work hard, pay taxes, buy a house, save money, and turn over any extra money to a financial planner—or an expert like Bernie Madoff.

Most people leave school not knowing even the basic differences between a stock and a bond, between debt and equity. Few know why preferred stocks are labeled *preferred* and why mutual funds are *mutual*, or the difference between a mutual fund, hedge fund, exchange traded fund, and a fund of funds. Many people think debt is bad, yet debt can make you rich. Debt can increase your return on investment, but only if you know what you are doing. Only a few know the difference between *capital gains* and *cash flow* and which is less risky. Most people blindly accept the idea of going to school to get a good job and never know why *employees* pay higher tax rates than the *entrepreneur* who owns the business. Many people are in trouble today because they believed their home was an *asset*, when it was really a *liability*. These are basic and simple financial concepts. Yet for some reason, our schools conveniently omit a subject required for a successful life—the subject of money.

In 1903, John D. Rockefeller created the General Education Board. It seems this was done to ensure a steady supply of employees who were always financially in need of money, a job, and job security. There is evidence that Rockefeller was influenced by the Prussian system of education, a system designed to produce good employees and good soldiers, people who dutifully follow orders, such as "Do this or be fired," or "Turn your money over to me for safe keeping, and I'll invest it for you." Regardless of whether this was Rockefeller's intent in creating the General Education Board, the result today is that even those with a good education and a secure job are feeling financially insecure.

Without a basic financial education, long-term financial security is almost impossible. In 2008, millions of American baby boomers began retiring at a rate of ten thousand a day, expecting the government to take care of them financially and medically. Today, many people are finally learning that *job security* does not ensure long-term *financial security*.

In 1913, the Federal Reserve was created, even though the Founding Fathers, creators of the U.S. Constitution, were very much against a national bank that controlled the money supply. Without proper financial education, few people know that the Federal Reserve is not federal, it has no reserves, and it is not a bank. Once the Fed was in place, there were two sets of rules when it came to money: One set of rules for people who *work for money*, and another set of rules for the rich *who print money*.

In 1971, when President Nixon took the United States off the gold standard, the conspiracy of the rich was complete. In 1974, the U.S. Congress passed the Employee Retirement Income Security Act (ERISA), which led to retirement vehicles like the 401(k). This act effectively forced millions of workers who enjoyed employer-provided defined benefit (DB) pension plans to instead rely on defined contribution (DC) pension plans and put all their retirement money in the stock market and mutual funds. Wall Street now had control of the U.S. citizens' retirement money. The rules of money were completely changed and heavily tilted in favor of the rich and powerful. The biggest financial boom in the history of the world began, and today, in 2009, that boom has busted.

Reader Comment

I remember when they stopped backing our money with gold. Inflation went crazy. I was only a teenager and had gotten my first job. Things I needed back then I had to buy myself—prices of goods went up, but not my parents' paychecks.

The discussions of the adults revolved around how this could have happened. They felt that this could be the downfall of our whole economic system. It took a while but here it is.

—Cagosnell

What Can I Do?

As mentioned, the conspiracy of the rich has created two sets of rules when it comes to money, old rules of money and new rules of money. One set of rules is for the rich and another set is for ordinary people. The people who are most worried by our current financial crisis are those playing by the old set of rules. If you want to feel more secure about your future, you need to know the new set of rules—the eight new rules of money. This book will teach you those rules, and how to use them to your advantage.

The following are two examples of old rules of money versus new rules of money.

OLD RULE: SAVE MONEY

After 1971, the U.S. dollar was no longer money, but rather a currency (something I talk about in my book *Rich Dad's Increase Your Financial IQ*). As a consequence, savers became losers. The U.S. government was allowed to print money faster than it could be saved. When a banker raves about the power of *compounding interest*, what he or she fails to also tell you about is the power of *compounding inflation*—or in today's crisis, the power of compounding deflation. Inflation and deflation are caused by governments and banks attempting to control the economy by printing and lending money out of thin air—that is, without anything of value backing the money other than the "full faith and credit" of the United States.

For years, people all across the globe have believed that U.S. bonds are the safest investment in the world. For years, savers dutifully bought U.S. bonds, believing that was the smart thing to do. At the start of 2009, thirty-year U.S. Treasury bonds were paying less than 3 percent interest. To me, this means there is too much funny money in the world, savers will be losers, and in 2009, U.S. bonds could be the riskiest of all investments.

If you don't understand why that is, don't worry. Most people don't, which is why financial education (or the lack thereof) in our schools is so important. This subject of money, bonds, and debt will be covered more fully later in the book—unlike in your high school economics class. It is worth knowing, however, that what used to be the safest investments, U.S. bonds, are now the riskiest.

NEW RULE: SPEND, DON'T SAVE

Today, most people spend a lot of time learning how to earn money. They go to school to get a high-paying job, and then they spend years working at that job to earn money. They then do their best to save it. In the new rules, it is more important that you know *how to spend your money*, not just earn or save it. In other words, people who spend their money wisely will always be more prosperous than those who save their money wisely.

Of course, by spend I mean *invest* or convert your money into long-lasting value. The rich understand that in today's economy you cannot become wealthy by sticking your money under a mattress—or even worse, in a bank. They know that the key to wealth is investing in cash-flowing assets. Today, you need to know how to spend your money on assets that retain their value, provide income, adjust for inflation, and go up in value—not down. This will be covered in more detail throughout this book.

OLD RULE: DIVERSIFY

The old rule of diversification tells you to buy a number of stocks, bonds, and mutual funds. Diversification, however, did not protect investors from a 30 percent plunge in the stock market and losses in their mutual funds. I thought it odd that many of the so-called "investment gurus," people who sang the praises of diversification, began shouting "Sell, sell, sell!" as the market fell. If diversification protected you, why sell all of a sudden at near market bottom?

As Warren Buffett says, "Wide diversification is only required when investors do not understand what they are doing." In the end, diversification is a zero-sum game at best. If you are evenly diversified, when one asset class goes down, the other goes up. You lose money in one place and make it in another, but you don't gain any ground. You are static. Meanwhile, inflation, a topic we will also discuss in detail later in the book, marches on.

Rather than diversify, wise investors focus and specialize. They get to know the investment category they invest in and how the business works better than anyone else. For example, when investing in real estate, some people specialize in raw land and others in apartment buildings. While both are investing in real estate, they are doing so in totally different business categories. When investing in stocks, I invest in businesses that pay a steady dividend (cash flow). For example, today I am investing in businesses that operate oil pipelines. After the stock market crash of 2008, the share prices of these companies dropped, making the cash flow dividends bargains. In other words, bad markets offer great opportunities if you know what you are investing in.

Smart investors understand that owning a business that adjusts to the ups and downs of the economy or investing in cash-flowing assets is much better than owning a diversified portfolio of stocks, bonds, and mutual funds— investments that crash when the market crashes.

NEW RULE: CONTROL AND FOCUS YOUR MONEY

Don't diversify. Take control of your money and focus your investments. During this current financial crisis I took a few hits, but my wealth remained intact. That is because my wealth is not dependent upon market values going up or down (aka *capital gains*). I invest almost exclusively for *cash flow*.

For example, my *cash flow* decreased a little when the price of oil came down, yet my wealth is strong because I still receive a check in the mail every quarter. Even though the price of the oil stocks, *capital gains*, came down, I'm not worried because I receive cash flow from my investment. I don't have to worry about selling my stocks to realize a profit.

The same is true with most of my real estate investments. I invest for cash flow in real estate, which means every month I receive checks—passive income. The people who are hurting today are real estate investors who invested for capital gains, also known as *flipping properties*. In other words, since most people invested for *capital gains*, counting on the price of their stock investments or their home to go up in price, they are in trouble today.

When I was a boy, my rich dad would play the game of Monopoly over and over again with his son and me. By playing the game, I learned the difference between *cash flow* and *capital gains*. For example, if I owned a property with one green house on it, I got paid $10 a month in rent. If I had three houses on the same property, I received $50 a month in rent. And the ultimate goal was to have one red hotel on the same property. To win at the game of Monopoly, you had to invest for cash flow—not capital gains. Knowing the difference between cash flow and capital gains at the age of nine was one of the most important lessons my rich dad taught me. In other words, financial education can be as simple as a fun game and can provide financial security for generations—even during a financial crisis.

Today, I do not need *job security* because I have *financial security*. The difference between *financial security* and *financial panic* can be as simple as knowing the difference between *capital gains* and *cash flow*. The problem is that investing for *cash flow* requires a higher degree of financial intelligence than investing for *capital gains*. Being smarter about investing for cash flow will be covered in greater detail later in this book. But for now, just remember this: It is easier to invest for cash flow during a financial crisis. So don't waste a good crisis by hiding your head in the sand! The longer this crisis lasts, the richer some people will become. I want you to be one of them.

Today, one of the new rules is to *focus* your mind and money, rather than to *diversify*. It pays to focus on *cash flow* rather than *capital gains* because the more you know how to *control cash flow* the more *your capital gains increase*, and so does your financial security. You might even become rich. It's basic financial education taught in the game of Monopoly and my educational game, CASHFLOW, which has been called Monopoly on steroids.

These new rules, *learn to spend rather than save* and *focus rather than diversify*, are just two of the many concepts that will be covered in this book, and they will be covered in more detail in future chapters. The point of this book is to open your eyes to the power you have to control your financial future if you have the proper financial education.

Our educational system has failed millions of people—even the educated. There is evidence that our financial system has conspired against you and others. But that is ancient history. Today, you control your future, and now is the time to educate yourself—to teach yourself the new rules of money. By doing so, you take control of your destiny and hold the key to playing the game of money according to its new rules.

Reader Comment

I think most people who are reading your books are looking for some sort of magic pill solution because that is the mind-set of society in America today, with their instant gratification desires. And I think you do a good job of letting people know that this is not a magic pill book. When you discuss the new rules of money, what you say is excellent in reshaping people's minds and how they should think.

—apcordov

My Promise to You

After President Nixon changed the rules of money in 1971, the subject of money became very confusing. The subject of money does not make sense to most honest people. In fact, the more honest and hardworking you are, the less sense the new rules will make. For example, the new rules allow the rich to print their own money. If you did that, you would be sent to jail for counterfeiting. But in this book, I will describe how I print my own money—legally. Printing your own money is one of the greatest secrets of the truly rich.

My promise to you is that I will do my very best to keep my explanations as simple as possible. I will do my best to use everyday language to explain complex financial jargon. For example, one of the reasons why there is a financial crisis today is because of a financial tool known as a *derivative*. Warren Buffett once called derivatives "weapons of mass destruction," and his description proved true. Derivatives are bringing down the biggest banks in the world.

The problem is that very few people know what derivatives are. To keep things very simple, I explain derivatives by using the example of an orange and orange juice. Orange juice is a derivative of an orange—just like gasoline is a derivative of oil, or an egg is a derivative of a chicken. It's that simple: If you buy a house, a *mortgage* is a *derivative* of *you* and the *house* you buy.

One of the reasons we are in this financial crisis is because the bankers of the world began creating derivatives out of derivatives out of derivatives. Some of these new derivatives had exotic names such as *collateralized debt obligations*, or *high-yield corporate bonds* (aka *junk bonds*), and *credit default swaps.* In this book, I will do my best to define these words by using everyday language. Remember, one of the objectives of the financial industry is to keep people confused.

Multilayered derivatives border on legal fraud of the highest order. They are no different than someone using a credit card to pay off a credit card, and then refinancing their home with a new mortgage, paying off their credit cards, and using the credit cards all over again. That's why Warren Buffett called derivatives weapons of mass destruction: Multilayered derivatives are destroying the world's banking system just as credit cards and home equity loans are destroying many families. Credit cards, money, collateralized debt obligations, junk bonds, and mortgages—they're all derivatives, just going by different names.

In 2007, when the *house of derivatives* began coming down, the richest people in the world began screaming "Bailout!" A bailout is used when the rich want the taxpayers to pay for their mistakes or their fraud. My research has found that a *bailout* is an integral part of the conspiracy of the rich.

One of the reasons I believe my book *Rich Dad Poor Dad* is the best-selling personal finance book of all time is because I kept financial jargon simple. I will do my best to do the same in this book.

A wise man once said, "Simplicity is genius." To keep things simple, I will not go into excessive detail or complex explanations. I will use real-life stories, rather than technical explanations, to make my point. If you want more detail, I will list a number of books that explain subjects covered here in greater depth. For example, Dr. Fuller's book *Grunch of Giants* might be a good book to read.

Simplicity is important because there are many people who profit from the subject of money being kept complex and confusing. It's easier to take your money if you're confused.

So I ask again, "Is the love of money the root of all evil?" I say no. I believe it is more evil to keep people in the dark, ignorant about the subject of money. Evil occurs when people are ignorant of how money works, and financial ignorance is an essential component of the conspiracy of the rich.

Reader Comments

I went to Wharton and am embarrassed to say that nothing in my course of study explained wealth creation this clearly. Everyone should read this book (and all of Robert's books) starting in high school.

—Rromatowski

Robert—I would say yes, the love of money is the root of all evil, for the same reason you say no. The evil of keeping the masses in ignorance about money is just a "derivative" of the evil love of money.

—Istarcher

Chapter 1

Can Obama Save the World?

Timeline of a Crisis

In August 2007, panic silently spread throughout the world. The banking system was seizing up. This set in motion a domino effect that threatens even now to bring down the entire world economy. In spite of massive government bailouts and stimulus packages estimated to be over $7 trillion to $9 trillion worldwide, some of the world's biggest banking and business institutions, such as Citigroup and General Motors, continue to wobble. Their long-term survival is in question.

The crisis threatens not only major corporations and multinational banking conglomerates, but also the security of hardworking families. Today, millions of people who thought they were doing the right thing by following the conventional wisdom of going to school, getting a job, buying a home, saving money, staying free of debt, and investing in a diversified portfolio of stocks, bonds, and mutual funds are in financial trouble.

In talking with people around the country, I find that they are concerned and scared, and a number of people are suffering personal depressions after losing their jobs, homes, savings, kids' college savings, and retirement funds. Many don't understand what is happening to our economy or how it will eventually affect them. Many wonder what caused this crisis, asking, "Is anyone to blame? Who can solve the problem? And when will the crisis end?" With that in mind, I think it's important to spend a moment reviewing the events leading up to our current crisis. The following is a brief and by no means comprehensive timeline highlighting some of the major global economic events that have led us to the precarious financial state we find ourselves in today.

August 6, 2007
American Home Mortgage, one of America's largest mortgage providers, filed for bankruptcy.

August 9, 2007
French bank BNP Paribas, because of problems with U.S. subprime mortgages, announced it couldn't value assets worth over 1.6 billion euros.

As global credit markets locked up, the European Central Bank injected nearly 95 billion euros into the Eurozone banking system in an effort to stimulate lending and liquidity.

August 10, 2007
A day later, the European Central Bank pumped another 61 billion euros into global capital markets.

August 13, 2007
The European Central Bank released another 47.6 billion euros, the third cash infusion totaling almost 204 *billion* euros in a span of three working days.

September 2007
Northern Rock, the largest mortgage broker and a large consumer bank in Britain, experienced a run on the bank by depositors. It was the first bank run in over a hundred years.

THE PRESIDENTIAL CAMPAIGN HEATS UP

As the financial crisis spread around the world in 2007, the U.S. presidential campaign—which was to be the longest and most expensive political campaign in history—picked up steam.

During the early part of the campaign, even though there were clear signs that the world economy was on the verge of collapsing, the major presidential candidates rarely mentioned the economy as an issue. Rather, the hot campaign topics were the war in Iraq, gay marriage, abortion, and immigration. When the candidates did discuss the economy, they did so dismissively. (This was never more apparent than when presidential candidate John McCain later famously remarked in late 2008, "The fundamentals of our economy are strong," as the Dow dropped a record 504 points that day.)

In the face of all the evidence of a mounting major financial crisis, where was our president? Where were our leading presidential candidates and financial leaders? Why were the media darlings of the financial world not warning investors to get out? Why were financial experts still encouraging investors to "invest for the long term"? Why were our political and financial leaders not sounding the warning call about this financial storm? Why didn't they at least have the wisdom to stand up and say, "It's the economy, stupid"? To quote a famous song, they were "blinded by the light." On the surface, everything seemed fine, as evidenced by the next event in our timeline . . .

October 9, 2007
The Dow Jones Industrial Average closed at a historic high of 14,164.

A YEAR LATER

September 2008
President Bush and the U.S. Treasury asked for $700 billion in bailout money to save the economy, over a year after the European Central Bank had already infused 204 billion euros into the economy in August 2007 and almost a year after the Dow hit its all-time high.

Toxic financial derivatives resulted in the collapse of Bear Stearns and Lehman Brothers and the nationalization of Fannie Mae, Freddie Mac, and one of the world's largest insurers, AIG.

Additionally, the U.S. auto industry revealed that it was ailing, and GM, Ford, and Chrysler asked for bailout money. Many states and city governments were also now asking for bailout money.

September 29, 2008

On a black Monday, after President Bush asked for bailout money, the Dow plunged 777 points. It was the biggest single-day point-based drop in history, and the Dow closed at 10,365.

October 1, 2008, through October 10, 2008

In one of its worst spans ever recorded, the Dow dropped 2,380 points in a little over a week.

October 13, 2008

The Dow began to exhibit extreme volatility, going up 936 points in one day, the best point gain in history, closing at 9,387.

October 15, 2008

The Dow plunged 733 points, closing at 8,577.

October 28, 2008

The Dow gained 889 points, the second best point gain in history, closing at 9,065.

November 4, 2008

Barack Obama was elected president of the United States with the campaign slogan, "Change We Can Believe In." He will take over a government that has by now committed $7.8 trillion in various forms to salvage the economy.

December 2008

It was reported that Americans lost 584,000 jobs in November, the biggest posted loss since December 1974. Unemployment was reported at a fifteen-year high of 6.7 percent, with nearly two million jobs lost in the United States alone in 2008. Additionally, it was reported that China, the world's fastest growing economy, lost 6.7 million jobs in 2008, an indication that the global economy was in severe distress and on the verge of meltdown.

Economists finally admitted the U.S. economy had been in a recession since December 2007. One year later, the economists finally figured it out?

Warren Buffett, who many consider the world's smartest investor, saw his company, Berkshire Hathaway, lose 33 percent of its stock value in a year. Investors took solace in the fact that the fund outperformed the market—by losing less than the average. That's comforting.

Yale and Harvard universities announced their endowment funds lost over 20 percent in a year.

GM and Chrysler received $17.4 billion in government loans.

President-elect Obama announced an $800 billion stimulus plan centered on massive infrastructure projects aimed at easing the record U.S. job losses—this was in addition to the $7.8 trillion already committed by the U.S. government.

December 31, 2008

The Dow closed at 8,776, down 5,388 points from its record high achieved just over a year earlier. It was the worst yearly performance for the Dow since 1931 and equated to $6.9 trillion in lost value.

Back to the Future

Faced with such an overwhelmingly bad economy, President Bush pushed through a landmark bailout plan aimed at saving the economy, saying, "This legislation will safeguard and stabilize America's financial system and put in place permanent reforms so these problems will never happen again."

Many people breathed a sigh of relief, thinking, "Finally, the government is going to save us!" The problem is those are *not* the words of President George W. Bush. Those are the words of his father, George H. W. Bush. In 1989, the first President Bush asked for $66 billion to save the savings and loan (S&L) industry. The $66 billion did not solve the problem; the S&L industry disappeared from sight. On top of that, the estimated $66 billion rescue package eventually cost taxpayers over $150 billion—more than twice the amount originally estimated. Where did all that money go?

Like Father, Like Son

Twenty years later, in September 2008, President George W. Bush asked for $700 billion and made a similar promise: "We'll make sure, as time goes on, this doesn't happen again. In the meantime, we got to solve the problem. And that's why people sent me to Washington, D.C." Why is it that a father and son said almost the same thing about saving the economy almost twenty years apart? Why was the first President Bush's promise to fix the system broken?

All the President's Men

The main campaign slogan of President Barack Obama was, *Change We Can Believe In*. Given that slogan, we must ask a question: Why did President Obama hire many of the same people who worked in the Clinton administration? That doesn't seem like change. It seems like status quo.

During the election, why did Obama consult Robert Rubin, who just recently resigned as head of Citigroup, a company on the verge of its own collapse and that has received some $45 billion in bailout funds, for advice on the economy? Why did he appoint Larry Summers to be director of the White House National Economic Council and Timothy Geithner, former head of the Federal Reserve Bank of New York, to be his secretary of the treasury? All of these men were members of the Clinton economic team and played a part in the repeal of the Glass-Steagall Act of 1933, an act that forbade banks from selling investments. Banks selling investments in the form of derivatives is a big reason why we are in this mess today.

In overly simple terms, the purpose of the Glass-Steagall Act of 1933, crafted during the last depression, was to separate savings banks, which had access to Federal Reserve funds, from investment banks, which did not. Clinton, Rubin, Summers, and Geithner succeeded in repealing Glass-Steagall in order to legitimize the formation of Citigroup, the biggest "financial supermarket" in U.S. history. Many people do not know this, but at the time of its formation, Citigroup was in violation of the Glass-Steagall Act.

The following is a comment by Kenneth Guenther, CEO of Independent

Community Bankers of America (the small bankers of America), made to PBS in 2003 about the formation of Citigroup:

> Who do they think they are? Other people, firms, cannot act like this...Citicorp and Travelers were so big that they were able to pull this off. They were able to pull off the largest financial conglomeration—the largest financial coming together of banking, insurance, and securities—when legislation was still on the books saying this was illegal. And they pulled this off with the blessings of the president of the United States, President Clinton; the chairman of the Federal Reserve system, Alan Greenspan; and the secretary of the treasury, Robert Rubin. And then, when it's all over, what happens? The secretary of the treasury becomes the vice chairman of the emerging Citigroup.

The most telling line is the last one: "The secretary of the treasury [Robert Rubin] becomes the vice chairman of the emerging Citigroup." As we've discussed, Robert Rubin was Obama's advisor during the presidential campaign.

President Obama's current secretary of the treasury is Timothy Geithner. He was undersecretary of the treasury from 1998 to 2001 under Treasury secretaries Robert Rubin and Lawrence Summers. Summers is Geithner's mentor, and many call Geithner a Robert Rubin protégé. Oh, what a tangled web we weave.

In other words, these same men are partially responsible for triggering this financial crisis. By allowing the combining of savings banks with investment banks, these guys accelerated the sale of the exotic financial derivatives that Warren Buffett called "weapons of mass financial destruction" and that have helped bring the entire global economy to its knees. How can there be change if the same people who expanded this financial mess remain in charge? What does President Obama mean when he promises change we can believe in?

Republicans, Democrats, and Bankers

One reason why Presidents Bush, Sr., and Bush, Jr., said almost the same words, that a bailout would save the economy and never happen again, is because they were elected to protect the system—not fix it. Could one reason that President Obama hired virtually the same financial team from the Clinton administration be because he was interested in protecting the same system—a system designed to make the rich get even richer? Only time will tell. Although President Obama was proud of the fact that he did not accept campaign money from lobbyists, the truth remains that his financial team is full of insiders who helped usher in the crisis they are now charged with fixing.

The only candidate who consistently mentioned the economy and the growing financial crisis during the early part of the 2008 presidential campaign was Representative Ron Paul of Texas, a true maverick Republican. Writing for Forbes .com on March 4, 2008, he stated, "Unless we embrace fundamental reforms, we will be caught in a financial storm that will humble this great country as no foreign enemy ever could." Unfortunately, not enough voters cared to listen.

Reader Comments

I voted for Obama because I believe he is a sincere and compassionate leader. And, no matter how intelligent he may be, or anyone working with him, you, Robert, have taught me to see that financial education in this country is scarce! I worry that the folks in charge simply do not have a very high financial IQ.

—virtualdeb

It seems that President Obama and his team are focused more on short-term tactical Band-Aids rather than long-term strategic goals. To date, all the "actions" taken by the new administration have been to plug the holes in the dike and shore it up a bit. There seems to be no attention to determining the underlying root cause and changing the foundation flaws that led to the current financial crisis.

—egrannan

The Roots of the Crisis

It is said that Mayer Amschel Rothschild, founder of one of the most powerful banking families of Europe, once observed, "Give me control of a nation's money supply and I care not who makes the laws." To understand today's financial crisis, it is important to understand the relationship between the U.S. government, the Federal Reserve System, and some of the most powerful people in the world. This relationship is depicted in the overly simple diagram below:

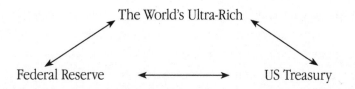

In 1913, the creation of the Federal Reserve System granted the very rich of the world the power to control the money supply of the United States and fulfilled the spirit of Rothschild's sentiments. Many people don't know or understand that the Federal Reserve System is not a government institution or a bank, nor does it have any reserves. Rather, it is a banking cartel run by some of the most powerful men in the financial world. The creation of the Fed was basically a license to print money.

Another reason the Federal Reserve System was created was to protect the biggest banks from failing by providing liquidity to those banks when they were in financial trouble, which protected the wealth of the rich, not of the taxpayers.

We see this in action even to this day. In 2008, when President Bush authorized $700 billion in bailout money, Secretary of the Treasury Henry Paulson, formerly of Goldman Sachs, in conjunction with the Federal Reserve, immediately handed out billions of dollars in TARP (Troubled Asset Relief Program) money to the biggest banks in the country, his friends, no questions asked.

The reality of the situation is that the TARP bailout money went straight from our pockets—taxpayers' pockets—into the pockets of the banks and corporations that helped create our financial mess in the first place. We were told the money was given to the banks with a mandate to lend it out, but our government was either unable or unwilling to enforce that mandate—or both.

In mid-December 2008, when *USA Today* asked banks what they were doing with the bailout money, JPMorgan Chase, a bank that received $25 billion in taxpayer money, replied, "We have not disclosed that to the public. We're declining to." Morgan Stanley, a bank that received $10 billion, replied, "We are going to decline to comment on your story." The Bank of New York Mellon responded, "We're choosing not to disclose that." The bank bailout money was really just a rich friend bailout, employed to cover those friends' mistakes and obvious fraud, not to save the economy.

The proof is in the pudding. As the *Wall Street Journal* reported on January 26, 2009, in an article entitled "Lending Drops at Big U.S. Banks," "Ten of the 13 big beneficiaries of the Treasury Department's Troubled Asset Relief Program, or TARP, saw their outstanding loan balances decline by a total of about $46 billion, or 1.4%, between the third and fourth quarters of 2008, according to a *Wall Street Journal* analysis of banks that recently announced their quarterly results." This is even as they scooped up $148 billion in taxpayer TARP funds intended to stimulate lending.

If President Obama really wants to make changes in Washington, he needs to change this cozy relationship between the Federal Reserve System, the U.S. government, and the rich and powerful. And maybe he will. But by putting President Clinton's financial team in his administration, it does not seem likely. It seems he will do as past presidents since Woodrow Wilson have done—protect the system, not change it.

Reader Comments

I must say that reading your first chapter has opened my eyes. I am only twenty-three years old and never fully understood what the Federal Reserve System was or what it did for our country. I have to say that it does not shock me; I am truly grateful that you have been honest and are not afraid to give the truthful definition of what a lot of things mean and stand for. It is however truly sad that taxpayers are affected by this and a lot of them do not even know or understand it!

—jacklyn

We hear the media speak of "the Fed" as if it is some mystical behemoth, when in reality, it is not what the general public thinks that it is. I had no clue that this was not a government or bank institution. It really worries me that this entity has almost limitless power with a lack of true oversight. The question becomes, how did they rise to such a prominent position?

—Kthompson5

By some estimates, the combined worldwide losses in commodities, stocks, bonds, and real estate are greater than $60 trillion. So far, the world's banks and governments have put up nearly $10 trillion in efforts to fix the problem. What about the other $50 trillion? Who will cover those losses? Where did that money go? Who will bail *us* out, the people who really lost money and now must pay for our own losses *and* the losses of the rich via bailout money paid for with our tax dollars?

The year 2013 will mark the hundredth anniversary of the Federal Reserve System. For nearly one hundred years the Fed has pulled off the biggest cash heist in the world. This cash heist is a bank robbery where the robbers do not wear masks, but rather business suits with American flag pins in the jacket lapels. It is a robbery where the rich take from the poor via our banks and our government.

While a student sitting in Dr. Buckminster Fuller's class in 1981, I was disturbed to hear him say, "The primary purpose for government is to be a vehicle for the rich to get their hands into our pockets." Although I did not like what he was saying because I only wanted to think great things about my country and its leaders, deep down inside of me, and based on my own experiences, I knew there was some truth in what he was saying.

Until that time, I had my own secret doubts about government. As a child, I often wondered why the subject of money was not taught in school. As a Marine pilot in Vietnam, I wondered why we were fighting the war. I also witnessed my dad resign his position as superintendent of education to run for lieutenant governor of the state of Hawaii because he was very deeply disturbed by the corruption he found in government. An honest man, my dad could not stomach what he witnessed after he became a high-ranking government official, a member of the governor's staff. So, although Dr. Fuller's words were not words I wanted to hear, because I do love my country and do not like criticizing it, his words were disturbing enough to become my wake-up call. In the early 1980s, my study began, and my eyes were opened to facts that many powerful people do not want us to see.

How Does This Affect Me?

In the big picture of personal finance, there are three financial forces that cause most people to work hard and yet struggle financially. They are:

1. Taxes
2. Debt
3. Inflation
4. Retirement

Take a moment and reflect briefly on how much these three forces affect you personally. For example, how much do you pay in taxes? Not only do we pay income tax, but also sales taxes, gasoline taxes, real estate taxes, and so forth. More important, to whom do our tax dollars go and for what causes?

Next, how much does the interest on debt cost you? For example, how much does interest on debt cost you on mortgage payments, car payments, credit cards, and college loans?

And then take a moment to think about how much inflation has affected your life. You may recall that not too long ago people began flipping houses because prices were going up so rapidly. During that same period, the prices of gasoline, a college education, food, clothing, and more were climbing steadily— but incomes weren't. Many people did not save because it was smarter to spend today rather than pay more tomorrow. That was inflation in action.

And finally, most people have money taken out of their checks and placed into retirement accounts like a 401(k) before they ever get paid. That money goes directly to Wall Street, where it is "managed" by someone the employee doesn't even know. On top of that, additional money is skimmed through fees and commissions. And, today, many people do not have enough money to retire because they have lost all their wealth in the stock market crash.

It is important to understand that these forces of taxes, debt, inflation, and retirement are kept alive by the Federal Reserve System's license to print money. Prior to the Federal Reserve, Americans paid very little in taxes, there was neither national debt nor much personal debt, there was very little inflation, and people did not worry about retirement because money and savings retained their value. Here is a brief and simple explanation of the relationship between the Fed and these four forces.

1. Taxes: America was relatively tax-free in its early days. In 1862 the first income tax was levied to pay for the Civil War. In 1895, the U.S. Supreme Court ruled that an income tax was unconstitutional. In 1913, however, the same year the Federal Reserve System was created, the Sixteenth Amendment was passed, making an income tax permanent. The reason for the reinstatement of the income tax was to capitalize the U.S. Treasury and Federal Reserve. Now the rich could put their hands in our pockets via taxes permanently.

2. Debt: The Federal Reserve System gave politicians the power to borrow money, rather than raise taxes. Debt, however, is a double-edged sword that results in either higher taxes or inflation. The U.S. government creates money, rather than raising taxes, by selling U.S. bonds, IOUs from the taxpayers of the country that eventually have to be paid for with higher taxes—or by printing more money, which creates inflation.

3. Inflation: This is caused by the Federal Reserve and the U.S. Treasury borrowing money or printing money to pay the government's bills. That's why inflation is often called the "silent tax." Inflation makes the rich richer, but it makes the cost of living more expensive for the poor and the middle class. This is because those who print money receive the most benefit. They can purchase the goods and services they desire with the new money *before* it dilutes the existing money pool. They reap all of the benefits and none of the consequences. All the while, the poor and the middle class watch as their buck gets stretched thinner and thinner.

4. Retirement: As stated, in 1974, the U.S. Congress passed ERISA. This forced Americans to invest in the stock market for their retirement through vehicles like the 401(k), which generally have high fees, high risk, and low returns, and gave Wall Street control over the country's retirement money.

Reader Comments

Living in Zimbabwe, which has had the highest inflation in the world of over 5,000 billion percent, I have come to understand the added advantage of not keeping money (currency). Basically, the price of a good changed three times in one day and there was need to lock down the value in the morning and resell the product in the evening, which meant a nice profit.

—drtaffie

I think the most evil of the three is inflation. It affects the poor and the middle class equally. The middle class pays more taxes than the poor, but everyone pays equally through inflation.

—kammi12

The Beginning of the End

I started this chapter with an important date: August 6, 2007. That was the day that American Home Mortgage, one of America's largest mortgage providers, filed for bankruptcy.

The reason this date is important is because it marked the point where debt had gone too far. The global system could not absorb any more debt. On August 6, 2007, the debt bubble burst, and today we have *deflation*, which is a much more serious problem than *inflation*—something we'll go over in more depth in future chapters.

To save the world, President Obama has to stop *deflation*. The primary tool he has for fighting *deflation* is *inflation*. This means he will have to employ massive amounts of debt and print more money out of thin air. And ultimately, this means higher taxes, debt, and, if he is successful, inflation.

Think of the global economy as a big hot-air balloon. Things were going along splendidly until August 6, 2007, when too much hot air—*debt*—caused a tear in the balloon. As the horrifying ripping sound spread, central banks of the world began pumping more and more hot air—*debt*—into the balloon in an attempt to keep it from crashing to the ground and causing a *depression*.

In his book *A Tale of Two Cities*, Charles Dickens famously wrote, "It was the best of times, it was the worst of times; it was the age of wisdom, it was the age of foolishness." Amazingly, things have not changed much since Dickens wrote that in 1859.

For some people, deflation makes these the best of times. The cost of living is going down as the prices of oil, real estate, stocks, and commodities drop and thus become more affordable. Apparently, Walmart isn't the only one rolling back prices. The central banks and governments of the world, hoping people, businesses, and governments will get deeper into debt by borrowing more money, are pumping trillions of dollars into the economy at interest rates near zero—virtually free money.

Holders of massive pools of money are waiting like vultures for the right moment to flood back into the market and pick clean the bones of dead and dying companies. For well-positioned investors, this is the opportunity of a lifetime to snatch up assets at a discount. For well-positioned businesses, now is the time to gain market share, as their competition goes under due to bankruptcy. These people see abundance.

For others, these are the worst of times.

The cost of living may be going down, but these people are unable to reap the benefits because they no longer have a job to cover even their basic living expenses, or they are so saddled with debt that they owe more money than their assets are worth—and the assets they have are really liabilities, such as their houses.

The central banks of the world are flooding the system with money, but it is not helping these people because they cannot get loans for cars or houses. As the money supply blows up like a balloon, their access to that money shrinks.

These people do not see the opportunity of a lifetime. They do not have pools of money waiting for the right deal. They see scarcity and feel fear. Many wonder if they will lose their jobs, homes, savings, and retirement, if they haven't already.

The difference between those who find it to be the best of times and those who find it to be the worst of times is simply knowledge and financial IQ. The great failure of our education system is that it does not teach people about how money really works, and what it does teach is antiquated and obsolete—the *old* rules of money. They teach you how to balance a checkbook, but they don't teach you how to grow a balance sheet—or even read one for that matter.

They teach you to save your money, but they don't teach you about inflation and how it steals your wealth. They teach you how to write a check, but they don't teach you the difference between assets and liabilities. One wonders if the system is intentionally designed to keep you in the dark.

In today's world, you can be an academic genius but still be a financial imbecile. This goes against the conventional wisdom, especially when we equate people who have high-paying jobs like attorneys or doctors with being financially and academically smart because they make a lot of money. But as we've seen, making lots of money doesn't mean you are financially intelligent, especially when you spend and invest that money unwisely—or turn your money over to people who do not care if you make or lose money. Always remember there is a big difference between job security and financial security, and true financial security requires a sound financial education based on the realities of the real world of money.

That is why I was *not* surprised when our economic crisis spread wider than just the mortgage defaults of subprime borrowers. The talking heads and our leaders appeared to be surprised. That is why our presidential candidates did not mention the problem during the campaign. They toed the line for as long as they could, assuring us that there was no crisis and that our financial problems were limited to poor people not paying their mortgages. As we now know, the problem was not just poor people with too much debt. The problem started at the highest levels of government and finance. Millions have lost much of what they spent their lives working for because they have no understanding of the new rules of money and how they affect our lives. And that is a systemic problem that can't be solved by one charismatic politician.

So here we come back to the question posed in the title of this chapter: Can Obama save us? The correct question should be: How can we save ourselves? The answer, and the key to our freedom from the tyranny of our economy, is knowledge. By educating yourself about money and how it works, you unlock the potential within yourself to break free from the mentality of scarcity and see the abundance all around you. For you, these truly can be the best of times.

Personally, I do not expect government or big business to save me. I simply watch what the powers that be *actually do,* more than what they say or promise, and I respond accordingly to those actions. Knowing how to respond, rather than follow, and taking confident action, rather than waiting to be told what to do, requires courage and financial education.

I believe our financial problem is too big and getting bigger. It is out of control. It is a monetary problem more than a political problem. It is a global problem, not just a U.S. problem. There is only so much Obama can do, and what he can do I fear may not be enough. Worst of all, the people really pulling the strings in the financial world do not answer to the president of the United States. They do not need his approval to do what they do. They are beyond the control of world governments and their elected leaders.

How Can We Save Ourselves?

When I am asked what I would teach if I were in charge of financial education for our school system, my answer is: "I would make sure the students understood the relationship between taxes, debt, and inflation before leaving the school system." If they understand that, they will have a more secure financial future. They would be able to make better financial decisions for themselves rather than expect the government or so-called "financial experts" to save them.

Reader Comment

*Because of things that I learned through financial education,
I have known for a long time that my 401(k) was not the great
investment it was touted to be, and today I'm better for having
that knowledge. I'm reminded of something else Robert said which
is, "It's not silver, gold, or real estate that make you rich; it's what
you know about silver, gold, or real estate that makes you rich."*

—dafirebreather

Ultimately, this book is about the relationship between taxes, debt, inflation, and retirement. These form the foundation for the new rules of money. This book will equip you to take control of your own financial future by giving you the knowledge necessary to understand these forces, and thus the new rules of money. And once you understand these things, you'll be in a position to opt out of the conspiracy of the rich and to live a life of true financial freedom.

Chapter 2

The Conspiracy Against Our Education

Why Money Is Not Taught in School

> *The purpose of the foundation [the General Education Board]
> was to use the power of money, not to raise the level of education
> in America, as was widely believed at the time, but to influence
> the direction of that education... The object was to use the
> classroom to teach attitudes that encourage people to be passive
> and submissive to their rulers. The goal was—and is—to create
> citizens who were educated enough for productive work under
> supervision but not enough to question authority or seek to rise
> above their class. True education was to be restricted to the sons
> and daughters of the elite. For the rest, it would be better to pro-
> duce skilled workers with no particular aspirations other than
> to enjoy life.*
>
> —G. Edward Griffin in *The Creature from Jekyll Island*,
> on Rockefeller's General Education Board, founded in 1903

The New School

I was nine years old when my suspicions about school began. At the time, my family had just moved across town to a new home in order for my dad to be nearer to his place of work. I was going to start the fourth grade at a new school.

We lived in the little plantation town of Hilo, on the Big Island of Hawaii. The main industry of the town was sugar, and about 80 percent to 90 percent of the population was descended from Asian immigrants brought to Hawaii in the late 1800s. I, myself, am fourth-generation Japanese American.

At my old elementary school, most of my classmates looked like me. At my new school, 50 percent of my classmates were white, the other half Asian. Most of the kids, white or Asian, were rich kids from well-to-do families. For the first time, I felt poor.

My rich friends had nice homes in exclusive neighborhoods. Our family lived in a rented home behind the library. Most of my friends' families had two cars. My family had one. A number of those families had second homes on the beach. When my friends had birthday parties, they were held at the yacht club. My birthday parties were at a public beach. When my friends began playing golf, they took lessons from the pro at their country club. I didn't even own golf clubs. I was a caddy at the country club. My rich friends had new bicycles, some even had their own sailboats, and they took vacations to Disneyland. My mom and dad promised we would someday go to Disneyland, but we never did. We had fun taking day trips to the local national parks to watch volcanoes erupt.

It was at my new school that I met my rich dad's son. At the time, he and I were in the bottom 10 percent of the class economically and, occasionally, academically. We became best friends because we were the poorest kids in the class and stuck together.

The Hope of Education

In the 1880s, my ancestors first began emigrating to Hawaii from Japan. They were sent off to work in the fields of the sugar and pineapple plantations. Initially, their dream was to work the fields, save money, and return to Japan as rich people.

My relatives worked very hard on the plantations, but the pay was low. On top of that, the owners of the plantations took money from the workers' paychecks to pay the rent for the houses that the plantation provided. The plantation also owned the only store, which meant workers had to purchase their food and supplies at the plantation store. At the end of the month, there was very little money left in their paychecks after rent and store charges were taken out.

My relatives wanted to get off the plantation as soon as possible, and to them a good education was their ticket out. From stories I've been told, my ancestors scrimped and saved to send their kids to school for a college education. The lack of a college education meant you were stuck on the plantation. By the second generation, most of my relatives were off the plantation. Today, my family boasts several generations of college graduates—most with at least a bachelor's degree, many with master's degrees, and a number with PhDs. I am on the low end of my family's academic pole: I only have a bachelor's of science degree—a BS degree.

The School Across the Street

Changing schools at the age of nine was a significant event in my life because of the new school's location. The following diagram shows the change in my social environment.

	S	My dad's office
	T	
Hilo Union School	R	Riverside School
	E	
	E	Our new home
	T	

Directly across the street from my new school, Riverside School, was Hilo Union School. Hilo Union School was the school for the kids whose parents worked for the plantations, many of whom belonged to the labor unions. Riverside School, on the other hand, was for the kids whose parents owned plantations.

In the fourth grade, I began attending Riverside School with the kids of plantation owners. In the 1950s, while walking to Riverside School, I would look across the street at Hilo Union School and see a school not segregated by race but by money. This is when my suspicion of school and the educational process began. I knew something was wrong, but I did not know what. If our home wasn't on the same side of the street as Riverside School, I might have gone to Hilo Union School instead.

From grade 4 through grade 6, I went to school with the kids who were the descendants of the plantation owners—the people and system my relatives wanted to escape from. All through elementary school, I grew up with these kids in school, played sports with them, and went to their homes.

Once elementary school was over, many of these friends were sent off to boarding schools. I went on to the public junior high school farther up the street. There, I joined the kids from across the street, the kids from Hilo Union School, and I grew more aware of the differences between kids raised in rich families and those raised in poor and middle-class families.

My dad was highly educated, and the head of the educational system in Hawaii. Not only did he make it off the plantation, but he was also very successful as a government employee. Although my dad went to school, had advanced degrees, and had a good job that paid well, as a family we were still financially poor—at least compared to the families of my rich friends. Every time I went to my rich friends' homes, I knew something was missing, but I did not know what. At the age of nine, I began to wonder why going to school did not make my mom and dad rich.

The Plantations

My relatives worked and scrimped to save for a good education so that their kids could get off the sugar plantation. I saw the relationship between Riverside School and Hilo Union School, and I experienced having rich friends who were descendants of plantation owners and having friends who were descendants of plantation laborers. In elementary school, the basic education is the same—yet something is missing, even today.

My relatives wanted their kids to get off the plantation. The problem was, and is, that in school we never learned to how to *own the plantation*.

So many of us go on to *work for the new plantations*—the big corporations of the world, the military, or the government. We go to school to get a good job. We are taught to work for the rich, shop at the stores of the rich, borrow money from the banks of the rich, invest in the businesses of the rich via mutual funds in our retirement plans—but not *how to be rich.*

Many people do not like hearing they are taught by our school system to be caught in the web, the web of the conspiracy of the rich. People do not like to hear that the rich have manipulated our system of education.

Hijacking the Education System

One of the greatest sins of our current educational system is that it does not teach you about money. Rather, it teaches you how to be a good employee and to know your station in life. Some would say this is by design. For instance, in his book *The Creature from Jekyll Island*, Griffin quotes from the first occasional paper of the General Education Board, entitled "The Country School of To-Morrow," written by Frederick Gates: "In our dream, we have limitless resources, and the people yield themselves with perfect docility to our molding hands. The present educational conventions fade from our minds; and, unhampered by tradition, we work our own good upon a grateful and responsive rural folk . . . For the task we set before ourselves is a very simple as well as a very beautiful one: To train these people as we find them to a perfectly ideal life just where they are . . ."

Keep in mind that the General Education Board was founded in 1903 by the Rockefeller Foundation—one of the most powerful and wealthiest foundations of its time. What we see here is an attitude that dates back over a hundred years, one of the elite rich of the United States, and even the world, seemingly orchestrating an education curriculum to meet their needs and not necessarily the needs of the student. This is important today, because although these attitudes are over a century old, they have not gone away, and they are the driving force behind your education, my education, and the education of your children. And they are the driving force behind the suppression of financial education even today. You do not need to know about money when you are destined to simply be a cog in someone else's money machine, or a worker on someone else's plantation.

After reading Dr. Fuller's *Grunch of Giants* in 1983, I began to understand why the subject of money is not taught in schools. Up until then, I did not have the courage to criticize the school system; after all, my father was the head of the education system in Hawaii. As the years went by, however, I began to run into others who had similar views on education and why schools do not teach us much about money.

One of the first people I came across who shared my suspicions about education is John Taylor Gatto, author of, among other books, *Weapons of Mass Instruction* and *Dumbing Us Down*. Mr. Gatto was named New York City Teacher of the Year three times and also New York State Teacher of the Year. In 1991, he quit the teaching profession in an op-ed piece in the *Wall Street Journal*, saying, "I can't teach this way any longer. If you hear of a job where I don't have to hurt kids to make a living, let me know. Come fall I'll be looking for work." He brought to my attention that our current system of education comes from the Prussian system, a system designed to create good employees and soldiers, people who blindly follow orders, waiting to be told what to do, including what to do with their money.

As Mr. Gatto said to me recently, "The school system was not designed to teach children to think for themselves. Nor was it developed to just support the present-day notion that we can all be free. In actuality, our current school system is based on a Prussian model that was developed to do just the opposite—to teach children to obey orders and do as they're told. Compliant and obedient students become employees who are content to work for the rich or become soldiers who sacrifice their lives to protect the wealth of the rich."

You can find out more about John Taylor Gatto at his website, *johntaylorgatto.com*. He continues to commit his life to educational reform.

Now, you may or may not believe that there was an intentional conspiracy against teaching about money in the school system. But what you cannot deny is that our schools should receive a failing grade when it comes to financial education. Whether purposefully or not, our system's lack of teaching and instruction on money is a driving force behind the financial oppression many people in our country face today. It is the lack of financial education that has so many highly educated people worried about today's global financial crisis. There are millions of people who have lost their retirement savings following the advice of financial salespeople. Too many people's eyes glaze over when they're forced to talk about their finances.

> **Reader Comment**
>
> *I agree with what you are saying, Robert. I taught primary school children for thirty years before I resigned. I was frustrated by the education system. I felt that we set up our youngsters to fail because we were educating them mainly in things that do not equip them for life. The ancient Greeks believed in teaching people to think. We train our young to do as they are told.*
>
> *—henri54*

Exchanging Freedom for Money

If people do not learn about money, they can end up exchanging their freedom for a paycheck—for a steady job and enough money to pay their bills. Some people spend their lives in constant fear of being fired. That is why, for millions of well-educated workers, job security is more important than financial freedom. For instance, when I was in the Marine Corps, I had the sense that some of my fellow pilots wanted to stay in the service for twenty years, not to fight for our country, but to receive a government paycheck for life. In the world of academia, many teachers dream of the security of tenure more than the pride of teaching.

The lack of financial education in our schools has resulted in millions of free people who are willing to let the government take more control over their lives. Because we do not have enough financial intelligence to solve our own financial problems, we expect the government to do it for us. In the process, we surrender our freedom and give the government more and more control over our lives and our money. Every time the Federal Reserve and the U.S. Treasury *bail out* a bank we are not helping the people; we are protecting the rich. A bailout is welfare for the rich. With each bailout, we surrender more of our financial freedom and our share of public debt grows and grows. Big government taking over our banks and solving our personal financial problems through government programs such as Social Security and Medicare is a form of socialism. I believe socialism makes people weaker and keeps them weak. In Sunday school, I was taught to teach people how to fish—not to give people fish. To me, welfare and bailouts are the purest form of giving people fish instead of teaching them how to provide for themselves.

Taxes, Debt, Inflation, and Retirement

As stated in Chapter 1, the four main forces that keep people struggling financially are taxes, debt, inflation, and retirement. I also stated that these four forces are directly connected to the Federal Reserve and the U.S. Treasury. Again, once the Federal Reserve was allowed to print money and increase the national debt, taxes, inflation, and retirement had to rise. Saying it another way, weakening people financially via taxes, debt, inflation, and retirement allows for a government's greater consolidation of power. When people are struggling financially, they are more willing to have the government save them, unwittingly exchanging their personal freedom for financial salvation.

In 2009, the percentage of Americans who own their homes is dropping. Mortgage foreclosures are at all-time highs. The number of middle-class families is dropping. Savings accounts are smaller, if they exist at all. Family debt is greater. The number of people officially below the poverty line is rising. The number of people who are working beyond the age of sixty-five is increasing. Bankruptcy is going through the roof. And many Americans do not have enough money to retire.

But this is not just a U.S. phenomenon. This is a worldwide personal financial crisis. The conspiracy of the rich affects every nation and all people of the world.

Regardless of whether you subscribe to a conspiracy theory, the facts remain that today the world is in the biggest financial crisis in history and people are looking for the government to save them. And regardless of whether you subscribe to a conspiracy theory, the fact remains that most people leave school without much knowledge about money, taxes, debt, inflation, and retirement and how these financial forces affect their lives.

Who Took My Money?

Take a moment to look at the financial realities many of us live with.

Realities	How they apply to rich and poor
School	Most people learn nothing about money at school. The rich learn about money at home.
Job	Most people get a job working for the rich.
Taxes	Taxes go to the companies that are owned by the rich and friends of political leaders in the form of bailouts. It is estimated that for every $1,000 in taxes you and I pay, less than $200 comes back as a benefit to us. The rich know how to play the system. They own the businesses, make more money, and pay a lower percentage in taxes than employees do.
National debt	When the government talks about trillion-dollar bailouts, it means that for generations to come our kids will be paying for these financial rescues of the rich. Our kids will pay for these bailouts in higher taxes and higher inflation.
House	Mortgage payments go to the banks of the rich. If you take out a $100,000 mortgage at 5 percent for thirty years, you will pay $93,000 in interest alone. This does not include fees, commissions, and service charges.
Retirement	Most people invest in stocks, bonds, and mutual funds for their retirement. Most of this money is invested in businesses of the rich. If the investment loses money, you lose money—and the financial planner, stockbroker, or real estate broker keeps the commission.
Cost of living	Who gets the money we spend for insurance, gasoline, telephone service, electricity, and other necessities of life? The rich. Who benefits if these necessities go up in price? The rich.

Reader Comment

I have noticed a real difference in the medical treatment between the social classes. You either have to be rich (self-insured or insurance provided) or very poor (free government care) to get treatment. I would be curious as to how many small business owners and entrepreneurs are actually affording "good" insurance. Not just some catastrophic plan. I believe the majority of people stay in a job they hate and never take the risks required to start their own business because of fear of losing health insurance for their family.

—Bryan P

The Biggest Lies About Money

My poor dad was a great man, an educated, hardworking, honest-to-a-fault teacher and public servant. Yet when it came to money, he was a liar. When he talked about work, teaching, and life, he often said statements like, "I'm not interested in money." Or, "I'm not doing it for the money." Or, "Money is not that important." Every time I heard him make such statements, I would shake my head. To me these were lies. One day I asked him, "If you're not interested in money, why do you accept a paycheck? Why do you often say, 'I'm not paid what I'm worth'? Why do you look forward to a pay raise?" He had no reply.

Like my dad, many people are uncomfortable with the subject of money. Many people lie or live in denial about the importance of money in their life. It is often said, "Never discuss sex, money, religion, or politics." These subjects are too volatile and primal in nature. That is why most people talk about the weather, sports, what is on TV, or the latest diet fad. These things are superficial—we can live with or without them. We cannot live without money.

Many people subscribe to the saying we discussed in the Introduction of this book, "The love of money is the root of all evil." What they fail to recognize is that, in the context of that saying, money itself is *not* the root of all evil. Many people believe that money has the power to corrupt, and it can.

Many people believe that if kids knew how to make money, they might not want to get a good education, and that, too, is possible. Yet living life takes money, and earning money is one of the facts of life. Most people spend most of their waking hours, and hence their lives, working for money. Many divorces and family breakups are caused by arguments about money.

Keeping people ignorant about money is evil because many people do evil things for money, such as work at a job they do not like, work for people they do not respect, marry people they do not love, take what is not theirs, and expect someone else—like their family or the government—to take care of them when they are capable of taking care of themselves.

Obsolete Ideas

The idea that *money is not important* is an obsolete idea.

Reader Comment

King Solomon, circa 850–900 BC, the wisest and wealthiest man of his age, wrote in Ecclesiastes 10:19, "A feast is made for laughter, wine will make you merry, but money answers all things!"

—drmlnichols

In very simplistic terms, humans have evolved through four basic societal ages. They are:

1. The Hunter-Gatherer Age: In prehistoric times, money was not important. As long as you had a spear, nuts, berries, a cave, and a fire, your needs were met. Land was not important because humans were nomads and followed the food. People lived in tribes with very little hierarchy. The chief did not live that much better than anyone else. During this age, there was only one class of people, and money was not important.

2. The Agrarian Age: Once humans learned how to grow crops and domesticate animals, land became important. Barter was the medium of exchange. Money was not important because even if you didn't have it, you could still survive. During this era, kings and queens ruled the land. The peasants who used the land paid taxes in the form of crops and animals to the family that controlled the land. The words *real estate* literally grew from the term *royal estate*. That is why we still use the word *landlord* in reference to the person to whom we pay our rent. During this age there were two classes of people: the royals and the peasants.

3. The Industrial Age: I believe the Industrial Age began in the 1500s. Christopher Columbus, seeking an ocean passage to Asia, defied the idea that the world was flat. Columbus was not looking for the New World, as many schools teach. He was looking for trade routes for resources like gold, copper, rubber, oil, lumber, furs, spices, industrial metals, and textiles, which were essential to the Industrial Age.

People moved off the farms and moved into the cities, causing a whole new world of problems and opportunities. In the Industrial Age, rather than the peasants paying the king, the new capitalists paid the employee. Instead of land, the new capitalists owned corporations.

Corporations were formed primarily to protect the rich, their investors, and their money. For example, before a ship sailed for the New World, the rich formed a corporation. If the ship was lost and sailors died, the rich were not responsible for the loss of life. All the rich lost was their money.

Today, it is more of the same. If a CEO runs the company onto the rocks, loads the company with excessive debt, pays the executives millions in salaries and bonuses, or steals the employees' retirement funds, the employees lose everything, but the rich are often protected from the losses and liabilities—even the crimes.

Even during the Industrial Age money was not important. That's because the rule of thumb between employee and employer was a job and paycheck for life—job security and financial security. For people of my parents' generation, money was not important because they had company and government pensions, a house that was paid for, and savings in the bank. They did not need to invest their money.

All that changed in 1974, when the U.S. Congress passed the Employee Retirement Income Security Act. This act led to what we know as 401(k), IRA, Keogh, and other retirement plans. In 1974, money became important, and people had to learn to manage their own money or die poor, living on Social Security, as my dad did after he lost his government job.

4. The Information Age: We live in the Information Age. In the Information Age, money is important. More specifically, *knowledge* about money is essential in the Information Age. The problem is that our educational system is still in the Industrial Age, and in the minds of most intellectuals and academics, money is not important. Most of these people are operating on old, outdated, and obsolete ideas of money. But money is important. Today money is a key aspect of life. Today *financial security* is more important than *job security*.

Reader Comment

Up until very recently, I have always equated job security with financial security; I never thought about it any other way than that. Now I know better.

—jamesbzc

Financial Education

Today, it is essential to have three different types of education. They are:

1. Academic education: This includes the ability to read, write, and solve basic math problems. *In the Information Age, one's ability to keep up with changing information is more important than what one learned yesterday.*

2. Professional education: This is knowledge of a trade in which to earn money. For example, one goes to medical school to become a doctor or to a police academy to join the police force. Today, it takes much more professional education to be financially successful. *In the Information Age, professional education is essential to job security.*

3. Financial education: Financial education is essential to financial intelligence. Financial intelligence is not so much about how much money you make, but how much money you keep, how hard your money works for you, and how many generations you pass your money on to. *In the Information Age, financial education is essential to financial security.*

Most school systems do a pretty good job with academic and professional education. They fail when it comes to financial education.

Why Financial Education Is Important in the Information Age

We also live in a world of information overload. Information is everywhere, on the Internet, TV, radio, in magazines, newsletters, computers, cell phones, schools, businesses, churches, billboards, and on and on. Education is essential to processing all of this information. That is why financial education is important.

Today, financial information is coming at us from all directions. Without financial education, a person is less able to process financial information into personal meaning. For example, when someone says a stock has a P/E of 6, or that a piece of real estate has a cap rate of 7 percent, what does that mean to you? Or when a financial planner says the stock market goes up an average of 8 percent a year, what does that make you think? Maybe you ask, "Is that information true, and is 8 percent a year a good or bad return?" Again, without education a person cannot translate information into personal meaning. Information without education is limited in value. This book is dedicated to adding to your financial education by teaching you the new rules of money, and how the new rules affect your life whether your realize it or not.

New Rule of Money #1: Money Is Knowledge

The first new rule of money is: *Money is knowledge.*

Today, you do not need money to make money. You simply need knowledge. For example, if a stock is priced at $100, on some stock exchanges you can *short* that stock, which means sell shares that you do not own. For instance, let's say I borrow 1,000 shares valued at $100 from the exchange, sell them, and put $100,000 in my account. Then the stock falls to $65, and I go back to the exchange, purchase 1,000 shares for $65,000, return for a full refund the 1,000 shares I borrowed at $100 a share, and keep the $35,000 difference, less fees, commissions, and transaction costs. That is in essence what it means to short a stock. To make this money all I needed was knowledge. First I needed to know that the concept of short selling existed, and second I needed to know how to use the method. I can do similar transactions in business and in real estate.

As this book progresses, I will use similar examples of money being made out of nothing—nothing but knowledge. Many of these examples will be real-life transactions that I've personally completed, and on top of these transactions creating money out of nothing but knowledge, my returns were also higher, gained with much less risk than investing in mutual funds, and resulted in little to nothing in taxes.

Today, in the Information Age, fortunes are won and lost in the blink of an eye as a result of good or bad information. As most of you know, many people recently lost trillions of dollars due to bad advice, bad information, and a lack of financial education. The frightening thing is that most of those people who dished out the bad financial advice are still handing out that same bad information. A famous biblical quote is "My people perish for lack of knowledge." Today, many people are perishing financially because they follow the old rules such as save money and get out of debt. Or they believe investing is risky, when it is the lack of financial education, experience, and bad financial advisors that is much more risky. Today, you can make money without money. You can also lose your life savings in a blink of an eye. That is what I mean when I say money is knowledge.

Reader Comments

I would say that this notion is correct, but I would also state emphatically that ACTION on knowledge is actually more important. That one knows how to short a stock, or build a website, or whatever, does not necessarily translate into that person taking the actions necessary to create wealth.

—ramasart

I would state the maxim in reverse, but the essence of this rule is that having the correct information is much better than simply having money. A rich man may not need to fear being broke, for he knows the tactics that may be exercised in order to regain his wealth. Conversely, the man who holds a significant amount of money today may live in great uncertainty because he does not know how to increase his holdings through new skills—new information that he has not been able to apply.

—dlsmith29

In Conclusion

It is bad enough that our schools do not teach students much, if anything, about money. But today, in 2009, many of the rich are fighting President Obama's economic stimulus plans to spend more on improving education. Only time will tell whether Obama's stimulus plan will work, but regardless, I do think spending more on education is vital to developing a strong economy, country, and free world.

I am an advocate for education. In Asian culture, the most respected professional is the teacher. Yet in Western culture, teachers are the lowest paid of educated professionals. I believe that if we valued education like we say we do, we would pay our teachers more money and build better, safer schools in bad neighborhoods. To me, it is a crime that in America our real estate taxes determine the quality of education a child receives. In other words, schools in poor neighborhoods receive less tax money than schools in rich neighborhoods. Talk about a conspiracy of the rich!

I also believe that if we truly valued education, we would teach people financial literacy because we would recognize that money is a central and important aspect of our existence. So while many so-called "advocates of education" deride my ideas, I simply ask: Why continue advocating a system that is designed to create cogs instead of freethinkers, and a system designed to suppress financial knowledge rather than create financially literate people who can prosper in a capitalist system?

Whether you believe as I do that there is a conspiracy in education, the fact remains that a sound education, one that includes financial education, is more important today than ever before. When I was a kid, if one of my classmates did not do well in school, he or she still could get a high-paying job working for the sugar plantation or a factory. Today, as factories close and jobs move overseas, a child who does poorly in school will probably do poorly in life. This is why the world needs better schools, safer schools, better-paid teachers, and more financial education.

In the Information Age, we are overloaded with data. Education gives us the power to translate that information into meaning, meaning we can use to make our lives better. Give us the power to solve our own financial problems rather than expect the government to solve our problems for us. Stop the bailouts and all the handouts. It is time to put an end to the conspiracy of the rich. It is time to teach us how to fish.

Chapter 3

The Conspiracy Against Our Money: The Bank Never Goes Broke

The Bank never "goes broke." If the Bank runs out of money, it may issue as much more as may be needed by merely writing on any ordinary piece of paper.

—Rule from the game of Monopoly

The Day the Dollar Died

On August 15, 1971, the U.S. dollar died. On that day, without authorization from Congress, President Nixon severed the relationship between the U.S. dollar and gold, and the dollar became Monopoly money. After that, the biggest economic boom in history began.

Today, in 2009, as the global economy collapses, central bankers of the world are creating trillions of dollars, yen, pesos, euros, and pounds by following Monopoly's rules for bankers.

The problem is that Monopoly is just a game. Applying Monopoly's rules in real life is a recipe for the destruction of society as we know it. As the noted English economist John Maynard Keynes once said, "There is no subtler, no surer means of overturning the existing basis of society than to debauch the currency. The process engages all the hidden forces of economic law on the side of destruction and it does it in a manner which not one man in a million is able to diagnose." Today, our economy is sick because the runaway printing presses of the Federal Reserve are flooding our monetary system with funny money that debauches our existing currency, and no one is able to diagnose the problem, just as Keynes warned so many years ago.

Reader Comments

Monopoly money...John Kenneth Galbraith once famously said, "The process by which banks create money is so simple that the mind is repelled."

—hellspark

I never knew that rule existed in Monopoly! Scary how true to life it is. The examples I think of are bank loans and credit cards.

—ajoyflower

Money from Nothing

One reason why people ignored the advice of Keynes, Nixon's 1971 change, and others on the destruction of money is because debauching the currency suddenly made people feel rich. Credit cards came in the mail, and shopping became the national sport. Many in the middle class became pseudomillionaires as their homes seemed to magically increase in value. They came to believe their retirement would be financed by profits in the stock market. People took out home equity loans to pay for family vacations. Rather than one car, families had a Mercedes, a minivan, and an SUV. Kids went to college and were strapped with student loans that take years to pay off. The middle class celebrated their newfound wealth by dining in fancy restaurants, dressing in designer clothes, driving Porsches, and living in McMansions—all financed by debt.

We are now coming out of the biggest economic boom in history. The problem is that the boom was caused by debt, not money; by inflation, not production; by borrowing, not working. In many ways it was *money for nothing*—because money *was* nothing. As Keynes would say, our money was debauched. We looked rich, but society as we knew it was collapsing.

After 1971, central bankers could create money by merely printing more paper. In today's digital age, bankers do not need paper to create money. As you read this, trillions of dollars, yen, euros, pesos, and pounds are being created electronically—out of thin air. According to the rules of Monopoly, you and I may go broke, but the Banker never does. After all, the global game of Monopoly must go on.

Witnessing the Change

In 1972, I was a Marine Corps pilot stationed on board an aircraft carrier off the coast of Vietnam. The war was not going well. We knew we were losing, but as Marines we could not dwell on that fact. As a Marine officer, my job was to keep my men positive and focused on living and, at the same time, ready to give their lives for each other and our country. I could not let my men see my doubts and fears, and they did not let me see theirs.

Keeping morale high was difficult because we knew the tide of battle had turned against us. We also knew that we were losing the war at home. Every time we saw pictures of student protesters burning draft cards and the American flag, we began to question who was right and who was wrong.

Some of the more popular rock songs of the era were against the war. The lyrics of one went, "War, what is it good for? Absolutely nothin'." Rather than let the lyrics get us down, my crew and I would loudly shout that line as we flew into battle. For some strange reason that song gave us the courage to do what we had to do and to face the ultimate reality—death.

The night before every mission I would go up to the bow of the aircraft carrier, sit alone, and allow the wind to separate my thoughts from my fears. I did not pray to live. Instead, I asked that if the dawn was to bring my last day, I wanted to choose how I would face death. I did not want to die a coward. I did not want fear to dictate my life.

That is why when I returned from the war I did not seek job security—I did not let the fear of financial insecurity dictate my life. Instead, I became an entrepreneur. When I lost everything after my first business failed, I did not let fear, frustration, and doubt stop me from doing what I needed to do. I simply picked up the pieces and got back to work rebuilding my business. Learning from my business mistakes was the best business school I could have attended. And I am still in that school today.

In recent years, while the stock and real estate markets were booming and fools were rushing in to invest, I did not let greed take over my logic. Today, during this economic crisis, I have the same fears as everyone else. However, I simply do not let fear stop me from doing what I must do. Rather than see only the crisis, I do my best to see the opportunities the crisis presents. That is a lesson I learned in the Vietnam War, and that, for me, was what war was good for.

There was something else war was good for. The Vietnam War gave me a ringside seat to witness one of the biggest changes in world history: the change in the rules of money.

A Letter from Home

In the war zone, mail call was the most important part of our day. Letters from home were treasured as a connection to the most important people in our lives.

One day, I received a letter from my rich dad. I rarely heard from him because he was not my real dad. He was my best friend's father. Since the age of nine, my rich dad was like a second father to me, and he was my financial mentor. His note began in bold letters: **"The rules of money have been changed."** Further on in the letter, he advised me to read the *Wall Street Journal* and follow the price of gold. President Nixon took the United States off the gold standard in 1971, he explained, stating more than once that the price of gold was at one time fixed at $35 dollars per ounce, but no longer. Once Nixon severed the link between the dollar and gold, gold's price started to rise. By the time I read his letter, gold was fluctuating from $70 to $80 an ounce.

At the time, I had no idea what he was so excited about. When I was a kid, my rich dad rarely talked about gold, except to say that it backed our money. What that meant, and its significance, went over my young head. Yet, just by the tone in his letter I received that day in Vietnam, I knew he was excited about the change Nixon made. His message was simply this: With our dollar separated from gold, the rich were about to play games with money like the world had never seen before. He explained, "As the price of gold goes up and down relative to the dollar, there will be the biggest booms and busts the world has ever seen. With gold separated from the dollar, we are entering a period of extreme financial instability. Inflation will go through the roof. The rich will get very rich and others will be wiped out." He closed his letter with, "The dollar is now officially Monopoly money, and the rules of Monopoly are now the world's new rules of money."

Again, I did not fully understand his message at the time. But now that I'm older and wiser, I believe he was saying that this was his time to become very rich. This was the opportunity of his lifetime—and he was right. My rich dad became very rich while the economy boomed. My poor dad clung to job security and missed the biggest boom in history.

Finally Reading the Rules

A few days later, I went to the officers' lounge, found a well-worn game of Monopoly, and took up a game with a group of pilots. Since I had played the game countless times, I did not bother to reread the rules. But as the game went on, I recalled rich dad's words about the rules of Monopoly being the world's new rules of money. Thumbing through the rule book, I came across the rule rich dad referred to. It stated:

> The Bank never "goes broke." If the Bank runs out of money, it may issue as much more as may be needed by merely writing on any ordinary piece of paper.

Today, thanks in part to my rich dad's simple warning, I know why we have a massive global financial crisis on our hands. For the rich and powerful, the rule change meant they could print money on any ordinary piece of paper. Our money had been debauched.

Prior to 1971, our money was golden because it was backed by gold. Today, our money is toxic, making the people and businesses of the world very sick. It is like drinking polluted water and wondering why you feel ill. By changing the rules of money, the rich could legally steal our wealth via the money system itself.

Real Life Education Begins

In 1972, I followed my rich dad's advice and read the *Wall Street Journal* religiously, looking for articles about gold. Thus began my education on gold and its relationship to money. I read every article I could find on the subject. But I didn't have to just read to learn these important lessons. Practical examples were on display all around me.

One day, I flew from my aircraft carrier to a small village outside of Da Nang, a major city in South Vietnam. Having a few hours to spend before we were scheduled to return to the ship, my crew chief and I walked into the village. He wanted to buy mangoes and papayas, exotic fruits we did not get back on the ship.

After selecting an assortment of fruits, he reached into his flight suit pocket and pulled out a wad of piasters, the paper money of South Vietnam. "No, no, no," said the fruit vendor, waving her hand. She was letting us know she would not accept "p," as the money was often called. My crew chief then pulled out a $50 bill and handed it to her. She reluctantly took the bill, scowling as she inspected the greenback suspiciously. Finally, she said, "OK, you wait," and ran to another stall, transacted something, ran back, and handed my crew chief the bag of fruit.

"What was that all about?" I asked my crew chief.

"She's getting ready to run," he replied. "She is planning to leave the country."

"How do you know?" I asked.

"She is choosy about her money," he replied. "She knows her country's money, the piaster, is worthless. Nobody outside of South Vietnam will accept it. Why would anyone accept the money of a country that will soon no longer exist? She also knows the U.S. dollar is dropping in value as the price of gold rises. That's why she ran to the other stall to change my money for gold."

Walking back toward the helicopter, I said, "I noticed she gave you change in piasters."

"I noticed that, too," my crew chief said, smiling. "I have a bag of fruit and a pocketful of p's, and she has gold. She may be just a fruit vendor, but when it comes to money, she's no fool."

Three weeks later my crew chief and I were flying north in search of an ancient gold mine, hoping to buy some gold. I thought that I could buy gold for a better price behind enemy lines. Risking my life and the lives of my crew, I found out that regardless of where I was in the world, the price of gold was the same. My real-world education in the new rules of money and the relationship between Monopoly money and gold was under way.

Public Concern

In 2009, as the economy worsens, there will be growing unrest. Even now, people know something is wrong. The problem is that they don't know what is wrong *exactly*. Again, as John Maynard Keynes said, "The process [of debauching currency] engages all the hidden forces of economic law on the side of destruction and it does it in a manner which not one man in a million is able to diagnose."

Today, people do what they have been taught to do; they go to school, work hard, pay their bills, save, invest their money in mutual funds, and hope that things will return to normal. That is why everyone is clamoring for his or her share of the bailout. Few people realize that the root of our problem *is* our money—the very thing they work for and hang on to. Few people realize that those who control the money supply want us to need more and more of their toxic money. The more we need money, the more money they can print. The more we need money, the weaker we become. The more we need money, the more we're headed toward socialism. Rather than teaching people to fish, the government *gives* people fish, and people become dependent upon government to solve their money problems.

Don't Bank on It

Ironically, the world is looking to the Federal Reserve and the U.S. Treasury to solve our money problems, even though those institutions are causing the problems. As we've discussed in this book, the Federal Reserve is not federal, and it is not American. The Fed is owned by some of the richest families in the world. The Federal Reserve is a banking cartel just as OPEC is an oil cartel. Few people realize it has no reserves because it has no money. It does not need a big vault to hold money. Why do you need to store money when Monopoly's rules for bankers apply? The Federal Reserve Bank is not a bank—that idea is as illusionary as our money.

Some people say the creation of the Federal Reserve was unconstitutional. They think the Fed's creation has harmed the world economy—and it has. There are others who say the Federal Reserve System is the best thing that has ever happened to the world. They say that it has helped bring wealth to the world like never before—and it has.

It does little good to question the motives of the Federal Reserve's founders. The reality is that today the Fed runs the game. Rather than ask what President Obama is going to do about the economic crisis, it is better to ask yourself, "What am I going to do?" Rather than ask if the trillion dollar stimulus package will work, it is smarter to ask yourself, Where does that trillion dollars come from? Is it sitting in someone's vault?

In very simple terms, the central banks of the world can only do two things. They are:

1. Create money out of thin air, just like the rules of Monopoly allow—something they are doing today by the trillions.

2. Lend money they do not have. When you borrow money from a bank, the bank does not need to have that money in the vault.

The Zero-Sum Game

Historically, every time governments have printed their own money, fiat money, that money eventually reverted to its true value: zero. That's because paper money is a zero-sum game. Will the same happen to the U.S. dollar, the yen, the peso, the pound, and the euro? Will history repeat itself?

Now, I can hear many proud, red-blooded Americans saying, "This will not happen in America. Our money will never go to zero." Unfortunately, it already has—many times. During the Revolutionary War, the American government printed a currency known as the "continental." After the government printed too many continentals, our money became a joke, giving birth to the phrase "not worth a continental." The same thing happened to the Confederate dollar. When I need a reminder of money going to zero, all I have to do is think about the woman fruit vendor in Vietnam and her aversion to the piaster. That was not that long ago. It's not ancient history.

Today, the entire world is running on Monopoly money. But what if the party is over? Will bailouts save us? Ironically, every time there is a bailout our national debt grows bigger, we pay more in taxes, the rich get richer, and our money's value edges closer to zero. Every time our governments print more money, our money becomes less valuable. We work harder for less and less, and our savings are worth less and less.

I am not saying today's Monopoly money will go to zero. I'm not saying it won't, either. Yet, if history does repeat itself, and if the U.S. dollar goes to zero, the worldwide chaos will be cataclysmic. It will be the biggest wealth transfer in world history. The rich will get richer. And the poor will most definitely get poorer. The middle class will be wiped out.

Apocalypse Now

As our financial crisis grows worse, the secrets about the new rules of money are harder to keep. This crisis is leading us to a financial apocalypse.

For many religious people, the word *apocalypse* is often used to refer to the end of the world. This is not the type of apocalypse I am referring to. The word *apocalypse* comes from the Greek word meaning "lifting of the veil." It is a term applied to the disclosure of something hidden from the majority of humankind. Simply said, apocalypse means "secrets are being revealed."

If you read *Rich Dad Poor Dad*, you may recall the subtitle of the book was "What the Rich Teach Their Kids About Money that the Poor and Middle Class Do Not." For many people, reading my book was an apocalypse, a lifting of the veil, a disclosure of something hidden from the majority of humankind. In 1997, when *Rich Dad Poor Dad* was first released, it caused a howl of protest because it stated, "Your house is not an asset." A few years later, as the subprime mortgage mess was revealed, millions of people lost their homes, and people around the world lost trillions of dollars investing in subprime mortgages and other forms of toxic debt, partly caused by bankers creating debauched money out of thin air. *Rich Dad Poor Dad* was not a book about real estate, as some would claim. It was a book about financial knowledge—knowledge handed down from a father to a son.

The Name of the Game Is Debt

In overly simple terms, after 1971, money became debt. For the economy to expand, you and I had to get into debt. That is why credit cards came in the mail and home equity loans were available to people who had less than stellar credit.

Technically, the money in your wallet is not money. It is an IOU. Our money is debt. The reason the current financial crisis is so severe is because the banker's rules of Monopoly money allowed our biggest banks and Wall Street to package debt and sell it to the world as assets. According to *Time* magazine, from 2000 to 2007, America's biggest export was debt. What the smartest and brightest minds in the banking and investment world were doing was not much different than when a poor person refinances his or her home to pay off credit cards.

If we as a people knew that our money was debauched, Monopoly money, we might not be in the financial mess we are in today. If people had a financial education, there would be more than one person in a million who could diagnose our financial problem. If people had more financial education, they would not blindly believe that their house is an asset, that saving money is smart, that diversification would protect them from risk, and that investing for the long term in mutual funds is a smart way to invest. But because of our lack of financial education, the powers that be are able to continue with their destructive monetary policies. It is to their benefit that you and I are in the dark. This is why the rich had to first take over our educational system before they could flood the world with debt. This is why our schools do not teach us about money.

Reader Comment

In reading this, I am reminded of what Henry Ford said about the Great Depression of the 1930s, and I paraphrase: that he was afraid that it might not last long enough, because his countrymen would not have had the time to learn from it.

—kuujuarapik

New Rule of Money #2: Learn How to Use Debt

Many people teach that debt is bad or evil. They preach that it is smart to pay off your debts and to stay out of debt. And to an extent they are right. There is good debt and bad debt. It *is* wise to pay off bad debt—or not get into bad debt to begin with. Simply said, bad debt takes money out of your pocket, and good debt puts money into your pocket. A credit card is bad debt because people use credit to buy depreciating items like big-screen televisions. A loan for an investment property that you rent out is good debt if the asset's cash flow covers the debt payment and puts money in your pocket.

Reader Comment

This is the key concept of getting rich. This is key! I do not pretend to be any great businessperson. I own a clinic, and I am a practicing professional. I operate mostly from the S quadrant, but I'm slowly increasing my B quadrant in terms of income and knowledge. I have learned firsthand how one piece of medical equipment can become a fabulous asset, even though it is financed with debt.

—grgluck

The people who preach the evils of debt do not understand that debt is essential to the American economy. Whether that is good or bad is debatable. What is not debatable is that without debt, our entire economy would collapse. That is why our government is issuing record numbers of bonds to raise money. That is why it is engaging in *deficit* spending like never before. The government's greatest fear is deflation, and the one way to combat deflation is by inflation. And the one way to create inflation is by debt.

I know President Obama promises change and hope. But given his choices of Tim Geithner as treasury secretary and former Treasury Secretary Larry Summers as head of the National Economic Council—the people who accelerated this crisis during President Clinton's administration—nothing is going to change if you and I do not get back into debt. If you and I stop borrowing, and the banks stop lending, there will be a crash and probably a depression.

The reason a prolonged credit freeze would lead to a depression is because the economy now grows by you and me getting into debt, not by goods produced. In 2003, President George W. Bush said, "It is in our national interest that more people own their own home." Obviously, he was encouraging the virtues of home ownership because he wanted more people to get into debt to save the economy. You may notice that today, when banks foreclose on a property, they do not want the house. Homes are not assets. You are the asset—or rather your ability to pay the interest on the loan is the asset.

Of course, living by the sword of debt also means dying by the sword of debt. By 2007, as the overwhelming mountain of credit card debt and home equity debt reached its peak, the United States and the world could not absorb any more debt. Today, millions of people are finding out why, in 1997, in *Rich Dad Poor Dad,* I stated, "Your home is not an asset."

In Gold We Trust

In 1957, the words "In God We Trust" were added to the U.S. dollar bill. In 1971, the dollar was severed from gold. According to a recent piece in *Vanity Fair*, the purchasing power of the dollar has dropped by 87 percent. As stated earlier, all fiat currencies, government-sponsored Monopoly money, have eventually gone to their true value—zero. In 1970, 1,000 dollars would have bought approximately 28 ounces of gold. By March 2009, with gold at approximately $900 an ounce, those 28 ounces of gold could be sold for around $25,000—even after the largest stock market crash in history.

In 1924, John Maynard Keynes, who warned against the debauching of money, dismissed gold as a "barbarous relic." Unfortunately, he did not realize how much the Federal Reserve and our government could debauch our currency once the rules of money were changed in 1971.

In 1952, the ratio of household debt to disposable income was less than 40 percent. In other words, if you had $1,000 after taxes, only $400 went to debt. By 2007, it was 133 percent. Since wages were not going up, people were living on credit cards and home equity loans. Today, Americans carry over $2.56 trillion in consumer debt.

Even our best and brightest bankers fell for the ruse. In 1980, bank debt was around 21 percent of the total output of the United States (GDP). By 2007, it was 116 percent.

In 2004, the Securities and Exchange Commission allowed the top five banks to print as much money as they needed to by dissolving the reserve limit of 12 to 1—just to save the economy. A reserve limit of 12 to 1 means for every dollar in the bank's accounts, the bank can lend out twelve dollars in debt. By allowing the top five banks to dissolve the 12-to-1 reserve limit, these banks could now effectively print money at will. Again, as the rules of Monopoly state:

> The Bank never "goes broke." If the Bank runs out of money, it may issue as much more as may be needed by merely writing on any ordinary piece of paper.

Unfortunately, allowing the biggest banks to print nearly unlimited amounts of money did not save the economy. It only made the problem worse.

New Rule of Money #3: Learn to Control Cash Flow

If you want to be financially secure and possibly rich, you will need to know how to control your personal cash flow as well as monitor the global flow of jobs, people, and money.

Running Money

The reason I wrote about the fruit vendor in Vietnam earlier in this chapter was to emphasize the relationship between money and "running" during economic crisis. On March 2, 2009, the Dow fell 299 points, to 6,763, down from a high of 14,164 points on October 9, 2007. In very simple terms, this meant that money was *running* out of the stock market, just as the fruit vendor was getting ready to run by exchanging her piasters and her dollars for gold. In 2009, using my rich dad's words, cash is *flowing* out of the stock market. The question is, Where is the money flowing?

The most important words in business and investing are *cash flow*. That is why the educational game I developed is called CASHFLOW. One of the most important things my rich dad taught me to do is control my *personal* cash flow and monitor the *world's* cash flow. He taught me to monitor global cash flow by observing three things.

1. Jobs: For years jobs have been flowing overseas. Today, in America, jobs are flowing out of Detroit as General Motors collapses. That means Detroit's economy is suffering.

2. People: Just as that Vietnamese woman was running, people today are running. They run toward areas where there are jobs. I like to invest in markets where people are moving to, not from.

3. Cash: The same Vietnamese woman wanted money that was global. That is why she exchanged her piasters and dollars for gold. The same is happening today. The stock market is crashing because cash is flowing out of equities into savings, mattresses, bonds, and gold.

Debt, Money, Cash Flow

Learning how to use debt is one of the most important skills a person can learn. And an important lesson is that debt is only as good as your cash flow. If I ran the educational system, I would teach students the differences between good debt and bad debt, and how to use good debt to make cash flow into their bank accounts rather than out of their bank accounts. To use good debt effectively requires financial IQ. Since our money is now debt, teaching people to use debt wisely would make our economy stronger.

In my book *Rich Dad's Increase Your Financial IQ*, I go into much detail on how I use debt with low risk and very high returns. Even as the economy collapses today, my investments with debt continue to have positive cash flow. One reason my investments remain strong is because my partners and I buy apartment houses where there are jobs—in areas where people and money are flowing. In simple terms, real estate is not worth much if there are no jobs, because jobs attract people, and where people are flowing, cash is flowing.

Reader Comment

What is most surprising, though, is that I learned nothing about cash flow in advanced accounting and finance classes while earning a master's in business administration. Wouldn't you think it would be something they would teach? I learned how to figure out the numbers, and where to place them when you are trying to keep track. They do not teach the SIGNIFICANCE of cash flow in building or creating wealth.

—drmbear

Hope vs. Education

Rather than hope that President Obama will save the world, I believe it is more intelligent to become smarter with your money. Since the first New Rule of Money is *Money is knowledge,* your knowledge of money must include learning to use debt and learning to control your personal cash flows, as well as monitoring the flows of jobs, people, and money throughout the world.

I created the CASHFLOW board game to teach the skills of taking control of your personal cash flow and using debt to have cash flow into your bank account—not out of it. CASHFLOW has been called Monopoly on steroids. There are three levels of the game:

Level #1: CASHFLOW for Kids, for children ages five to twelve
Rather than use words and numbers, CASHFLOW for Kids uses colors and pictures to teach children basic fundamentals about money and cash flow and how to use them wisely.

Level #2: CASHFLOW 101, the fundamentals of investing
This game teaches the differences between assets and liabilities and using debt wisely. It combines accounting principles with investing principles.

Level #3: CASHFLOW 202, technical investing
This game teaches the principles of investing in up and down markets. As you know, millions of people lost trillions of dollars when the market crashed. CASHFLOW 202 teaches you how to profit in up markets as well as down markets.

You can find out more about the games from my website RichDad.com. There are also thousands of official and unofficial CASHFLOW Clubs all over the world where you can learn how to play the game for free or at low cost.

Official CASHFLOW Clubs subscribe to an online service from the Rich Dad Company. They also offer our standardized ten-step curriculum designed to increase your financial IQ and are asked to adhere to the principles of the Rich Dad Company. If there is not a club in your area you may want to start your own club, because teaching is one of the best ways of learning.

In Conclusion

Finally, always remember the bank never goes broke—but you and I can. But there is good news! A bank can print its own money, and so can you and I. In later chapters I will show you how I print my own money by using my financial intelligence, often using debt, and by controlling cash flow.

Chapter 4

The Conspiracy Against Our Wealth

Are You Prepared for the Coming Depression?

Question: *How many years did the Great Depression last?*

A. 25

B. 4

C. 16

D. 7

The answer to this question depends on the measurement you use. If you use the stock market as a measurement, the last depression lasted twenty-five years. In September 1929, the Dow hit an all-time high of 381. By July 8, 1932, the market had lost a staggering 89 percent of its value. On that day, the volume on the New York Stock Exchange contracted to around one million shares traded, and the Dow sank to a low of 41 points. That low was the bottom of the bear market, and from there the market soared bullishly—even in the middle of a depression. Still, even with a bull market, it took twenty-five years, from 1929 to 1954, for the Dow to pass its high of 381.

In the recent past, we witnessed another all-time high in the Dow. In October 2007, the Dow soared to 14,164. A little over a year later, the Dow was almost 50 percent lower. If 1929 to 1954 is any indication, the Dow may break 14,164 again in 2032.

On March 10, 2009, the Dow shot up over 379 points to 6,926 in one day—making in that day nearly the same point gain made from 1932 to 1954 after the last depression. Wall Street celebrated, even though it was reported earlier in the week that more than 650,000 jobs were lost in February.

As I write, people are saying, "The worst is over. The bottom has finally come." Fed Chairman Ben Bernanke says he is hopeful the recession will be over by fall 2009. But the March 10 stock market rally was caused by Citigroup reporting a profitable first two months of 2009 via a "leaked" memo—even though it has billions in toxic debt. I wonder what these guys are smoking.

Even in the middle of the market's recent optimism, the specter of possible depression still hangs over the financial world. I tend to not be as optimistic as some about the short-term prospects of the U.S. and global economies. Don't get me wrong: I am *not* hoping for a depression. Far from it. No one in his or her right mind wants another Great Depression. But if this recession slides into a depression, it might be best to start preparing now, because not all depressions are alike and not all depressions are depressing.

Rich and Poor Experiences of the Depression

My rich dad and my poor dad were in elementary school at the start of the Great Depression. That experience affected the course of their lives forever. One dad became very rich from the lessons he learned during the depression. The other remained poor and financially timid for the rest of his life.

POOR DEPRESSION

My poor dad's father—my grandfather—lost everything in the Great Depression. He lost his business and priceless beachfront real estate on the island of Maui, Hawaii. My grandfather was an entrepreneur, so he did not have a steady paycheck to protect the family. When my grandfather's business failed, my dad's family lost everything. The Great Depression was a terrible experience for my dad.

The financial hardship of the Great Depression caused my poor dad to embrace the ideas of having job security, saving money, buying a house, staying out of debt, and securing a government pension. He did not want to be an entrepreneur. He wanted the security of a government job. He did not believe in investing, because he saw my grandfather lose everything in the stock market and in real estate. My dad held on to those values all his life. For my poor dad, *security* was more important than *wealth*. His memories of the last depression stayed with him all his life.

Reader Comment

My grandmother, who was an adult during the Great Depression, reused everything, including paper towels. She'd dry them like dishrags and reuse them until they had shredded into tiny pieces. On the rare occasion of dinner out, she'd stuff all the bread and butter into her handbag. Those were breakfast the next morning!

—Rromatowski

RICH DEPRESSION

My rich dad's family struggled financially even before the Great Depression. His father was ill for years and passed away shortly after the depression started. Early in life, my rich dad became the man of the house and the sole provider of income. As he was a young man without an education and with few job prospects, the Great Depression forced my rich dad to become an entrepreneur as a teenager. He took over the family store and grew the business.

Although his family struggled, my rich dad did not ask for government support. He did not ask for welfare. The depression caused my rich dad to grow up faster, and he learned to do well financially. The lessons of the depression turned him into a rich man.

Socialist vs. Capitalist

My poor dad grew up to become a *socialist*. He was school-smart but not street-smart. He strongly believed the government should take care of people for life.

My rich dad grew up to become a *capitalist*. He did not finish school, but he did become street-smart. He believed in building businesses that provided stable income for his family and his workers' families. He believed that people should learn to take care of themselves. As a capitalist, he believed in teaching people to fish.

Socialism Taking Control

Socialism took control during the last depression. Massive government welfare programs were created. Rather than teaching people to fish, we gave people fish—even rich people. If the United States were a true capitalist nation, we would let the economy fall, not prop it up with bailout upon bailout. Bear markets, market crashes, and depressions are the economy's way of hitting the reset button. Recessions and depressions correct the mistakes made and reveal the crimes committed during the boom times.

Today, instead of hitting the reset button, we hand out trillions of dollars to the incompetent, the fraudulent, and the obsolete. Bear markets exist to clean out the faults, scams, and inefficiencies that grew from a preceding bull market. Rather than let the bear market do its work, we let the government pay billions of dollars in bailout money to bankers who loaded the world with fraudulent debt, when we should be sending those bankers to jail. Businesses like General Motors that grew too fat and lazy during the good times to compete in the bad times are saved from bankruptcy. Executives who are firing thousands of workers are given cash bonuses and golden parachutes as the businesses they were entrusted with protecting and growing instead contract and, as the company's share price drops, investors lose their money.

That is *not* capitalism. Today's bailout government is socialism—for the rich. In many ways, it is worse than Marxism or communism, because at least those systems had the illusion of being for the people. Those systems at least preached the redistribution of money from the rich to the poor, even if they didn't practice it. Our bailouts, however, take money from the poor in the form of taxes and give it to the rich. I am not pointing the finger at President Obama. This cash heist has been going on for years. It has become a practice for the very rich to use our government to take from the poor and middle class and to give to the rich. Today, we've made it a practice to tax those who produce and to reward the lazy, the crooked, and the incompetent.

History Repeats

It has been said that a depression comes along approximately every seventy-five years. If this is true, then the coming depression should have started around 2005. One of the reasons depressions are hard to pin down is because there is no real working definition for a *depression*. Economists only define *recessions*.

One reason why we may not have gone into a depression earlier is because the Federal Reserve and the U.S. government have manipulated the money supply to keep the economy afloat. They are doing the same thing today. If they do a good job, the economy will be saved. If they fail, that failure may lead to a depression.

Better Definitions

It took until 2008 for economists to finally declare we were in a recession, after we had been in a recession for a year. During that year, Lehman Brothers failed, the stock market crashed, big banks accepted billions of dollars in bailout money, the automakers went broke, people lost their homes and their jobs, and California prepared to hand out IOUs because it was out of money. In spite of all this financial bad news, it took a year for economists to figure out that we were in a recession. I wonder how long it will take for them to declare a depression. Obviously, we need better definitions of *recession* and *depression*—or at least better economists! Personally, I have simple definitions of *recession* and *depression*. To quote the old saying: *If your neighbor loses his job, we are in a recession. If I lose my job, we are in a depression.*

In 2008, more than two million Americans lost their jobs. In February 2009 alone, more than 651,000 jobs were lost.

The Depression that Never Ended

Stepping back and looking at the past seventy-five years, you can make a case that the last depression never ended. Many of today's financial problems stem from issues from the last depression that were never solved. The problems were simply pushed forward onto our generation. For example, Social Security was created in 1933, and the price for that government program will explode, as 75 million baby boomers began retiring in 2008. A solution created to combat the last depression has grown into a mega-problem today. Social Security also led to the creation of Medicare and Medicaid, which are financial problems five times bigger than Social Security. The Federal Housing Administration led to the creation of Fannie Mae and Freddie Mac, and those two agencies are at the center of today's subprime mess. In other words, stepping back and looking over the past seventy-five years, the last depression never ended; the socialist solutions created to keep it at bay just keep getting more expensive.

Fixes or Farces?

Following is a short summary of government solutions created to address the Great Depression.

1. Social Security, Medicare, and Medicaid: Today these creations are a $65 trillion problem and growing.

2. The Federal Deposit Insurance Corporation (FDIC): The FDIC protects bankers more than it protects savers. Because deposits are insured, the FDIC rewards bankers who take greater risks, punishes bankers who are prudent, and covers up banking fraud. Deposit insurance gives savers a false sense of security while their savings are put at greater risk. The FDIC helped cause the banking crisis and credit meltdown. I'll write more about this in the next chapter.

3. The Federal Housing Administration (FHA): The FHA led to politics taking control of housing, as well as the creation of Fannie Mae and

Freddie Mac, two government-sponsored enterprises that are at the heart of the subprime mess and have cost the taxpayers billions of dollars. Today, Fannie Mae is proving to be a financial problem even bigger than AIG.

4. Unemployment insurance: Unemployment insurance was created in 1935. Typically, a person can receive insurance benefits for twenty-six weeks. When things get really bad, the federal government can extend the number of weeks for which a person can collect benefits. In June 2008, Congress added thirteen more weeks just as the number of layoffs accelerated.

5. The Bretton Woods Agreement: In 1944, just as World War II was about to end, a meeting of international banking leaders was held at a resort in Bretton Woods, New Hampshire—the United Nations Monetary and Financial Conference. This conference resulted in the creation of the International Monetary Fund (IMF) and the World Bank. While popular perception is that these two agencies were created for the good of the world, they have actually resulted in a lot of harm—foremost of which is the spread of a fiat monetary system throughout the world.

In 1971, when the dollar was severed from gold, the IMF and the World Bank required the rest of the world to separate from the gold standard, as well, or be excluded from their club. Today's global crisis spread because the world economy is floating on Monopoly money.

Robert's Note

In 1944, the world essentially adhered to the dollar standard, making the U.S. dollar the reserve currency of the world. This meant that the world had to trade in U.S. dollars, just as the U.S. citizen has to pay his or her taxes in U.S. dollars. The reason the United States is such a rich country today is because we can pay our debts and trade with U.S. dollars we've printed—legalized counterfeit money. If other countries like Argentina or China were allowed to have their currencies as the reserve currency of the world, they too would be rich. The danger of this all is that if the dollar loses too

> much credibility, countries like China may indeed choose to create a new reserve currency. If that happens, America is toast. We will not be able to live off counterfeit money any longer.

6. Make-work programs: During the last depression, government work programs were created. One of them was the Civilian Conservation Corps (CCC). This government program paid unemployed people to carry out various conservation programs initiated by the government. There was also the Works Progress Administration (WPA). This government program paid people to complete civic construction projects such as bridges and was engaged in large arts, drama, media, and literacy projects. At one point it constituted the largest employment base in the United States.

In 2009, the world's governments are again sponsoring make-work programs. The primary reason governments sponsor make-work programs is to keep people fed. If people are not fed, history shows they begin turning on their governments. The greatest fear of government officials is political unrest, which can lead to revolution.

The last depression never ended. The problems were pushed forward, and today, they have grown bigger, more expensive, and dangerous.

Two Types of Depression

Throughout history there have been two basic types of depressions:

1. Depressions caused by *deflation*
2. Depressions caused by *inflation*

The last depression in the United States was caused by deflation. Conversely, Germany's last depression was caused by inflation.

Same Depression, Just Different Money

One of the reasons the U.S. depression was caused by *deflation* was because the U.S. dollar technically still had real value. It was money backed by gold and silver: *receipt money.* Receipt money was basically a paper receipt for gold or silver supposedly held in the vault of the U.S. Treasury.

After the stock market crashed in 1929, fear spread, Americans hung on to their dollars, the economy deflated, businesses closed, people lost their jobs, and depression set in. The government did not print money to solve the problem because it was technically illegal to do so—although the government did stretch some rules. Savers were winners in this case because money was scarce and still had tangible value. A depression was caused as *deflation* set in.

The reason the German depression was caused by *inflation* was because Germany's money was no longer real money. It was Monopoly money, IOUs from the government—*fiat money* created out of thin air.

Since the German Reichsmark was merely Monopoly money—a piece of paper with some ink on it, backed by nothing—the German government just kept the printing presses running. It was the German government's way of solving its financial problems. Savers were losers because money was worth less and less as more and more of it was pumped into the system. A depression was caused as *inflation* set in.

There is a popular story about a woman who took a wheelbarrow filled with German Reichsmarks to the bakery to buy a loaf of bread. When she came out of the bakery to get her money, she found her wheelbarrow was stolen but the thieves had left her Reichsmarks behind. This comical story illustrates the devastating effects of hyperinflation.

Preparing for the Next Depression

So the question is: If there is a depression coming, do you think this one will be like the *U.S. depression* or the *German depression?* In the next depression, will cash be king or will cash be trash?

PREPARING FOR A U.S.–TYPE DEPRESSION

Most people are preparing for a repeat of a U.S.–style depression. These people feel secure hanging on to cash in savings, receiving a steady retirement check from the company they work for and a Social Security check from the government, reducing debt, cutting back on living expenses, and living a more simple life.

Although these people are well prepared for a U.S.–style depression, they will be wiped out if we have a German-style depression. Many mutual fund managers feel smart today because they got out of the market early and are now flush with cash. But what happens if a German-style depression is on the horizon? Will cash still be king? Will they still be smart?

PREPARING FOR A GERMAN-TYPE DEPRESSION

A few people are preparing for a German-style depression. These people are accumulating gold and silver coins, some cash, and investments that adjust for inflation. Examples of such investments are oil, food, gold and silver stocks, and government-sponsored housing.

> **Reader Comment**
>
> *I live in Metro Detroit, and the next depression is already here. It's neither an American nor a German depression, but a wiping out of the middle class and its way of life.*
>
> —cindyri

What's on the Horizon?

Personally, I see a German depression coming—not a U.S.–style depression. Here are a few reasons why I say this.

1. The Warburg effect: One of the original founders of the Federal Reserve was Paul Warburg, who represented the Rothschild and Warburg families of Europe. He was a member of M. M. Warburg and Company, which had offices in Germany and the Netherlands. His brother Max Warburg was the financial advisor to the kaiser before World War II and was director of the Reichsbank of Germany. Both Warburgs were anti-gold. They argued for an elastic money supply that could be expanded and contracted to accommodate the needs of business. They were for fiat money. Of course, this generally leads to inflation, which is a silent tax on the middle class and savers. The devastating result of the Warburg monetary philosophy was historically displayed in Germany. Max, a Jewish man, fled Germany in 1938—but only after hyperinflation had set in. The brothers' philosophy of currency is playing out today in America as the Fed pumps trillions of dollars into our economy.

It is also important to note that prior to 1913, there was no income tax in America. The income tax was established to provide the government with enough cash to pay the interest due the Federal Reserve. So, in essence, the Fed is responsible for both the silent tax of inflation and the overt income tax that takes money out of our pockets and puts it into the pockets of the rich.

2. Printing our way out of debt: The 1929 crash was triggered by stocks being bought on margin. The 2007 crash was set off by real estate on margin. The main difference, however, is that, as discussed earlier, the U.S. government *could not* print its way out of deflation in 1929 because the dollar was still pegged to gold. Today, the dollar is a free-floating currency backed by nothing but the good faith and credit of the U.S. government. Now that the government has the authority to print debts into oblivion, what do you think it's going to do?

3. Fool's gold: Roosevelt asked the American public to turn in their gold in 1933, for which they were paid $20.22 per ounce in paper money. He then raised the price of gold to $35 an ounce. In other words, for every $20.22 in gold that was turned in, the public was cheated out of about $15, a 58 percent heist. If anyone was caught holding gold coins, the punishment was a $10,000 fine and ten years in jail. One reason for doing this was to get the public used to paper money as the sole currency of the world. Another reason was to cover up the fact that the U.S. government had printed too many paper dollars and did not have enough gold in reserve to back them—in other words, the U.S. government was broke.

In 1975, President Gerald Ford allowed the American public to own physical gold once again—only after Nixon had permanently severed the link between the dollar and gold. Who cared about gold when those who controlled our government and our banks could now print money at will?

Today, most people are only used to paper money. Most Americans have no idea where to buy gold and silver coins, or even why they should be buying gold and silver coins. All they can see are jobs disappearing, their home values declining, and their retirement savings going down with the stock market. Many desperately want government bailout money, which probably means they are unknowingly choosing hyperinflation over deflation.

3. A world of wheelbarrow money: As stated earlier, the 1944 Bretton Woods meeting created the World Bank and the IMF. These agencies are extensions of the Federal Reserve and other European central banks. The IMF and World Bank required the world's banks to shift their money to fiat currency, currency not backed by gold and silver, similar to pre–World War II Germany's currency. In other words, the United States, the IMF, and the World Bank began exporting Germany's type of monetary system, *wheelbarrow money*, to the world.

Up until 1971, the U.S. dollar was the primary currency used by the IMF. Since the dollar was redeemable in gold at $35 an ounce, the amount of international money that could be created was limited. To operate as a true world central bank, the IMF needed to be able to issue unlimited amounts of funny money. On August 15, 1971, President Nixon signed an executive order stating that the United States would no longer redeem the dollar for gold. In 1971, the U.S. dollar became true Monopoly money for the world.

The World's Money Is Wheelbarrow Money

Today, all of the world's major currencies are basically Monopoly money—wheelbarrow money. So again, we need to ask ourselves: Will the next depression be *a U.S. deflationary depression* or *a German hyperinflationary depression*? Will cash be king or will cash eventually become trash? Will savers be winners or will savers be losers? Will pensioners win or lose? Will prices come down or will prices go higher?

Robert's Note

Presently, the Fed and the Treasury are trying to stop deflation. Deflation is much worse than inflation, and much harder to stop. That's why we're seeing bailouts and stimulus packages. If these tactics are successful, we will return to an inflationary economy. But, and this is a big but, if on the off chance the economic stimulus packages don't work, this will lead to printing massive amounts of money, which in turn lead to hyperinflation. Hyperinflation, if it were to happen, can be just as bad as a depression. This has happened most recently in Zimbabwe, where it reportedly takes a billion Zimbabwean dollars to buy three eggs. If the unthinkable happens and the United States goes into hyperinflation, it means the death of the U.S. dollar. If that happens, the world economy will collapse. That is what our leaders fear most.

Step one in preparing for the coming depression is to know your history, check the facts, look into the future, and make your own decision. Then decide if you choose to follow my poor dad's depression formula or my rich dad's. Today, as times get bad, I keep in mind that my rich dad got richer and my poor dad remained poor, both influenced by the same depression.

Reader Comment

Right now cash is still king, because the rest of the world's currencies are still pegged to the U.S. dollar. As the Fed continues to print money, the dollar will become less and less attractive as a reserve currency. Then the other countries will seek to unpeg their currencies from the dollar and peg them to something more stable like gold (perhaps). That's when we will experience hyperinflation.

—deborahclark

Exporting Debt

It may well be that there is no depression. It may be that President Obama has the power to unify the world, and that the world can go on forever printing money out of thin air. Maybe the countries of the world will continue to accept the United States' number-one export—debt—in payment for their goods and services. As long as the world is willing to accept our debt, T-bills, and bonds as money, the merry-go-round will keep turning. But if the world stops accepting the U.S. dollar, the music will stop, and the depression that follows will be greater than the last great depression.

On Wednesday, March 18, 2009, the Fed announced to the world it was injecting another $1.2 trillion into the economy. Does this mean you should fasten your seat belt for a takeoff or brace yourself for a crash landing? This means the Fed is now truly printing money, just as the German government did during the last depression. In a normal economy, when the U.S. Treasury offers bonds, countries such as China, Japan, England, and private investors buy the bonds. *But when the Fed buys our bonds, this means the United States is truly printing money.* This means the economy is still collapsing like a hot-air balloon with a tear in it.

As you may know, Fed Chairman Ben Bernanke is a student of the last depression. He has often stated he would keep the economy afloat by printing money. He once said he would drop money from a helicopter to save the economy, hence his nickname "Helicopter Ben." This move on March 18, 2009, is confirmation of his intentions—inflation at any price. If he goes too far and overinflates the money supply, we will see a German-style depression.

New Rule of Money #4: Prepare for Bad Times and You Will Only Know Good Times

When I was in Sunday school, I was told a story about a pharaoh of Egypt who had an unsettling dream. In his dream, he saw seven fat cattle being eaten by seven skinny cattle. Disturbed, he searched for a person who would interpret his dream. Finally, he came upon a young slave boy who told him his dream meant the world would have seven years of abundance followed by seven years of famine. The pharaoh immediately began preparing for famine, and Egypt went on to become a powerful nation, feeding that part of the world.

After reading Dr. Fuller's book *Grunch of Giants* in 1983, I began preparing for today's financial crisis. Today, my wife and I, our company, and our investments continue to prosper simply because we are always preparing for bad times. That is why New Rule of Money #4 is: *Prepare for bad times and you will only know good times.* You can read more about this later in the book.

Only Good Times

My generation—the baby boom generation—and their kids have only known the biggest economic boom in history. The baby boomers do not know what a depression is. For the most part, all they know are good times. The baby boomers were blessed by being born into a massive economic boom, a boom that began in 1971 when all the world's money became Monopoly money. Many people in my generation made wheelbarrows full of money. After the crash of 2007, many of my generation lost their wheelbarrows of money. But worse than being out of money, they may be out of time.

I am afraid my generation and their kids are not prepared for the economic decline, a depression that may be coming. If a person has only known an *expanding economy,* he or she may not be prepared for life in a *deflating* or *hyperinflating economy.*

A good exercise is to find people who experienced the last depression and take them to lunch. I have gone to lunch with survivors of both the German and U.S. depressions. It's a great way to start preparing for the next depression. How are you preparing?

Reader Comment

First off, I do believe that this is right around the corner on some level, and I do believe that the majority of people will be caught off guard because they've always lived in a time of economic expansion, the same as me. I see hard assets as being the way to survive the next depression. Ideally, you'll be earning cash flow from one hard asset now to be able to invest in physical gold and silver, which would hopefully be enough to offset the loss of cash flow or the value of money when USD is no longer worth anything.

—dkosters

Chapter 5

The Conspiracy Against Our Financial Intelligence

The Best Way to Rob a Bank

Question: *What is the difference between a banker and Jesse James?*

Answer: Jesse James robbed banks from the outside. Bankers rob them from the inside.

Question: *What is the best way to rob a bank?*

Answer: The best way to rob a bank is to own one.

—William Crawford, Commissioner of
California Department of Savings and Loans

People Are Smart

Just as people do, money evolves. One of the reasons so many people are in financial crisis today is because our money evolved but we did not evolve with it. One reason why we did not evolve is because there has been a conspiracy against our financial intelligence. Our evolution has been stunted.

When it comes to money, most people are smart. Even a ten-year-old child knows the difference between a $5 bill and a $50 bill. If offered the choice between the $5 and the $50, most kids would go for the $50.

To diminish our natural financial smarts, we had to be financially dumbed down. This was achieved through banking, a complex and confusing system by which money is created. In many ways the modern monetary system makes no sense to a logical person. For instance, how can it create trillions of dollars out of thin air?

Reader Comment

How many times have you been asked to initial "here, here, and here" without really looking at the details of what you were initialing or just had the person asking you to initial explain it to you briefly? This practice is often said to make things simpler for the client; however, most of the time it just makes the clients simpler.
                                                                    —dafirebreather

---

Financial Fairy Tales

When I was a child I believed in fairy tales, but by the time I was seven or eight, I knew fairy tales were just stories for little kids. So when the president of the United States asks us to believe in *hope* while at the same time the Federal Reserve prints trillions of dollars out of thin air, I begin to wonder if our leaders expect the people of the world to believe in golden geese. Apparently, our leaders have stumbled upon a magical goose that lays golden eggs, creating wealth out of thin air. Let's hope our story doesn't end the way the fable of the golden goose does.

The Magic Show

When I was a kid, I also believed in magic. Eventually, I learned there was no such thing as magic—just tricks, just sleight of hand. Unfortunately, this is really how money is created today—by sleight of hand. It is a magic show. The U.S. Treasury issues a bond in the form of a T-bill, the Federal Reserve writes a magic check for the bond, and the check is deposited into commercial banks, which then issue checks to regional banks, which then issue checks to smaller banks.

But this is not the full bag of tricks. The real magic is that the money supply increases at each bank. For every dollar a bank receives, it can in effect print even more money thanks to the sleight of hand known as *fractional reserve banking*, something we'll discuss in more detail later in this chapter. Every bank can do this trick. All a bank has to do is find people like you and me who are desperate for money and are willing to sign our life away by borrowing the magic money—and the more desperate you are, the higher the interest rate.

All banks, big or small, are effectively granted the license to print money. You don't need a mask to rob banks. All you need to do is own one.

People have a tough time understanding money today. If you are an honest, hardworking person, it probably doesn't make much sense to you how banks create magic money. The conspiracy of the rich diminishes our financial intelligence through a monetary system that honest people don't understand. Owning a bank is not only a license to print money—it is also a license to steal money, legally.

I am not calling your banker a crook. Most bankers are honest people, too, and have no idea how this robbery is accomplished. Many bankers are unaware of how they are used to steal the wealth of their customers. Bankers are not much different than a financial planner or real estate agent who reaches out to shake your hand, saying, "How may I help you?" Most bankers are simply doing a job, earning a living like the rest of us. It is the *system of money creation* that steals our wealth. The same system also makes some people very rich.

The Evolution of Money

Money evolved as human society grew more sophisticated and required a more sophisticated means of transacting business.

The following section describes in very simple terms the evolutionary stages of money—how it evolved from real money to magic money.

1. Barter: One of the first monetary systems was barter. Barter is simply trading a product or a service for other products and services. For example, if a farmer had a chicken and needed shoes, the farmer could trade chickens for shoes. The obvious problem with barter is that it is slow, tedious, and time-consuming. It is hard to measure relative values. For example, what if the cobbler did not want a chicken? Or if he did, how many chickens were his shoes really worth? A faster, more efficient means of exchange was needed, so money evolved.

On a side note, however, if the economy continues to slide downward and money remains tight, you will see barter increase. One good thing about barter is that it is hard for the government to tax barter transactions. The tax department does not accept chickens.

2. Commodities: To speed up the process of exchange, groups of people came to agree on tangible items that *represented* value. Seashells were some of the first forms of commodity money. So were stones, colored gems, beads, cattle, goats, gold, and silver. Rather than trade chickens for shoes, the chicken farmer might simply give the cobbler six colored gems for the shoes. The use of commodities sped up the process of exchange. More business could be done in less time.

Today, gold and silver remain the commodities that are internationally accepted as money. This is the lesson I learned in Vietnam. Paper money was *national*, but gold was *international*, accepted as money even behind enemy lines.

3. Receipt money: To keep precious metals and gems safe, wealthy people would turn their gold, silver, and gems over for safekeeping to people they trusted. That person would then issue the wealthy person a receipt for his or her precious metals and gems. This was the start of banking.

Receipt money was one of the first financial *derivatives*. Again, the word *derivative* means "derived from something else"—just as orange juice is derived from an orange and an egg is derived from a chicken. As money evolved from a tangible item of value into a derivative of value, a receipt, the speed of business increased.

In ancient times, when a merchant traveled across the desert from one market to the next, he would not carry gold or silver for fear of being robbed along the way. Instead, he carried with him a *receipt* for gold, silver, or gems in storage. The receipt was a derivative of valuables he owned and held in storage. If he purchased products at his faraway destination, he would then pay for his products with the receipt—a derivative of tangible value.

The seller would then take the receipt and deposit it in his bank. Rather than transfer gold, silver, and gems back across the desert to the other bank, the two bankers in the two cities would simply balance or reconcile the trading accounts between buyer and seller with debits and credits against receipts. This was the start of the modern-day banking and monetary system. Once again, money evolved and the speed of business increased. Today, modern forms of receipt money are known as checks, bank drafts, wire transfers, and debit cards. The core business of banking was best described by the third Lord Rothschild as "facilitating the movement of money from point A, where it is, to point B, where it is needed."

4. Fractional reserve receipt money: As wealth increased through trade, bankers' vaults became filled with precious commodities such as gold, silver, and gems. Bankers soon realized that their customers had little use for the gold, silver, and gems themselves. Receipts were much more convenient for transacting business. Receipts were much lighter, safer, and easier to carry. To make more money, bankers transitioned from storing wealth to lending wealth. When a customer came in wanting to borrow money, the banker simply issued another receipt with interest. In other words, bankers realized that they did not need their own money to make money. Bankers began effectively printing money.

The financial term *in kind* is derived from the German word *kinder,* which simply means *child*. This is where the word *kindergarten* comes from—literally, a garden of children. The financial term *in kind* was created when a borrower used cattle as collateral, security, to borrow money from the banker. If the borrower's cattle had calves while being held as collateral, the banker kept the calves as a part of the loan agreement. This was the start of interest payments, or as bankers say, *payments in kind*.

Since bankers made money from interest payments, payments in kind, it was not long before bankers began making more loans for more money than they had in their vault. This is where the magic show begins. This is where the bankers pull rabbits out of hats. For example, they might have had $1,000 in gold, silver, and gems in their vault, but they could have $2,000 in receipts in circulation that could lay claim to that $1,000 in valuables. In this example, they created a *fractional reserve* of 2 to 1—two dollars in receipts for every one dollar in gold, silver, and gems in their vault. The amount of money in the bank was only a fraction of the receipts in circulation. The bankers collected interest on money they technically did not have. If you and I did this, it would be considered fraud or counterfeiting—yet it is perfectly legal for banks to do.

With more money in circulation, people felt richer. There was no problem with this expanded money supply as long as everyone didn't want his or her gold, silver, and gems back at the same time. In modern terms, economists would say, "The economy grew because the money supply expanded."

Before central banks, such as the Federal Reserve, many smaller banks issued their own money. Many of these banks went bust when they got greedy and began lending out much more *fractional receipt money* than they had in gold, silver, and gems in their vaults, and they were unable to cover withdrawal requests. This is one reason why central banks, such as the Bank of England and the Federal Reserve, were created. They wanted only one form of money—their money—and they wanted to regulate the fractional reserve system.

Even though central banks were vigorously opposed by the Founding Fathers—the signers of the U.S. Constitution—the Federal Reserve was created in 1913 with the blessing of President Woodrow Wilson and the U.S. Congress and marked the beginning of the super-rich entering into a partnership with the U.S. Treasury. All money in the United States was now controlled by this partnership. No other banks could issue their own money. This is why the statement by Mayer Amschel Rothschild almost a century earlier was so prophetic, "Give me control of a nation's money supply and I care not who makes the laws."

Today, President Obama and the U.S. Congress are trying to solve the financial crisis by changing or enforcing the rules. But, like Rothschild, the conspiracy of the rich does not care about the rules. All the banking cartels controlling the world's central banks care about is how much bailout and stimulus money the president and Congress will pump into the struggling economy. All the cartels want is the *interest* payments on that money, the trillions of dollars in magic money created for bailout and stimulus programs.

Today, in 2009, as the president and Congress talk about a new $800 billion round of bailout money, a whole series of government operations have been invented to inject cash into the economy, most of them completely secret, with strange names such as Primary Dealer Credit Facility or the Commercial Paper Funding Facility. We rarely hear about these operations in the media. But through these newly created operations, the Fed has pumped in at least $3 trillion in loans and as much as $5.7 trillion in guarantees for private investments.

So who has more power? Fed Chairman Bernanke or President Obama?

Reader Comment

Here is a very intriguing question, indeed. As I read more and more into this subject, I've come to the conclusion that the Federal Reserve is little more than a socialist entity that was created by the government to control money. As such, I don't think it is which entity has more power that concerns me, but rather that together they have more power over the people.

—rdeken

This is *intergenerational* bank robbery by bankers. Regardless of whether a person agrees or disagrees with the idea of a conspiracy, the reality is that trillions of dollars of magic money, plus interest, will have to be paid for by future generations. We leverage our children's future to pay for our mistakes today.

5. Fiat money: When President Nixon severed the U.S. dollar from the gold standard in 1971, the United States no longer needed gold, silver, gems, or anything else in its vaults to create money.

Technically, prior to 1971, the U.S. dollar was a *derivative of gold*. After 1971, the U.S. dollar became a *derivative of debt*. Severing the dollar from gold was bank robbery of ungodly proportions.

Fiat money is simply money backed by government's good faith and credit. If anyone messes with the government and central bank's monopoly on money, the government has the power to put that group or person in jail for fraud and counterfeiting. Fiat money means all bills payable to the government, such as taxes, must be paid in that nation's currency. You cannot pay your taxes with chickens.

Shaving Coins

When money was commodity money, especially gold and silver coins, it was pretty easy to know when you were being robbed. In early Roman times, con men would try to trick people by shaving the edges of coins. That is why most Roman coins are irregular and oddly shaped. And that is why many modern coins have grooves on their edges. If you receive a U.S. quarter whose edges are smooth and irregularly shaped, you would immediately know that someone had filed some metal from the coin and that the coin was worthless. Someone had stolen your money. When it comes to money, people are smart—but only if they can see, touch, and feel it.

Debasing Coins

Another way Romans were cheated was by debased currency. That means, rather than pure gold or silver coins, the government mint would blend gold or silver with *base metals* such as nickel or copper, diluting the gold and silver content of the coin. The coin was physically worthless and inflation increased. *Inflation is a derivative of money going down in value.*

In 1964, the U.S. government did the same thing the Roman government did when it took our silver coins and turned them into *base metal coins*. That is why, today, you see a copper tinge along the grooved edges of coins. While the grooves prevented people from shaving the edges of the coins, the government was metaphorically shaving the value from the coins by taking the silver out of them. After 1964, no one shaved coins because coins were no longer valuable.

In 1964, I was in high school and immediately began gathering as many old silver coins as I could get my hands on. I didn't really know why I was doing this; I simply felt compelled. I knew that something was changing and that I had better hang on to real silver rather than coins. Years later, I found out that I was responding to Gresham's law. Gresham's law states that when bad money enters into circulation, good money goes into hiding. Just like the Vietnamese fruit vendor I wrote about in an earlier chapter, I was responding to a change in the money system. I was exchanging bad money for good money and putting the good money—the silver coins—into my coin collection. I still have some of those same silver coins today.

The Invisible Bank Robbery

Today the shaving and debasing of our money continues, just not in physical form. Since money is invisible, a derivative of debt, bank robberies by bankers have become invisible. This means most people cannot see how their banks steal their money.

Following are two of the ways modern bankers rob banks.

1. Fractional reserve banking: Assuming a 12-to-1 reserve limit (the ratio can change depending on economic conditions), when you deposit $100 in your bank, your local bank is allowed to lend up to $1,200 in loans tied to that $100. When that happens, your money has been shaved and diluted, and inflation increases.

For example, let's say the bank pays you 5 percent interest per year on your $100, equating to $5 per year in interest payments to you. The bank can then extend $1,200 in loans at 10 percent interest, generating $120 in interest payments to them. The bank has robbed you of your wealth by debasing your money through fractional reserve, and it has made $120 in interest on your $100. You have made $5.

The fractional reserve banking system is the modern and hidden way of shaving and debasing coins. It is a modern-day bank robbery that very few people can see because every bank, even your neighborhood bank, can create money out of thin air in that manner. When your banker receives your savings, he says, "Thank you." He can seemingly print more money like magic. When the banker lends out more money than you deposited, the money supply expands and inflation increases.

In June 1983, clever investment bankers got the idea of packaging thousands of mortgages, securitizing them, and calling them a collateralized debt obligation (CDO), a derivative of debt. They then sold CDOs all over the world as an alternative to government and corporate bonds.

Rating agencies such as Moody's and Standard and Poor's blessed this repackaged debt with investment-grade ratings, and insurance companies like AIG, Fannie Mae, and Freddie Mac insured the transactions with credit default swaps. The reason these quasi-insurance companies used the word *swap* rather than *insurance* is because a company is required to have money behind the insurance policy. *Swaps* have no money backing them, which is a major reason why companies such as AIG crashed when the mortgage market crashed. It would be like finding out the insurance company that insured your car is broke—after you have an accident.

As demand for these CDOs grew, mortgage bankers scrambled to supply the demand. Eventually, they found new customers to whom to give loans, poor people starving for money and willing to buy a new home with nothing down or to refinance their old home and pull out all of their equity. A new word entered the national vocabulary: *subprime.*

Everything was fine until the subprime borrowers could not make their monthly payments, and the house of debt began to crumble in 2005. This financial mess stems from the Federal Reserve System granting banks the power to lend money they do not have, via the fractional reserve banking system.

The problem is that the federal government stood ready to pick up the tab on these derivatives, an exposure estimated to be over $600 trillion.

The government picking up the tab leads to the second way modern bankers rob their own banks: deposit insurance.

2. Deposit insurance: Deposit insurance protects the bankers—not savers. In America we have the Federal Deposit Insurance Corporation (FDIC) to protect our savings, but its primary purpose is to protect big banks like Citigroup, Bank of America, and JPMorgan Chase—the very banks that helped cause this crisis.

When savers line up en masse to withdraw their savings, it is known as a *bank run*. The FDIC exists to make sure that runs don't happen on banks. During the Savings and Loan Crisis of the 1980s, savings were insured up to $50,000. When the savings and loans got into trouble, deposit insurance was increased to $100,000. When the financial crisis of 2007 began, the insurance was increased to $250,000. These increases were put in place to create confidence that even if a bank fails, depositors won't lose their money. From 2007 to 2009 there have been very few runs on the banks even though the number of failed banks is increasing. One reason is because savers feel secure that the FDIC will protect them.

Although the FDIC does a lot of good, it also protects incompetent, greedy, and dishonest bankers. By giving a sense of security—a financial backstop—the FDIC rewards bankers for taking greater and greater risks with depositors' money. And while the FDIC claims the banks pay for their insurance, the truth is that the FDIC does not have enough money to cover today's losses—so the taxpayer will have to cover them, in the form of bailouts. The bankers get away with billions of dollars. We get stuck with the bill.

Not All Banks Are Equal

Today, we hear the word *bailout* over and over. In reality, not all banks are bailed out. *Bailouts are only for the biggest banks.*

If a smaller bank goes bust, the FDIC generally uses a *payout* to fix the situation. For example, if you and I owned a small bank, and we made too many bad loans, the FDIC would simply close the bank, pay off the depositors, and we and our investors would lose the equity we put in to start the bank. A *payout* is often the remedy for small bankers with no political clout.

A second option is a *sell-off.* A sell-off occurs when a large bank steps in to take over a struggling bank. This has happened a number of times during the recent financial crisis, most notably with JPMorgan's purchase of Washington Mutual. It is an easy way for a larger bank to gain market share. The FDIC takes over the troubled bank on Friday and reopens it on Monday as a branch of the bigger bank. Again, this is a *sell-off,* not a bailout.

Bailouts are generally reserved only for big banks and bankers with political clout—and for banks that took the greatest risk and thus have the greatest chance of severely damaging the economy, banks that are *too big to fail.* As Irvine Sprague, a former director of the FDIC, writes in his book *Bailout,* "In a bailout, the bank does not close, and everyone—insured or not—is fully protected, except management which is fired and stockholders who retain only greatly diluted value in their holdings. Such privileged treatment is accorded by the FDIC only rarely to an elect few."

This means bailouts are only for the rich. If a big bank such as JPMorgan Chase or Citibank gets in trouble, the taxpayers pay for all losses. This means the $250,000 limit does not apply. If a bank in Europe has millions on deposit, or a rich man from Mexico has millions in savings, their money is 100 percent covered. Taxpayers pick up the tab.

If you and I took the risks that the biggest banks did, we would lose everything. We would not be bailed out. In overly simple terms, the FDIC is a smoke screen protecting the biggest banks. If a big bank gets caught, the government bails it out.

Mistakes Were Made

In 2009, former Federal Reserve Chairman Alan Greenspan came forward and admitted to the world that mistakes were made. What he did not say was who was going to pay for them. Of course, we already knew—the taxpayer.

To date, more than $180 billion in taxpayers' money has gone to AIG. Only when it was revealed that $165 million of that bailout was used to pay bonuses to executives for *losing* money did anger from taxpayers reach Fed Chairman Bernanke, Treasury Secretary Geithner, and President Obama, who suddenly promised to look into the matter. Many wanted to know to whom the bonuses went.

But a more important question is: Why should an *insurance* company like AIG receive bailout money in the first place? Isn't bailout money reserved for banks? The *Wall Street Journal,* citing confidential documents, reported that $50 billion of AIG bailout money went to firms such as Goldman Sachs, Merrill Lynch, Bank of America, and a number of European banks. In other words, the reason AIG received bailout money is because it owed the biggest banks in the world a lot of money and didn't have the cash to pay up. In the last quarter of 2008, AIG posted the biggest loss in corporate history—some $61.7 billion. That is $27 million for every hour.

A Bigger Failure than AIG

At the time this book went to press, AIG was the most expensive bailout in the country's history. But a bigger bailout will probably be Freddie Mac. Just as the business of the FDIC is to insure our savings, one of Freddie's primary businesses is insuring mortgages. As more workers lose their jobs, Freddie will also accrue more losses. As of March 2009, Freddie had taken back more than 30,000 homes. Maintaining each of these homes costs about $3,300 a month. It is estimated that the bailout of Freddie Mac will be much more expensive than AIG.

Back to the Future

In Chapter 1 of this book, I quoted the words of President Bush, Sr., reassuring us that "this legislation will safeguard and stabilize America's financial system and put in place permanent reforms so these problems will never happen again." He was speaking about the bailout of the savings and loan industry in the late 1980s and early 1990s. Today, you and I know these problems *did* happen again.

During the Savings and Loan Crisis, Senator John McCain was implicated with the failure of Lincoln Savings and Loan and the loss of billions of dollars. Bill and Hillary Clinton were implicated with the failure of Madison Guaranty Savings and Loan. And the Bush family was directly involved with the failure of Silverado Savings and Loan.

Senator Phil Gramm, in 1997 and 1998, helped repeal the Glass-Steagall Act, an act that was written during the last depression to prevent savings banks from mixing savings and investments. Once the Glass-Steagall Act was gone, the bank heist took on epic proportions. It is interesting to note that Senator Gramm, the chairman of the Senate Banking Committee, collected $2.6 million in campaign contributions from the banking, brokerage, and insurance industries. Fed Chairman Greenspan, President Clinton, and his Treasury secretaries Robert Rubin, Larry Summers, and Tim Geithner (today's Treasury secretary) were all part of repealing the Glass-Steagall Act, which led to the formation of Citigroup. Coincidentally, Rubin immediately left the White House to become the head of that newly formed company.

My point is this: Big bank robberies require political clout, and that is why our politicians have been slow to react to these bailouts. In a system so corrupted, how can there be change we can believe in?

Reader Comments

I'm not certain that's the right question. I don't know that we can change the system, so perhaps we should be asking how we can take advantage of the system as it exists.

—Rromatowski

This is the best quote I keep in mind. "Be the change you want to see in the world." –Mahatma Gandhi

—justemailme

National Ruin

Back in 1791, Thomas Jefferson was very much against a central bank for the very reasons we are all experiencing today. It was Jefferson who pointed out that the Constitution did not grant Congress the power to create a bank or anything else. He went on to say that even if the Constitution had granted such a power, it would be an extremely unwise thing to utilize because allowing banks to create money could only lead to national ruin. In fact, it was not uncommon for Jefferson to compare banking to the dangers of standing armies.

Repeating from an earlier chapter what John Maynard Keynes said about debauching our money supply: "There is no subtler, no surer means of overturning the existing basis of society than to debauch the currency. The process engages all the hidden forces of economic law on the side of destruction, and does it in a manner which not one man in a million is able to diagnose." In other words, it's hard to diagnose something you cannot see. Today, the banks are robbing us of our wealth right under our noses, a hidden theft that is only exposed once you have the knowledge to know what to look for.

New Rule of Money #5: The Need for Speed

At the beginning of this chapter we talked about how money has evolved from barter to digital money—money at the speed of light. Today, one reason why we have people making billions and others still working for $7 an hour is a difference in speed. Today, the faster a person can transact business, the more money he or she will make. For example, a typical medical doctor can see one patient at a time. A high school kid with a global web business, transacting business to unlimited customers 24/7, can potentially earn much, much more than a medical doctor. The difference, as I will talk about in the next chapter, is that one type of work is metaphysical (web business) and the other is physical (medical doctor). One type of work creates wealth exponentially; the other creates wealth linearly.

Many people are financially struggling today because they are simply too slow—they cannot make money faster than the banks are printing it. When it comes to financial transactions, most people are still in the Stone Age, getting paid by the hour, by the month, or per transaction, working for commissions, as is the case with real estate agents or stockbrokers. Those who will succeed in the future will be entrepreneurs who understand how quickly business and money are changing, and who have the ability and flexibility to quickly change and adapt.

Postscript

For More Detail on the Global Monetary System

If you would like greater detail on the monetary system, here are two excellent books I recommend.

1. ***The Creature from Jekyll Island* by G. Edward Griffin:** This is a thick yet easy-to-read book on the history of the conspiracy. I have read it three times, and each time the book opened my eyes up to a world only one in a million know about. This book goes into greater detail on how the Federal Reserve came to be and how money is really created. Much of Griffin's findings track directly with my findings. Originally published in 1994, the book reads as if it were written today, and seems more like a crime novel than a nonfiction book on global economics.

2. ***The Dollar Crisis* by Richard Duncan:** This book completes the global picture on the conspiracy. *The Dollar Crisis* explains what is happening in the world economy today as a result of the meeting held on Jekyll Island that led to the formation of the Federal Reserve. Duncan's book explains how the U.S. dollar is causing booms and busts in Japan, Mexico, China, Southeast Asia, Russia, the European Union, and elsewhere.

Both books are excellent and written by brilliant authors. The two books offer a more complete and in-depth picture of why and how we got into this global financial crisis.

Time to Move On

This ends Part One of *Rich Dad's Conspiracy of the Rich*. In Part Two, you will learn how to do well in a world that is *booming* as well as *busting*. While millions are sitting on their rooftops, surrounded by a flood of debt, hoping someone will save them, a few people are moving on and so is this book.

Now that you know some of the historical causes of this crisis, it is time to focus on *personal solutions* rather than what caused the global problems.

Part Two will focus on beating the conspiracy at its own game.

PART TWO

FIGHTING BACK

*Beating the Conspiracy at Its Own Game: Why Winners Are
Winning, and Why Losers Are Losing*

The Importance of History and the Future

When I am asked, "What would you teach people about money to increase
their financial intelligence and financial literacy?" my reply is, "I'd begin with
history, because through the lens of the past you can better see the future." If
you learn nothing else from Part One, learn that only by studying history can
you be prepared for the future.

Part One of *Rich Dad's Conspiracy of the Rich* is about the financial
history of the United States and how that history is repeating itself today.
It is about how the rich and powerful have manipulated our lives via central banks, multinational corporations, wars, education, and government
policies.

Over the course of history, the actions of the rich and powerful have
done both much good and much harm. I don't fault the rich for looking out

for their interests or their family's interests. Rather than placing blame, I studied the history of the rich, learned their game, and lived my life aware of their rules of money—and created some of my own rules along the way. Most people who know the rules of the game of the rich are *not* in financial trouble today. For the most part, it is only those people who have a low financial intelligence and live by the old rules of money who are hurting financially.

In Part One of this book, I also wanted you to understand that the Fed often protects only the biggest banks in the name of protecting the economy—banks deemed *too big to fail.* In fact, it's my belief that the Fed exists to protect big and powerful banks.

You may have noticed that the Fed saved the banks implicit in this crisis but did not fire the bank executives—many of whom were instrumental in creating the crisis. This is not so with other industries hurt by the downturn. The administration "fired" Rick Wagoner but not the heads of the banks. Why? The government has not gone after Moody's or Standard & Poor's, the rating agencies that gave subprime debt an AAA rating—the highest credit rating available. It was this AAA rating that caused foreign governments and pension plans to invest their money in toxic assets. Again, why? And only after much public pressure did AIG, the giant insurance agency that insured the toxic assets, reveal to whom the billions in bailout money it received went—the biggest banks, such as Goldman Sachs, Société Générale of France, Deutsche Bank of Germany, Barclays of Britain, UBS of Switzerland, Merrill Lynch, Bank of America, Citigroup, and Wachovia.

In Chapter 3, I talked about the word *apocalypse* and how it was derived from the Greek word meaning "lifting of the veil." For me, the process of writing *Rich Dad's Conspiracy of the Rich* is incredible. I'm continually struck by the fact that even as I write about financial history, history itself is being made. Literally, a financial apocalypse is happening before our eyes as this book unfolds. The veil is being lifted on the greed and incompetence of Wall Street and politicians. On April 14, 2009, Goldman Sachs announced it was returning the TARP money it received in the wake of better-than-expected earnings and a $5 billion stock sale. But as University of Maryland Professor Peter Morici pointed out on a CNBC segment aired that evening, the systemic problem of banks gambling on derivatives is not fixed. Rather, he noted that Goldman Sachs was hoping to come off as a model citizen and to continue business as usual. But, he commented, the whole notion that "you don't really need to regulate them and stop them from writing derivatives on top of derivatives on top of derivatives and paying Blankenfeld [sic] $72 million a year is madness." That is an example of the veil being lifted. That is a financial apocalypse.

The fact of the matter is that Goldman Sachs is doing well financially not because of sound financial decisions but because, as the *New York Times* reports, it was bailed out by the Fed via payments to AIG. That is because the Fed is not in the business of saving the weak and poor, just the weak and rich. Little banks do not receive bailouts. Nor do small businesses. Nor do people who pay their mortgages faithfully—even at the expense of other bills.

Rich Dad's Prophecy Is Coming True

Another important financial apocalypse that needs to occur is one regarding pensions and retirement: Simply stated, the concept of a secure retirement is a dying reality. The Pension Benefit Guaranty Corporation (PBGC), the insurance arm behind government pensions, announced in April 2009 that public pensions are hundreds of billions short of funds due to the crash in the stock market. This means state governments have to increase taxes to ensure that government workers can retire. In other words, state governments are in trouble because they promised benefits they could not afford. This is further proof that the traditional idea of the pension is dead and will not be resuscitated.

In 2002, I wrote about this pension crisis in my book *Rich Dad's Prophecy*, which was about the coming of the biggest stock market crash in history—a crash that, despite the recent havoc in the markets, I believe may not have fully come. The cause of the prophesied crash is a flaw in the 401(k) retirement plan, a plan blessed by Congress in 1974 as an attempted fix to the dying pension system. At the time of the book's publication, the stock market was breaking records left and right, at least numerically. There was little doubt in the establishment's mind that the stock market and mutual funds would solve the retirement problem for many Americans. As would be expected, the Wall Street media trashed the book.

But today, we see the market has at times been down nearly 50 percent from its record highs, and as stated, I would not be surprised to see it fall much farther in the near future. No one is laughing now. I believe the market will crash harder than it already has because the 401(k) plan was a primary catalyst for pushing the retirement money of the baby boomers, the biggest generation in U.S. history, into the stock market, which created immense demand for stocks and mutual funds. As the baby boomers retire, they will need to begin drawing on that money in order to live—which means they will be selling stocks, not buying them. And when there are more people selling than buying, the market goes down. This means that today those who are forty-five or younger and have retirement plans connected to the stock market are in trouble. Many people believe they are safe because the stock market will recover. But the market will not recover; it will only continue to fall when baby boomers retire in earnest between 2012 and 2016. The idea of a comfortable retirement is becoming a myth for young and old.

Ancient History Comes Alive

I have one final point about history. The Founding Fathers opposed central banks like the Federal Reserve. President George Washington experienced the pain of government-made money when he had to pay his troops with the continental, a currency that eventually went to its true value—zero. Thomas Jefferson adamantly opposed the creation of a central bank. Yet today central banks control the financial world, and we've granted them the power to solve our financial crisis for us, the very crisis they helped create.

Simply said, a central bank can create money out of nothing and then charge us interest on money it did not earn. That interest is paid via taxes, inflation, and, today, deflation, which results in the loss of jobs and value in our homes. The policies of the Fed aren't abstract realities. They are powerful actions that determine your financial well-being in both open and hidden ways.

Anyone who purchases a home knows that for the first years most of your mortgage payment goes to the bank to pay down interest, and that very little goes toward reducing the principal. The bank effectively receives interest payments for money it did not earn but rather created out of thin air. Chapter 5 is a very important chapter because it talks about the fractional reserve system, how the banking system allows the bank to lend out, for example, $12 for every $1 you put into savings. Allowing banks to effectively create money out of thin air via the fractional reserve system robs us of our wealth by devaluing our dollars. Today, the central banks of the world are printing trillions of dollars, which will be paid by us via debt, taxes, and inflation.

A Government-sponsored Cash Heist

When the Federal Reserve was created in 1913, a deal was cut between the bank and the U.S. Treasury—a government-sponsored cash heist. Without a solid understanding of history and how money is created, true financial education is not possible. To simply say to a child, "Get a job, save money, buy a house, and invest for the long term in a well-diversified portfolio of stocks, bonds, and mutual funds" is a script right out of the central banker's operating manual. It is a success myth propagated by the super-rich.

So this book has covered a lot of ground in terms of history and has presented a number of facts surrounding the conspiracy of the rich, and all for a purpose: to equip you with the historical knowledge necessary to answer the question, What can I do to beat the conspiracy at its own game? The answers to this question comprise the second half of this book.

This Fed's for You?

Today, many people grumble, criticize, and complain about big banks, politicians, and the financial crisis. To me that is a waste of time. As G. Edward Griffin states in his book *The Creature from Jekyll Island*, "Bailout is the name of the game." In other words, what you see today is the real game of the Federal Reserve System. The system was designed to allow big banks with political clout to make a lot of money, fail, and then be bailed out by the taxpayers. In the process the rich get richer and the poor get poorer. This Fed is not for you. It's for the rich and powerful.

Reader Comment

I was most surprised by how much money was going out the back door of AIG to big banks such as Goldman Sachs. Also about the smoke screens that are out in public while the bigger heists are happening behind the scenes. Yesterday, I watched the tax protests on TV. I found it interesting that nobody had any signs saying to stop printing money; they mostly said stop taxing our children (which I agree with). Nobody seems to see the real tax of inflated currency supply via the Federal Reserve.

—herbigp

Should the Fed Be Abolished?

Some people want to abolish the Federal Reserve System. My question is, What would replace it? How much chaos would that cause? And how long would that take?

Rather than rail against the Fed, you should ask, How can I minimize the effects of the Fed on my personal financial situation? Personally, I decided to study the game of the rich and play the game according to my rules. In 1983, after reading Dr. Fuller's *Grunch of Giants*, I took what I had learned from my rich dad and applied that knowledge to playing the game of the rich differently. If I had not begun preparing years ago for this crisis, I, too, might have been an aging baby boomer watching my pension dissolve and my home decline in value, fearing I would soon lose my job, my pension, and my health insurance. And worst of all, I might have become dependent upon the government via Social Security and Medicare, just like my poor dad.

Part One of this book was about history and how history is repeating itself today. Now that you are equipped with the knowledge of history necessary to clearly see the future, Part Two will focus on the future and how you can prepare to beat the conspiracy at its own game by offering you new rules of money that will help you thrive despite the conspiracy of the rich.

Part Two begins with Chapter 6, which is a brief commentary about the present economy, asking the question, Is the economy coming back to life?

From Chapter 7 on, this book will be about how I personally prepared and am now preparing for the future—and how you can, too. You'll learn how to beat the conspirators at their own game—how you can opt out of the conspiracy of the rich.

Reader Comment

Throughout history some have prospered in every economy. If some can do it, I can do it. You and a few others have chosen to make it your life's work to lead the way. I am pleased to be learning from your example and plan to in turn help as many others as I can.

—deborahclark

Chapter 6

Where We Are Today

Is the Economy Coming Back?

On March 23, 2009, the Dow jumped 497 points, capping one of the biggest market rallies in history. In less than two weeks the Dow had advanced 1,228 points.

As I write this in April 2009, Wall Street is still rallying. Some think the worst is over and are rushing back into the stock market. Others think the rally is a *bear market rally*, or as I like to call it, a *sucker's rally*. A sucker's rally sucks in people who think the market has bottomed and hope to snatch up cheap stocks, catching the next elevator ride up. And the elevator does go up—for a little while, but then without warning the bear cuts the elevator cable. Greed turns into panic as the elevator falls even faster than it went up.

Today, people are asking, "Is the crisis over? Is the economy coming back?"

My reply is, "No, the economy is not coming back. The economy has moved on, and the people asking if it's coming back are being left behind."

Before moving on to the practical applications in Part Two of *Rich Dad's Conspiracy of the Rich*, this chapter will explain how the world came out of the last depression, in spite of government intervention, and explore the implications of that past for our present. By knowing a little about history, the present will become clearer, and you will be better able to see the future.

Reader Comment

The economy will not come back to be exactly what it was; it will change and evolve as it always has. Positive or negative—only time will tell, but we are all here to prepare ourselves for prosperity no matter which way the economy as a whole goes.

—Jerome Fazzari

The New Economy in 1954

As we discussed earlier in the book, the U.S. economy didn't recover from the Great Depression until 1954, when the Dow finally reached its previous high of 381. A few reasons why the economy improved in 1954 are:

1. The World War II generation was settling down. When the war ended, soldiers came home, went to college, got married, and had kids. By the 1950s a housing and baby boom was on.

2. The first credit card was introduced in 1951, and shopping became a national sport. With the advent of the suburbs, shopping centers sprang up like weeds.

3. Interstate highways were built, and the auto industry boomed. Drive-ins became the place where kids hung out, and the fast-food industry was born. In 1953, McDonald's began franchising and became the shining star of the new fast-food industry.

4. Television became a national phenomenon, and the baby boomers were the first generation raised by TV. Entertainment came to life on *The Ed Sullivan Show*, and sports stars became the new mega-rich. Advertising took on a whole new dimension in people's daily lives.

5. Boeing introduced the 707, and the jet age arrived. Being a pilot or a flight attendant suddenly became a glamour job. Larger airports were built to accommodate increased demand for air travel, and mega-airports became an industry unto themselves. Hotels and destination resorts sprang up to meet the demand of road-weary travelers, and tourism thrived. My rich dad became very rich as lower fares and faster travel brought tourists to Hawaii.

6. Workers could expect company pensions and healthcare for life. Without the expense of retirement savings and healthcare premiums, workers could spend money more freely.

7. China was a poor communist country.

8. America was the new financial and military power.

Fifty-five Years Later

In 2009, many of the factors that spurred on the new economy fifty-five years ago are now fading:

1. Baby boomers are retiring and beginning to collect Social Security and Medicare alongside their World War II–generation parents.

2. The suburbs are ground zero for the subprime mess. As suburbs struggle, major shopping centers face trouble and retailers close their doors while online shopping is taking off.

3. Our highways and bridges are in need of major repair. The auto industry is dying and outdated. An old saying goes, "As GM goes, so goes the nation." That saying is truer today than ever.

4. Television networks are losing advertisers—many of which are leaving for the web.

5. Major airlines such as Pan American are history, and giants such as United Airlines are on life support. Today, people can sit at their desk and visit with people all over the world via the Internet.

6. People are living longer, but many are overweight and in poor health. Diabetes is the new cancer, and our medical system is going broke. The high cost of healthcare is causing many businesses to close, which costs more jobs.

7. Pension plans are going broke. Few workers have company pensions or healthcare coverage after they retire. This will be a disaster for government programs as 78 million baby boomers become dependent upon America's Medicare and Social Security systems.

8. China will soon be the richest country on earth. China is now asking that the U.S. dollar no longer be the reserve currency of the world. If that happens, America is toast.

9. America is now the biggest debtor nation on earth, and its military is overextended.

So, again, is the economy coming back? I don't think so. The boom economy that pulled us out of the last depression is dying. Millions of people are being left behind as they wait for the old economy to come back. Unemployment is rising as people's jobs are becoming obsolete, often replaced by technology or outsourced to a nation with a cheaper labor pool. This means there will be an even greater divide between the haves and have-nots, the rich and the poor. The middle class will shrink like the polar ice caps.

The Future of America

Many of us have seen, either in person or on television, poverty and the shantytowns where the very poor live. No matter how many times I see poverty, it never fails to make me pause and wonder how to solve this issue.

If you ever have a chance to go to Cape Town, South Africa, please do. Cape Town is one of the most beautiful cities in the world. It is a rich and modern city. It is exciting and vibrant. And I believe you can see the future of the world in Cape Town. Driving in from the airport, all you see are miles and miles of shantytowns and hundreds of thousands of people barely surviving on the boundary of civilized life. When I drive past the shantytowns and approach gorgeous Cape Town, I often wonder if I am looking at the future of America. I wonder if one day our middle class will be living in shantytowns.

Reader Comments

As an older baby boomer looking at retirement on my horizon, I feel mostly pessimistic. It is hard to imagine recouping my losses before my health gives out. I am concerned about what quality of life I will have in my older age, especially since we are living longer.

—jeuell52

Because I love a challenge, I am optimistic and very curious about the future. Americans will bounce back in a new way. It will take time and a complete mind shift, I imagine.

—annebecker

The Crash of 1987

Today, one reason the middle class is losing ground and the gap between rich and poor is growing can be found in the differences between the crash of 1987 and the crash of 2007.

On October 19, 1987, I was on a flight from Los Angeles to Sydney, Australia. When the plane landed in Honolulu to refuel, I stepped off the plane to call a friend from a payphone in the terminal.

"Did you hear the stock market crashed?" my friend asked.

"No, I didn't," I replied. "I've been flying."

"It's a big one," he said. "The Dow dropped 23 percent today. A lot of people were wiped out."

"That's not good for those people, but it's good news for me," I replied. "It's time to get rich."

From 1987 to 1994, my wife, Kim, and I worked hard at building our business and investing all the money we had. Many friends and relatives thought we had lost our minds. They were in hiding and waiting for the economy to come back. Instead of investing, they were stuffing their money in mattresses. By 1994, Kim and I were financially free and in position to make tremendous profits as the next bull market took off in 1995. Many of our friends that did nothing are still in financial trouble to this day.

Reader Comment

Yes, I remember 1987 . . . it was the time I decided to become more independent and resigned my job to start contracting. I rolled my Super over into a private fund at the suggestion of my accountant. I remember questioning why it was all going into one managed fund, and not split up into two or three. He said it wasn't really worth it for "such a small amount." That was a few months before the market crash and my hard-earned (ten years' worth) of Super was halved in an instant. My financial intelligence training hadn't even begun.

—10 billion

The Crash of 2007

The crash of 2007 is different than the crash of 1987. I do not know if the markets will come back the way they have in the past. Many of the industries that caused the last boom in 1954 are now dying. This time things are different.

The big difference between the 1987 crash and the 2007 crash is the rise of the Internet. The Internet is changing everything. Along with a toxic dollar and bankrupt government, the Internet is one of the primary causes of people being left behind, causing unemployment to increase.

I believe the Internet is bringing a shift to the world a million times more profound than Columbus discovering America in 1492. Just as explorers like Columbus opened the world to new wealth, the Internet is opening even larger worlds of wealth to today's explorers.

Yet there is significant difference between Columbus and the Internet.

People could see the changes that Columbus brought. They could see ships, cargoes of plundered wealth, and drawings of natives and their land.

We cannot see the world of the Internet with our eyes. *The world of the Internet is invisible, and we have to see it with our minds.* And that is why people are being left behind. They cannot see the changes that are remaking their world. In their blindness, they are becoming obsolete.

Are You Becoming Obsolete?

Dr. Buckminster Fuller once said that when change went invisible, the speed of that change would increase exponentially—a concept he termed in an article *accelerating acceleration*. An example he used was the rapid advance of aviation technology. Think about how amazingly fast flight technology has expanded in the past century. In 1903, the Wright Brothers flew the very first sustained airplane flight. In 1969, we put the first man on the moon. And now today, we have space shuttles that travel 17,320 miles per hour and that will soon be capable of flying to Mars. That is an example of accelerating acceleration. Technology, and how that technology affects business, is changing at such a rapid pace it is nearly impossible to keep up.

During one of his lectures in the early 1980s, Bucky Fuller talked about a new technology that would explode before the end of the decade. By tracking the rate at which technology advanced, he claimed he could predict the future. One particular statement from his lecture stuck with me. He said, "We are entering the world of the invisible." Clarifying, he said, "When you lie on your back and look up at the clouds, you do not see the clouds moving. Only after closing your eyes for a while, and then looking up again, do you notice the change."

Dr. Fuller was concerned. His message was that soon millions of people would be out of work. They would be put out of work by technology and inventions that operated well outside their vision. I remember his words well: "You cannot get out of the way of things you cannot see moving toward you," he said.

As an example of what he was speaking of, he talked about the evolution from horses to automobiles. He said, "Humans could see the automobile. They could see that change. If a car came toward them, they could get out of the way." Because they could see the car, they could adapt and make changes to their lives. But future inventions, he claimed, would be invisible. So humans would not see what was changing their lives. He finished his point by simply stating, "Humans are being run over by what they cannot see."

Today, people are being run over and made obsolete by technological innovations they cannot see and that they do not understand. Millions of people are unemployed because their skill set is no longer needed. They are obsolete.

Business at High Speed

In the 1970s, when I began my first business, I soon became a multimillion-mile traveler with United and Pan American Airlines. Today, I get more business done sitting in my office and using the web to reach more people in less time, and with less energy—all for a lot less money. While I make more money, the airlines suffer, because business travelers like me have found a faster, less expensive way to transact business with people all over the world.

In 1969, I graduated from the U.S. Merchant Marine Academy at Kings Point, New York. At the time, we were the highest paid graduates in the world. Many of my classmates graduated and immediately began earning $80,000 to $150,000 a year if they sailed on freighters in the Vietnam War zone. That was not a bad starting pay for twenty-two-year-old kids.

After graduation, I sailed for Standard Oil on a tanker for a few months. But when my brother joined the military to go and fight in the Vietnam War, I quit my high-paying job and volunteered to fly for the Marine Corps. My income went from nearly $5,000 a month to $200 a month. It was a shock.

Today, some of my classmates are still sailing. Many make about $400,000 a year and will retire on about $200,000 a year. Not a bad return on their college education.

Instead of going back to sailing after the war or flying for the airlines, I chose to become an entrepreneur. Today, I'm reaping the benefits of that choice.

There are two primary differences between my classmates and me. The first difference is that most of my work is 90 percent mental and most of theirs is 90 percent physical. They have to sail ships to get paid. I make money even when I'm sleeping. The second difference is the rate of transaction speed. My classmates work five days a week and get paid by the month. I work 24/7, 365 days a year, and I get paid by the minute. Even if I stopped working, money would still come in. I will explain how I do this in upcoming chapters.

Once I understood what Dr. Fuller meant by accelerating acceleration, I took decisive action to stay ahead of the curve. I have no plans to become obsolete. I'm not waiting for the economy to come back. I'm working hard staying ahead of the accelerating economy.

Pavlov's Dogs

As we discussed throughout Part One, the seeds of today's financial crisis were planted, in my opinion, with the hijacking of the U.S. education system in 1903. Today, we still do not have adequate financial education in our schools.

During the dark days of American slavery, slaves were forbidden to be educated. In some states, it was a crime to teach slaves to read and write. An educated slave class was a dangerous slave class. Today, we fail to teach kids to be financially literate. It is another way of creating slaves—wage slaves.

Immediately after leaving school, most kids begin to look for a job, save money, buy a house, and invest for the long term in a well-diversified portfolio of mutual funds.

Now that millions are losing their jobs, what do they do? They go back to school to get retrained, look for a new job, try to save money, pay their mortgage, and invest for their retirement in mutual funds. And they teach their kids to do the same.

Ivan Pavlov won a Nobel Prize in 1904 in Physiology and Medicine for his research on the digestive system of dogs. Today, when we hear the term *Pavlov's dogs*, it refers to conditioned response. Going to school to get a high-paying job, saving your money for a house, and investing in a diversified portfolio of stocks and mutual funds is an example of a conditioned response. Many people cannot articulate why they do these things. They simply do it because it is what they were taught, a conditioned response.

Employee to Entrepreneur

In 1973, I returned from the Vietnam War and found my poor dad at home, alone and unemployed. He had run for lieutenant governor of Hawaii and lost. Although he was a smart, well-educated, and hardworking man, he was finished at age fifty. He was a star in the education system but ill-equipped for the world of business and politics. He could survive in school but not on the street.

His advice to me was to go back to school, get my PhD, and then get a job with the government. Although I loved my dad dearly, I knew his life was not my life. Leaving his home, I drove to Waikiki and at the age of twenty-seven once again became an apprentice of my rich dad. That was one of the smartest decisions I have ever made. I was breaking a conditioned response of an employee to become an entrepreneur.

History is full of success stories of those who ignored conditioned responses and forged their own path. The Wright Brothers and Henry Ford never finished high school. Bill Gates, Michael Dell, and Steve Jobs never finished college. Sergey Brin of Google suspended his PhD studies at Stanford. Mark Zuckerberg started Facebook in his dorm room at Harvard, traveled to California, and never returned to finish his education. All of these world-changers dropped out of school because they no longer needed to look for a job. They had an idea and the courage to act on that idea. They started businesses and created jobs for others. Today, entrepreneurship is exploding all over the world. More important, the most successful entrepreneurs understand that we are in the information age. They have the vision to see the changes happening that most do not.

The Future Will Be Different

Today, we have a new generation that is going to change the future. This generation is composed of kids born after 1990. These are kids who have only known a world with the Internet. They are not the same as people born before 1990; they were born into a different world and will create a different future. What the future will look like, I do not know exactly—I just know the future they see is not the future I see.

What I do know is that the gap between the rich and poor will continue to expand. The idea of a high-paying job for life is becoming ridiculous as low-wage countries compete globally and as companies exchange ideas across oceans at the speed of light. Jobs tend to migrate to countries with the lowest cost of labor. I predict that young entrepreneurs equipped with low-cost PDAs and access to the Internet will soon rise out of shantytowns and transform the world. The rich and complacent will find their world of luxury disturbed as young and hungry entrepreneurs change the future of the world—some from shantytowns.

In the Industrial Age, the rich nations of the world controlled the world's natural resources such as oil, metals, lumber, and food. As the Information Age grows, no longer will the rich and powerful nations have a monopoly on the world's true natural resource—our minds. In the invisible world of the Internet, the geniuses of the world will be unleashed, and class lines that are centuries old will be erased. A new mega-rich will rise.

New Economy, New Wealth

With the arrival of the new economy, there will be an explosion of new wealth. There will be new millionaires and billionaires. Money will be made at ultrahigh speed. The question is, Will you be one of the new rich, or one of the new poor? Back in the 1950s, my rich dad saw the new economy and took action. My poor dad was crushed by the new economy. He chose financial security rather than financial freedom—and in the end, he had neither.

So, Where Are We Today?

The stock market will eventually come back, but remember that it took from 1929 to 1954 for the market to return to the all-time high of 381. When the stock market does come back, there will be new companies making up the Dow. New blue chips will dominate. The real estate market will eventually come back when populations grow and jobs finally return. But there will be new families living in the old mansions. And there will also be many more homeless people.

But the old economy, the economy as we knew it, is not coming back. The economy has moved on. The old economy born around 1954 is dying. A new economy is being born, an economy that will be led by kids born after 1990, young people who only know the invisible, high-speed world of the web.

Smart Person, Wrong Business

While Donald Trump and I were working on our book *Why We Want You to Be Rich*, a book about the shrinking middle class, Donald said something to me that hit home: "I have a lot of classmates who were much smarter than me, but I make more money than they do. One reason is because I am an entrepreneur and they became employees working for big companies. Another reason is because they went to work for the wrong industry. They went to work for dying industries."

Listening to his words, I reflected upon my own life. If I had followed my poor dad's advice, I, too, would have been an employee in dying industries. Today, graduates from the U.S. Merchant Marine Academy have a difficult time finding jobs. The reason the U.S. Merchant Marine Cadet Corps is dying is the same reason General Motors is dying. The pay for Merchant Marine officers is so high that the shipping companies have moved their ships to countries with lower wages. The labor unions priced themselves out of a job.

As Donald and I sat in his office overlooking Central Park and Fifth Avenue, I realized I would not be sitting where I was if I had followed my poor dad's advice—a philosophy he developed from his experience in the last depression. As the possibility of a new depression looms, rather than feel fear, Donald and I are preparing for the challenges and tough times ahead. We have gone through tough times before, and each time we have come out smarter and even richer.

Crystal Ball

In April 2009, as I write this, the world is feeling better about the economy. People are becoming more optimistic. The stock market is rallying. Cash is flowing out of gold and savings accounts, and back into the stock market. As stated earlier, I believe it is only a bear market rally—a sucker's rally—one of the most vicious of all market rallies, but I could be wrong.

I feel the worst is not yet over for the following reasons.

1. Old industries are dying. Many older people depend upon the dividends paid by these old companies. In this crisis, with earnings dropping, many businesses are cutting dividends. GE cut its dividend by 68 percent and JPMorgan cut its by 86 percent. That means if you are a retiree who was living on $1,000 a month from GE's dividend, today you're receiving $320 instead. If you were living on dividends from JPMorgan, you're living on $140 rather than $1,000.

2. Taxes will rise. As the United States continues to print trillions of dollars, our kids and grandkids will pay for this mess with rising taxes. Taxes often punish producers and reward the crooked, lazy, or incompetent.

For instance, the White House announced a cap on tax-deductible charitable donations, which will most negatively affect the wealthy. In 2006, four million Americans earned gross incomes of $200,000 or more. They accounted for less than 3 percent of all Americans, yet they donated 44 percent of all charitable donations. This cap on tax deductions means many charities will close, and millions more will need government help, which will cause the government to again raise taxes.

There is a growing mood in this country to "get" the rich. This sentiment is embodied in the action of Congressman Jerry McNerney (D-CA), asking for a 90 percent tax rate on wealthy people. The mobs are out to punish the working rich—those who pay taxes, create jobs, and make charitable donations. The real rich, those who influence the politicians and the Federal Reserve, are untouched.

3. The United States is the biggest debtor nation in the world. The gross domestic product (GDP) of the United States is over $14 trillion. The total dollar sum of all the bailout programs rolled out early this year is about half that amount.

4. China is threatening the reserve status of the U.S. dollar. In March 2009, China began talking in earnest about abandoning the U.S. dollar as the world's reserve currency. In the long run, this means the United States may not be able to pay its bills with Monopoly money.

5. The U.S. consumer is loaded with debt and strapped for cash. About 70 percent of the U.S. economy is spurred by consumer spending, according to the Bureau of Labor Statistics, and almost every country in the world relies on the power of the U.S. consumer for the strength of their economy. U.S. consumers have stopped spending, which means the world suffers. Without much in savings, the average American cannot withstand a long recession. If the recession lingers and the U.S. consumer runs out of money, the world will slide into a depression.

6. Unemployment is rising. Every business in the world, big or small, is trying to reduce overhead. One of the quickest and easiest ways to do this is to reduce payroll liability by laying off employees.

As of March 2009, the official unemployment rate was 8.5 percent. During that month, approximately 694,000 jobs were lost in the United States, according to the Bureau of Labor Statistics. However, that unemployment statistic does not count the unemployed people who haven't looked for a job in thirty days, or those working part-time jobs while waiting for full-time work. When you add those people into the official number, the real unemployment rate was 19.1 percent, according to Shadowstats.com. During the Great Depression, unemployment reached 24 percent. At this rate, we will be there soon.

7. Technology is invisible and relatively inexpensive. Today, businesses can do more business with fewer employees and thus become more profitable. This will lead to more unemployment.

8. Our school systems have not prepared students for the Information Age. Technology and its applications are changing so fast that college graduates are not equipped to succeed in the marketplace. Today, most college graduates are obsolete the minute they receive their diploma.

9. Frugality is now cool. For thirty years, people went into debt in order to look rich. It was hip to sport the latest designer handbag or drive an expensive car. Today, the opposite is true. People are proud to be frugal and are spending money more wisely. This will only add fuel to the economic crisis. As you know from Part One of this book, the only way the economy can expand is by us getting into debt. Being frugal may be cool, but it will not help the economy. When we as a country stop spending, unemployment rises and small businesses fail.

An Old Joke

There is an old joke that goes like this: Two friends were walking in the woods when a bear suddenly jumped out and came at them.

"Do you think we can outrun the bear?" one friend asked.

To which his friend replied, "I don't have to outrun the bear. I only have to outrun you."

In my opinion, this is like the world we live in today. Many businesses will fail, and the strong will survive and emerge stronger. Unfortunately, many of my fellow baby boomers are not prepared for the future. Many have taken life too easy for too long. Many are in poor health and without sustainable wealth. Many have no health insurance just as government hospital programs are running out of money.

I believe we are entering a long and hard financial winter. The good news is that spring will come, flowers will bloom, and new life will be born. Eventually, we will come out of this financial crisis, but unfortunately, millions of people will be permanently left behind. For their sake, I hope the president can save them.

In my opinion, it matters little what the politicians do to save the economy. In the end, they are going to save the rich in the name of bailing out the economy.

What really matters is what *you* are going to do to save yourself. You do not need to outrun the bear; you just have to outrun those who are waiting to be saved.

There is good news for those who are ready to move on into a brave new world: This is the best of times for those willing to study, learn quickly, work hard, and not join the chorus of negative people. Learn from the past to succeed in the future. This is your time to become rich—if you want it to be.

Before going further with Part Two, let's review the five new rules of money we have covered so far. They are essential to beating the conspiracy at their own game.

New Rule of Money #1: Money is knowledge. Today, traditional assets do not make you rich or financially secure. You can lose money on businesses, real estate, stocks, bonds, commodities, and even gold. Knowledge makes you rich and a lack of knowledge makes you poor. In this brave new world, it is your knowledge that is the new money.

Part Two is about increasing your financial knowledge.

New Rule of Money #2: Learn how to use debt. After 1971, the U.S. dollar switched from being an asset to being a liability—debt. Debt exploded because the banks could create more money by creating more debt. Our current subprime mess was caused by subprime borrowers and subprime banks. Obviously, both the poor *and* the rich need to learn to use debt better.

Debt is not bad. *Misuse* of debt is bad. Debt can make you rich, and debt can make you poor. If you want to get ahead financially, you need to learn to use debt, not abuse it.

Part Two is about learning how to use good debt to make your life richer and to position yourself to be financially secure.

New Rule of Money #3: Learn to control cash flow. After the dollar became debt, the name of the game was getting you and me into debt. When you are in debt, your cash flows *from* you *to* others. Today, many people are in financial trouble because they have too much cash flowing out of their pockets and very little money flowing into their pockets. If you are going to be financially secure, you need to learn to have more cash flowing into your pockets.

Part Two of this book will be about taking control of your cash flow, both going in and going out.

New Rule of Money #4: Prepare for bad times and you will only know good times. The last depression made my rich dad very rich and made my poor dad very poor. One dad saw the depression as an opportunity, and the other saw it as a crisis.

My generation, the baby boomers, has only known good times. Many are not prepared for the bad times. I am doing well today because I began preparing for bad times over twenty years ago. By preparing for bad times, I do well in good times.

Part Two is about you doing well in bad times, and doing even better in good times.

New Rule of Money #5: The need for speed. Money evolved from barter to digital money as the world's financial system picked up speed. Today, slow people are left behind. A well-positioned person can transact business 24/7. Rather than making money by the month, people can make money by the second.

Self-Examination

As we move into Part Two of *Rich Dad's Conspiracy of the Rich*, it's important to ask yourself:

1. Are you being paid by the month, the hour, the minute, or the second?
2. Are you earning money eight hours a day or 24/7?
3. If you stop working, will money continue to come in?
4. Do you have multiple sources of income?
5. If you are an employee, are you working for an employer who is being left behind?
6. Are your friends and family moving forward or being left behind financially?

Reader Comment

I attended a few courses and read books on wealth and personal development, but I didn't know how to create passive income. I have learned the lesson of passive income the hard way. I am self-employed, and last November I had an operation on my foot. I couldn't work for three months, and during that time I relied on my savings. The experience has taught me the importance of passive income. I am now busy buying property and looking for investment opportunities.

—henri54

Only you can *honestly* answer those questions. Only you know if you are *financially* satisfied with your own life. Only you can *daily* make changes in your life.

If you are ready to make changes and plan for a brighter financial future, then the rest of this book is for you.

Chapter 7

What's the Name of Your Game?

Question: *What advice do you have for the average person?*

Answer: Don't be average.

The 90-10 Rule

Most of us have heard of what is commonly referred to as the 80-20 rule. The principle states that, for many events, about 80 percent of the effects come from 20 percent of the causes. It is also known as the Pareto principle, *the rule of the vital few*. It is named after an Italian economist, Vilfredo Pareto, who noticed that 80 percent of the land in Italy was owned by 20 percent of the people—the vital few. In business, a good rule of thumb is that 80 percent of your business comes from 20 percent of your customers—so take good care of them.

My rich dad took this rule a step further. He believed that 90 percent of all money is earned by 10 percent of the people. He called it the 90-10 rule of money. For example, if you look at the game of golf, I would say that 10 percent of the golfers earn 90 percent of the money. In America today, approximately 90 percent of the wealth is owned by 10 percent of the people.

If you want to win the game of money, you cannot be average. You need to be in the top 10 percent.

Financial Advice for Average People

One reason why 90 percent of people are financially average is because they follow average advice, for example:

1. "Go to school."
2. "Get a job."
3. "Work hard."
4. "Save money."
5. "Your house is an asset and your biggest investment."
6. "Live below your means."
7. "Get out of debt."
8. "Invest for the long term in a well-diversified portfolio of stocks, bonds, and mutual funds."
9. "Retire, and the government will support you."
10. "Live happily ever after."

Reader Comments

My late father, who was a judge and then an investment banker, told me that the stock market was the only way to go. He also said real estate was a stupid investment, with a huge downside. He was not a believer in passive income. He died last year and his estate was settled early this spring. His net worth decreased 87 percent from the time of his death until his estate was settled. The legacy he so desperately wanted to leave for his children had vanished.

—FredGray

> *My dad always says, "There is nothing wrong with being average."*
> *I never really understood that statement. I feel you should try your*
> *best, and as a result you will not be average.*
>
> —arnei

Fairy Tales of Money

I added "Live happily ever after" because I call the above financial advice *the fairy tales of money*. And everyone knows that it's only in fairy tales that people live happily ever after. These are the same fairy tales the World War II generation believed. But these fairy tales are not reality.

Many people my age, the Vietnam War generation, including some of my friends who were once well off but are in financial trouble now, are in trouble today because they believed in these fairy tales. Many of my fellow baby boomers are hoping and praying the stock market goes back up so they can afford to retire.

Today, there are college kids afraid that they won't find a job when they leave school. They too believe in these fairy tales, especially "Go to school" and "Get a job."

The conspiracy wants us to believe in the ten fairy tales. By following the fairy tales, 90 percent of us become pawns in the game of the rich. Most people only know the ten fairy tales, not the reality of money, and therefore few people know the name of the game.

What's the Name of the Game?

For the conspirators, the name of the game is *cash flow*—to be in the 10 percent who collect the cash flow from the other 90 percent. The conspirators want you to believe in the ten fairy tales because that is how the cash flows from you to them.

Now, I can hear some of you saying, "Foul! All you're doing is promoting your own game, CASHFLOW." And I am promoting my game. I'm proud of my game and the accolades it's received. In fact, it's been called Monopoly on steroids. Yet CASHFLOW is not just a board game; it really is the game of the conspiracy. The entire goal of the conspiracy is to get your money to flow from your pocket into the pockets of the conspirators.

Just as a fish cannot see water, most people cannot see the conspiracy. Yet, just like fish are engulfed by water, we are all submerged in the conspiracy. Rich or poor, educated or uneducated, working or unemployed, we are all involved in the game of cash flow. The difference, however, is that some are playing the game, and some are pawns in the game.

To help you to better understand the game of cash flow, the following are examples of how the cash flow game is played in real life.

EXAMPLE #1: A GOOD EDUCATION IS NOT ENOUGH

Many students, or their parents, are deeply in debt with college loans. Additionally, in college, students are able to sign up for credit cards, which contribute to more bad debt piling up. When a student takes out loans and signs up for a credit card, cash flows out of the student's pocket for years to pay off the debt from the loans and credit cards. The conspiracy loves students because students are a great source of cash flow. They are usually financially naïve, and often think of credit cards as free money. Many students learn that that isn't true the hard way—and of course, most never learn. School is a great place to train people to have cash flow out of their pockets and into the pockets of the rich.

Students graduate heavily in debt, enter the job market, find a good job, rack up more debt, and watch their cash flow to the government via income taxes. The more they earn, the higher the percentage they pay in taxes. To save money, they eat at McDonald's, and cash flows to McDonald's. They deposit their paycheck in their bank, and cash flows to the bank in the form of fees each time they use an ATM to get *their* money. They buy a car, and cash flows to the car company, finance company, gas industry, auto insurance, and, of course, to the government for an auto license. They buy a house, and cash flows out of their pockets to pay for the mortgage, insurance, cable TV, water, heat, electricity, and government for property taxes. Every month cash flows to Wall Street to invest in mutual funds for retirement plans, and cash flows from mutual funds to fund managers in the form of commissions and fees. Later in life, when people are old and feeble, cash flows to the nursing home.

And when they die, cash flows to pay taxes on what they left behind. For most people, their entire lives are spent trying to keep up with their outgoing cash flow.

The reason 90 percent of people struggle financially is because cash is always flowing out to someone or something else—flowing to the 10 percent who know the name of the game. The harder the 90 percent work and the more they earn, the more cash flows out to the 10 percent.

This is the story of my poor dad. He worked very hard. He went back to school for higher degrees and specialized training. He made more money and saved some of it, but he never got control of his outgoing cash flow. When he lost his job and was forced to stop working, no cash flowed in—yet he still had to honor his outgoing cash flow obligations. He was in real financial trouble.

School does not teach kids about cash flow. If schools do have financial education classes, they usually only teach kids to save money in a bank and to invest in mutual funds—again, training them to send their cash to the rich.

If I ran the school system, I would have classes on how to control outgoing cash flow and how to create incoming cash flow. This concept will be covered in more detail in the following chapters.

EXAMPLE #2: WHAT CAME FIRST, THE CELL PHONE OR CASH FLOW?

The answer, of course, is cash flow. There would never have been a cell phone without cash flow—no matter how useful one is. Cash flow is the single driving force behind innovation. Once investors realized the opportunity cell phones presented for cash flow, money was raised for the development of a global cell phone network. Without the opportunity to produce cash flow, no one would have been interested in developing the network.

Every time you use your cell phone, cash flows from your wallet to the wallets of the cell phone businesses. They are in the cell phone business, but *the name of the game is cash flow.*

Today, there are many great products, services, or businesses that could save the world, but without cash flowing from the consumer to the rich, those products or businesses are not funded. If you are going to launch a new product or start a new business, you must be very aware of cash flow. If your business only provides enough cash flow for you, chances are that your business will not attract investors or grow.

EXAMPLE #3: THE STOCK MARKET CRASHED

When the stock market began to crash in 2007, that meant cash was flowing out of the market to other assets. As the market crashed, it's a safe bet that 90 percent of investors lost money because they were too slow in moving it. They were slow because they were told the financial fairy tale about investing for the long term in a well-diversified portfolio of mutual funds.

The 10 percent who don't believe in financial fairy tales, however, had already moved their money to safer harbors such as gold, which rose briskly as the market crashed. As cash flowed out of the stock market, mutual fund investors lost and gold investors won. The same thing happened in real estate when the housing bubble burst and cash flowed out, leaving homeowners with lower-valued homes.

Knowledge Is the New Money

The game of cash flow is one reason why new rule of money #1 is *Money is knowledge.* Without financial education in schools, students graduate educated on a variety of subjects but unaware of the game of cash flow—what I believe to be the most important subject of all. Most students graduate and work hard to have incoming cash flow, but they have very little control over it. Every month, more and more money flows out than flows in, which causes them to work harder or get deeper into credit card debt.

Job security is very important for most people because they have little control over their outgoing cash flow. That is why so many financial pundits advise, "Cut up your credit cards and live below your means." This is financial advice for the 90 percent who need to control outgoing cash flow to the 10 percent—the 10 percent who know how to have cash flowing in even when they aren't working.

When it comes to investing, the average investor has very little control over cash flow. In today's traditional retirement plans, cash flows out of work-ers' paychecks before they even touch it and into their 401(k) pension plan. The mutual fund companies then take investors' money and legally siphon out *cash flow* via hidden fees and expenses.

For years, I have been critical of mutual funds. They are horrible invest-ment vehicles designed for financially average people. Over the years, many financial experts have fought back against me because they are sponsored by mutual fund companies. On TV programs and in popular financial publica-tions, you will see these mutual fund pushers offering the same old advice: Invest in a well-diversified portfolio of mutual funds for the long term. This is average advice for average investors; it is not good advice.

One of my heroes is John Bogle, founder of the Vanguard Group. As the inventor of the index fund, which keeps fees low by reducing management overhead, he, too, is an outspoken critic of traditional mutual funds. In an interview with *SmartMoney*, he said that the mutual fund investor puts up 100 percent of the money, takes 100 percent of the risk, and earns only 20 percent of the gains—if there are gains. The mutual fund companies take 80 percent of the profits via fees and expenses. To make matters worse, in 2009, because so much cash has flowed out of the stock market, mutual funds are beginning to raise fees and expenses. This means more cash flow-ing out of investors' pockets.

In his book *The Battle for the Soul of Capitalism*, Bogle also says that mutual fund companies and bankers talk about the magic of compounding interest, but they fail to talk about the power of *compounding costs*, which lower your net returns significantly. I have tremendous respect for Bogle for taking on one of the most powerful forces of the conspiracy, the mutual fund industry. It seems to me that few publications or television channels have the courage to criticize the industry because they do not want to lose the adver-tising revenue that comes from mutual funds.

New Rule of Money #6: Learn the Language of Money

When a student goes to medical school, he learns the language of medicine and is soon speaking of diastolic pressure versus systolic pressure. When

I went to flight school, I had to learn the language of a pilot. I soon spoke words such as *altimeter, aileron,* and *rudder.* When I shifted to helicopters, I used different words, such as *cyclic, collective,* and *rotors.* I could not have succeeded as a pilot if I did not know these words.

In Sunday school, I was taught the phrase "And the word became flesh." In other words, you become your words.

In 1903, when I believe the conspirators took over our school system, they took away the language of money and replaced it with the language of schoolteachers, words such as *algebra* and *calculus,* words rarely used in the real world. The main reason 90 percent of the population struggle financially is because they were never taught the language of money.

Reader Comment

We think in language, and therefore we cannot conceptualize what we have no language to describe. This is why knowing the language of money, and having command of that language, is the way we learn the concepts of what money really is and how it works. It is how we can come to make our own financial decisions instead of being led by "experts" or blindly following conventional advice. It is how we can transcend the mind-set of, "I'm not smart enough to do this; it's beyond my understanding." If you learn the language, then you can gain understanding and control your own outcomes.

—buzzardking

Joining the 10 Percent

When you learn the language of money, you learn the language of the conspiracy. By investing a little time every day to learn the words of money, you have a better chance of being a part of the 10 percent—the vital few. More important, by learning the words of money, you will lessen your chances of being fooled by the false prophets of money—the same false prophets who advise you to save money, buy a house, get out of debt, and invest for the long term in a well-diversified portfolio of mutual funds.

The good news is that it does not cost much to teach kids the vocabulary of money; no massive increase in educational funding is necessary—just some common sense. If schools simply taught students the language of money, financial struggle and poverty would be reduced. If more kids learned the language of money, there would be more entrepreneurs who would create new jobs, instead of the government trying to create jobs.

The remainder of this book will give you some of the basic words about money and investing that you need to know to join the 10 percent.

Words Form Our Attitudes, and Attitudes Form Our Reality

Life is an attitude. If you want to change your life, first change your words, which will in turn change your attitude. The following are some common attitudes about money.

"I'll never be rich" are the words of a person with a poor person's attitude. The chances are he will struggle financially all his life. When a person says, "I'm not interested in money," he actually drives money away from him. When I hear, "It takes money to make money," I reply, "No, money begins with words, and words are free." When someone says, "Investing is risky," I reply, "Investing is not risky. Lack of financial education and listening to poor financial advice is risky." My words reveal a different perspective and a different attitude toward money and investing than someone with a poor person's attitude.

Knowledge Begins with Words

Since money is knowledge, it follows that knowledge begins with words. Words are the fuel for our brains, and words shape our reality. If you use the wrong words, poor words, you will have poor thoughts and a poor life. Using poor words is the same as using bad gasoline in a good car. The following are examples of how words affect us.

WORDS OF A POOR PERSON

It is easy to tell whether a person is poor just by their words. For example:

1. "I'll never be rich."
2. "I'm not interested in money."
3. "The government should take care of people."

WORDS OF A MIDDLE-CLASS PERSON

The middle class employs a different set of words.

1. "I've got a high-paying, secure job."
2. "My home is my biggest investment?"
3. "I'm investing in a well-diversified portfolio of mutual funds."

WORDS OF A RICH PERSON

Just like the poor and the middle class, the rich have words that set them apart.

1. "I'm looking for good employees to work for me."
2. "I'm looking for a cash-flowing hundred-unit apartment house to buy."
3. "My exit strategy is to take my company public via an IPO."

Can you tell the difference between these words? What kind of reality does each set of words reveal? Repeating the lesson from Sunday school, "And the word became flesh." We do become our words.

Capital Gains vs. Cash Flow

In the following chapters, I will introduce you to a few basic terms that a person who wants to be in the 10 percent must know.

Two very important such terms are *capital gains* and *cash flow*. As stated earlier, the most important term is *cash flow*, because cash flow is the name of the conspiracy's game. The reason why 90 percent of people lost money when the real estate and stock markets began crashing in 2007 is because instead of playing the game of cash flow, they played the game of *capital gains*. People who play the game of capital gains are often hoping the price of their home will go up or that the stock market will go up. However, someone who invests for cash flow does not really care if the market or the price of a house goes up or down.

Another important term that is related to capital gains and cash flow is *net worth*. Often you will hear someone brag about his net worth because he bought an expensive house or owns a large number of expensive stocks. The problem with net worth is that, in markets like the one we are currently in, it is *worthless*.

Net worth is often measured by capital gains. For example, if you buy a house for $1 million, technically that is part of your net worth, but if you cannot sell it for $1 million and instead have to sell it for $500,000 and your loan is for $700,000, your net worth is worthless.

And it's not just individuals who think this way. Today, the term *mark to market* is simply another way of saying *net worth* for corporations and banks. Companies loved mark to market when the economy was strong, because it made their balance sheets look good. Now that the market is tanking, however, mark to market is putting many companies under as their net worth becomes worth less and less every day.

Rather than use net worth, I use cash flow to measure my wealth. The money my investments bring in every month is true wealth—not some perceived notion of value that may or may not be true.

During this financial crisis, my wife, Kim, and I are doing well financially because our business and our investments focus on *cash flow*. The reason we were able to "retire" early in life, Kim at thirty-seven and me at forty-seven, is because we made the conscious decision to invest for cash flow. In 1994, we had approximately $120,000 in annual cash flow (passive income) from our investments. Today, our annual cash flow is over ten times that amount, even during this financial crisis, because we continued to invest for cash flow.

One of our neighbors across the street is among the richest people in Arizona. About five years ago, he came over to our home and thanked us for our games and books. With a smile on his face he said, "I play your game

CASHFLOW with my kids and grandkids. I am finally able to explain to them what I do. For years, my kids and grandkids wondered why I did not have a normal job like their friends' parents. For years, I could never explain to them what exactly I did."

Four Green Houses

When I was nine years old, my rich dad began my financial education by playing the game of Monopoly with me. For many years, we played the game together for hours at a time. When I asked why we played the game so often he said, "The formula for great wealth is found in this board game."

"So what is the formula?" I asked.

"Turning four green houses into one red hotel," he replied.

When I was nineteen, I returned from going to school in New York to find that my rich dad had purchased a massive hotel, right smack-dab on Waikiki Beach. Over the course of ten years, from age nine to nineteen, I had watched my rich dad grow from a small businessman into a major player in the Hawaii market. The secret to his success was that he invested for cash flow.

When I was a young boy, rich dad would teach his son and me the finer distinctions of the game of Monopoly. For example, he would pick up a card and ask, "How much income do you receive if you have one green house on your property?"

I would reply, "Ten dollars."

"And how much would you receive if you had two houses on the same property?"

I would say, "Twenty dollars."

I understood basic math. Having $20 was much better than having $10. That was rich dad's way of training his son and me to focus on *cash flow*—not *capital gains*.

Focus on Cash Flow

After 1971, when Nixon took the dollar off the gold standard, inflation began to creep into the economic system. People knew something was wrong, but without much financial education, they did not know what was wrong. In

1980, gold hit $850 an ounce and silver went to $50 an ounce as inflation blasted off.

Under President Reagan, Federal Reserve Chairman Paul Volcker put his foot down and raised the federal funds interest rate to 20 percent in an effort to kill inflation. A new word entered the common vocabulary: *stagflation*, which meant the economy was stagnant (people and businesses weren't making more money) yet inflation was growing (things were getting more expensive).

I remember going into restaurants and seeing menus where prices were crossed out repeatedly. They were increased almost on a monthly basis. Business stalled, yet prices kept going up to pay for rising costs.

Even though home mortgage rates were high, around 12 percent to 14 percent, home prices were starting to skyrocket. I bought a condo in Waikiki in 1973 for $30,000 and sold it for $48,000 two years later. I purchased three condos on the island of Maui for $18,000 each and flipped them for about $48,000 each, making around $90,000 in about a year, nearly six times what I had been making as a Marine pilot. I thought I was a financial genius.

Thank God my rich dad sat me down and talked some sense to me. The next phase of my financial education began. I was no longer a little ten-year-old boy playing Monopoly with rich dad. I was now in my mid-twenties, and I was playing Monopoly for real.

Patiently, rich dad reminded me of the differences between *capital gains* and *cash flow*. It was a good reminder. Every time I flipped a property, I was investing for *capital gains*. Rich dad informed me that the tax laws were different for capital gains and cash flow, just as they are today. "Invest for *cash flow*," were rich dad's words. "Remember the lessons I taught you years ago from Monopoly. Investing for *capital gains* is gambling."

Just as when I was a child, he took out a deed card from Monopoly and said, "How much do you receive for one green house?"

Taking the card in my hand I said, "Ten dollars." Even though I was now nearly thirty years old, I recalled his lesson on the differences between capital gains and cash flow; lessons I had learned as a little boy, but had forgotten as an adult.

"Good," said rich dad patiently. "And how much for two green houses?"

"Twenty dollars," I replied.

"Good," said rich dad sternly. "Don't ever forget that. Invest for cash flow, and you'll never worry about money. Invest for cash flow, and you will not be wiped out in boom and bust markets. Invest for cash flow, and you'll be a rich man."

"But," I began, "it's easier to make more money with capital gains. Real estate prices are skyrocketing. Finding investments that create cash flow is hard."

"'I know," said rich dad. "Just hear what I am saying. Don't let greed and easy money interfere with becoming a rich and financially wise man. Never confuse *capital gains* with *cash flow*."

Reader Comment

When I was younger my father set me up with some property investments that I sold a long time ago. I went to work and invested in the mutual funds like everyone else. I was playing the CASHFLOW game and realized how important it is to have investments creating cash flow for myself. I didn't realize how well I would have done to hold on to the income property and purchase more. If I did it when I was younger I would be in a very strong position now. I have begun purchasing income properties again.

—miamibillg

Cash Flow Is Harder

After 1971, prices increased, but wages did not keep up with inflation. At the same time, jobs were being exported overseas. Knowing something was wrong with our money and wanting to get rich quick, people began investing for capital gains. Intuitively understanding that the dollar was becoming worthless, people stopped saving money and began investing in things that appreciated with inflation. Some things they invested in were art, antiques, old cars, Barbie dolls, baseball cards, and vintage wine—but the stock market and real estate were the most popular investment classes for capital gains investors. Many people became very rich borrowing money and investing in this way. Today, however, many of these same people are the new poor. This time their bets didn't pay off.

In 1929, just before the market crashed, people were borrowing money to buy stocks on margin—basically taking out loans to buy stocks. They were betting on capital gains. In 2007, people were again betting on capital gains with borrowed money—this time with houses and stocks. And this crash is just as devastating.

Crisis of Capital Gains

In 2009, most of the investors crying the blues are investors who invested for capital gains. If they had focused on cash flow, they might not have been as affected by this crisis. They might not be so worried now about their retirement, sending their kids to college, or losing their job.

Between 2007 and 2009, the stock market lost over 50 percent of its value—a value measured in capital gains.

According to Bloomberg.com, since January 2007, the Case-Shiller Home Price Indices in twenty big American cities had fallen every month over two years. In some cities, such as San Diego, Miami, and Las Vegas, the decline was as much as 33 percent. Recently, it was reported in the *Arizona Republic* that my city, Phoenix, earned the distinction of being the first major metropolitan area where home prices had dropped over 50 percent from their highs. Again, Case-Shiller is measuring capital gains—the price of an asset at one particular time versus the price of that asset at another particular time.

Millions of baby boomers my age are praying that both the housing and stock markets will come back before they retire so they won't have to work through their retirement. But again, they are praying for capital gains. They are not actively taking control of their incoming cash flow. They are putting their faith in the market.

Investing for Cash Flow

My real estate investment company owns a lot of real estate in Phoenix. But my company isn't hurting. We're doing fine because we invest for cash flow. We rent apartments. We rarely flip properties. We beat the conspirators by playing the same game they play, the game of cash flow, the same game I learned from my rich dad while playing Monopoly.

Monopoly is *not* a game about flipping. Monopoly is *not* a game about buying low and selling high. It is *not* about diversification. Monopoly is about focus, planning, patience, and long-term control. The first objective is to control one of the four sides of the board game. The second objective is to improve the properties on the side you control, adding green houses and eventually a red hotel. The ultimate investment strategy is to have only red hotels on your side of the board. Then you sit and wait as the other players round the corner hoping not to land on one of your properties. The final objective is to bankrupt the other players and take all their money. In 2009, many people are going bankrupt in the real game of Monopoly.

I Would Have Been Richer

I would have made a lot more money if I had invested for capital gains, and if I flipped real estate. It was hard to invest for cash flow while everyone else was investing for capital gains. In 2009, however, I appreciate rich dad's lessons more and more. I know why he insisted on teaching me to focus on cash flow and not to get sucked in to the frenzy of buying low and selling high.

Today, I have four main sources of cash flow, which I will talk about in upcoming chapters. They are:

1. **My businesses:** Regardless of whether I work or not, cash flows in. Even if the business were to close, cash flow would still come in.
2. **Real estate:** My wife and I own real estate that has cash flow income every month.
3. **Oil:** I do not invest in oil companies. Instead, I invest as a partner in oil drilling. When we hit pay dirt, I receive checks for oil and natural gas sold every month.
4. **Royalties:** My books are licensed to approximately fifty publishing houses. Every quarter, I am paid a royalty from those publishing companies. Additionally, my board games are licensed to approximately fifteen game companies. I am paid a quarterly royalty payment from those companies as well.

Cash Flow for Average People

Most people understand that it's important to have cash flow coming in every month. The problem is that they don't understand the difference between good cash flow strategies and average cash flow strategies. Good cash flow strategies provide passive income that is taxed as little as possible and that you can control. Average cash flow strategies provide passive income that is taxed at the highest income bracket and that you have little to no control over. The following are some examples of *average* cash flow strategies.

1. Savings: Interest from savings is a form of cash flow. Today, the interest rates on short-term bonds are less than zero. If you are lucky, a bank may pay you 3 percent interest on your savings.

There are two problems with cash flow from savings. One is that the 3 percent interest is taxed as ordinary income—the highest tax possible, which means your 3 percent interest is really 2 percent net taxes. Second, the Federal Reserve is printing trillions of dollars to bail out the big banks. In the late 1970s, the bailouts were only in the millions. By the 1980s, bailouts were measured in billions. In 2009, the bailouts are in the trillions.

This will result in inflation, and possibly hyperinflation. If inflation is higher than 2 percent per year, you actually lose money by collecting interest from banks in the form of savings account interest. Understanding the relationship between bailout money and inflation is one example of the importance of knowing history: By knowing a little history, you can understand how fast your savings can lose value. You get paid 3 percent (2 percent after taxes) on your savings as the central banks print trillions of dollars.

2. Stocks: Some stocks pay dividends, which are a form of cash flow. Millions of retirees live on dividends from their stocks. The problem with dividends is that during this crisis many firms cut dividends. During the first week of April 2009, Standard and Poor's announced that 367 firms cut dividends by $77 billion in the first quarter of 2009. That was the worst payout since the S&P started tracking dividend payments in 1955. This meant the recession was spreading right where it hurt, to retirees who were once well off in the pocketbook.

3. Pensions: Pensions are a form of cash flow. The problem is that the federal Pension Benefit Guaranty Corporation (PBGC) shifted most of its $64 billion in assets from bonds to stocks and real estate, just in time for the crash. This means the geniuses behind the PBGC shifted out of cash flow from bonds, presumably because the income from bonds was perceived as too low, and into stocks and real estate, hoping for larger profits from capital gains. This means many pension plans are now in deep financial trouble.

Additionally, the concept of the pension is ancient history for most people. Most companies do not provide a pension anymore, or have drastically reduced the range of their pension program. Now it is mostly government and labor union employees who can count on a pension. Most people have to figure out some other way to generate cash flow for their retirement.

4. Annuities: Annuities are also a form of cash flow. Let's say you turn over $1 million to an insurance company. In exchange, it agrees to pay you a percentage of interest on that money for the rest of your life.

The problem is that annuities are often backed by commercial real estate that you have no control over—commercial real estate and other financial instruments that were bought by large institutional-type investors, many of which are public companies, for capital gains and not for cash flow. The problem with public companies investing for capital gains is that by standard accounting rules, they must mark down their assets to market and raise more capital to cover those losses. This hurts the insurance companies and your annuity returns—all you have to do is look at AIG.

Why Don't More People Play the Game of Cash Flow?

Recently, I went to a conference on investing and listened to different speakers present on different investments. One speaker was a financial planner who was advising people to rebalance their stock and mutual fund portfolios, which to me is ridiculous. *Rebalancing* is another way of saying *invest for capital gains*. He then said, "I know some of you have lost money in the market. But don't worry. The stock market will come back. Remember, on average, the stock market goes up approximately 8 percent per year, so I recommend you continue to invest for the long term." I had to leave when

I saw people in the audience nodding their heads in agreement with him. I wondered how people could be duped so easily.

The conspirators need your cash flowing to them. That is why they train their salespeople such as financial planners and stockbrokers to say things like the stock market goes up 8 percent per year. They use the lure of capital gains to draw your cash flow into their pockets.

Real estate agents use a similar sales pitch. They often say, "You'd better buy now before prices go up." The idea of buying before prices go up is buying on the expectation of capital gains. Again the salesperson uses the lure of capital gains to get your cash flow. That's the game. The moment you sign that mortgage, cash flows from you to them.

Why Doesn't Everyone Invest for Cash Flow?

There are a number of reasons why most people invest for capital gains, and not cash flow. Some of the reasons are:

1. Most people do not know the difference.

2. When the economy was growing, it was easy to play the capital gains game. People automatically assumed their house and stock portfolio would go up with inflation.

3. Cash-flow investing requires more financial sophistication. Anyone can buy something and hope the price will increase. Finding cash-flowing deals takes knowledge of both potential income and expenses, and how to project the performance of the investment based on those variables.

4. People are lazy. They live for today and ignore tomorrow.

5. People expect the government to take care of them. This was my poor dad's attitude, and he died a poor man. For my poor dad, it was easier to expect someone else take care of him. Today, there are over 60 million Americans, my fellow baby boomers, who are about to follow in my poor dad's footsteps.

If you don't want to follow in my poor dad's footsteps, the next chapters are for you.

In Conclusion

The way to beat the conspiracy is to first know the name of the game, and the name of the game is cash flow. Once you know the name of the game, you need to learn the terminology—the language of money. One way to learn the language of money is to play my board game, CASHFLOW. You can start with CASHFLOW 101, which will teach you basic financial concepts. From there you can move on to CASHFLOW 202, which is for advanced financial learning. But in the end, the goal is to prepare you for the real game of cash flow that happens all around you, every hour of the day.

As we discussed, two very important terms are *cash flow* and *capital gains.* In simple terms, 90 percent of the people play the game of capital gains. Only 10 percent play the conspirators' game of cash flow. Therefore, only 10 percent win. Do you want to be a winner or a loser? Do you want to be average or excellent? If you want to win at the game of cash flow, then the rest of this book is for you.

Chapter 8

Print Your Own Money

Cramer vs. Stewart: The Clash of Comedic Titans

The Daily Show with Jon Stewart is a very popular news satire program that is broadcast on Comedy Central. Although the program is supposed to be political satire, many viewers use the program as their primary news source. Many people feel that the mainstream news has become tainted and think satire about the news is more honest.

Jim Cramer has his own television program, *Mad Money*, which airs on CNBC, one of the leading financial news channels broadcast around the world. Cramer is brilliant, entertaining, and does his best to make financial news entertaining. He and Jon Stewart have similar shows on different subjects. Cramer's is about money, and Stewart's is primarily about politics.

On March 12, 2009, Jon Stewart invited Jim Cramer onto his program for a showdown. That night, Stewart was not being funny. He was angry and spoke for millions of people, expressing their frustration with the entire financial industry, including financial news reporting.

Stewart summed up the general feeling of the American public today, saying that CNBC and the financial news media could help educate Americans, showing the idea that there are two markets: one for the long term that average Americans invest in and are encouraged to invest in, and another, fast-paced market that exists away from the public eye. That market, Stewart said, "is dangerous, it's ethically dubious, and it hurts that long-term market. So what it feels like to us—and I'm talking purely as a layman—it feels like we are capitalizing your adventure by our pension and our hard-earned money."

Reader Comments

I do not trust that what the mainstream media says about the financial crisis is credible enough to take action in my portfolios. I actually don't think they are intentionally misleading, but are sharing knowledge from their narrow perspective.

—hattas

I know from experience as a professional trader that the quickest way to lose money is to trade while watching the financial news networks.

—gone17

A *Cash Heist of Your Pension*

Again, history sheds some light on what is happening today. In 1974, Congress passed the Employee Retirement Income Security Act (ERISA), which led to the 401(k), and one of the biggest cash heists in history was under way.

As stated earlier in this book, many people who lived through the last depression were leery of the stock market. Both my rich dad and my poor dad wanted nothing to do with it. They thought the stock market was rigged and that investing in it was gambling. In 1974, ERISA effectively forced millions of people back into the stock market, even if they knew nothing about investing. Prior to 1974, most companies paid for workers' pensions. Pushing workers into the stock market was better for a company, however, because it no longer had to pay those workers a paycheck for life via a pension plan. The 401(k) plan saved the company money, but if a worker did not invest in the stock market, or if the stock market crashed, the worker would not have any money to retire on. This was one reason why the stock market boomed

in the 1970s, and a whole new profession known as financial planning was
created.

My rich dad would have agreed with Jon Stewart's sentiment about there
being two markets—a long-term investment market and a transactional market
that gambles investor money. When the 401(k) program was implemented in
the United States, my rich dad warned me to stay clear. His warning led me to
write *Rich Dad's Prophecy* in 2002, and to later collaborate with Donald Trump
to write *Why We Want You to Be Rich—Two Men, One Message* in 2006.

Donald and I are not against the stock market. We have both founded
publicly traded companies. Rather, we are advocates for responsible financial education. The reason we are so passionate about responsible financial
education is because there are many people and organizations that practice
the exact opposite. They take advantage of the financially illiterate to make
a buck with so-called news and education. As Jon Stewart alluded to in his
interview with Jim Cramer, CNBC, as a leading financial news network, fails
to educate the masses about the real game being played with their money.

Being a former hedge fund manager, Jim Cramer is, in my opinion, an
expert at the game of the conspiracy. As you may know, hedge funds often
prey upon mutual funds like sharks feed on tuna. Although Cramer promised
Stewart during the interview that he would repent and do a better job at
offering financial education, in my opinion, so far I have seen no change—
just more excuses and accusations. But really, how can he change? His very
livelihood is dependent on the hidden game of the conspiracy.

The Shark and the Tuna

About five years ago, my brother and his wife had a baby. They asked if I
would open a 529 education plan for the child's college education. I was more
than happy to help but wanted to be sure I wouldn't throw my money away.
Immediately, I called my stockbroker, Tom, and inquired about the plan.

"I could open an account for you," he said, "but I know you won't like it."

"Why?" I asked.

"Because most 529 plans can only invest in mutual funds," said Tom. "And
I know you know the games mutual funds play."

"Thanks," I said. "I'll find something else."

Thank God I did not open that account. I would have lost over 40 percent of my investment during the 2007 market crash. As Jon Stewart pointed out, there are two games going on. One game is for long-term investors in stocks, bonds, and mutual funds (the tuna), and the other game is for short-term investors like hedge fund managers and professional traders (the sharks).

Even if the market had not crashed, I still would not have invested in the 529 plan because of its reliance on mutual funds. As we discussed in detail in Chapter 7, mutual funds help themselves to the money of unsophisticated investors through fees and expenses. I know the 529 education plan offers a few tax incentives, but those tax incentives hardly make up for the cash being heisted out of the account via fees and expenses, nor would the tax incentives make up for the losses incurred just because of market volatility. Mutual funds are simply an unintelligent investment designed for the financially unintelligent.

Turning Down $4 Million

In 2001, when *Rich Dad Poor Dad* took off, a major mutual fund company asked me to endorse their family of mutual funds. The company offered me $4 million over four years for my endorsement. As tempting as the offer was, I turned them down.

Among the reasons why I turned them down was that I did not wish to endorse a product I didn't believe in. Also, I didn't need their money—as nice as it would have been to have. In the following chapters you will find that making $4 million is not that difficult if you have a solid financial education. I knew that my true wealth was in my financial knowledge, not cash. I knew I could make that $4 million and more by using my intelligence and operating businesses I believed in. Turning down $4 million was difficult, but selling my soul was not worth the money.

As a caveat, I am not against the concept of mutual funds. I am, however, against the high fees and hidden expenses of mutual funds that rob investors of their money. On top of that, there are thousands of mutual funds, but less than 30 percent of them actually beat the S&P 500. In other words, all you have to do is invest in an S&P Index Fund and you will beat over 70 percent of all mutual fund managers—all with less money and higher returns.

As stated in the previous chapter, mutual funds are generally for average to below average investors, the C students in the world of financial intelligence. A- and B-level investors do not need them.

The Power of Words

As we recapped in Chapter 7, new rule of money #1 is *Money is knowledge*, and new rule of money #6 is *Learn the language of money*.

One reason so many people lose so much money in bad investments is because our schools fail to teach us even the basics of financial education. This lack of financial education leads to a misunderstanding of the language of money. For example, when a financial planner recommends you *invest for the long term*, a sophisticated investor would question the definition of *long term*. As Einstein discovered, everything is relative.

One of the reasons Jon Stewart was upset with Jim Cramer is because Cramer is a *trader*. As a general rule, traders are very short-term investors. For a short-term trader, investing for the long term might be a day—or even an hour. The traders are in and out of markets, often ripping into the profits of the investors saving for a safe retirement or their kid's college education. Rather than use the words *long term*, a sophisticated investor would use the words *exit strategy*. A smart investor knows it's not about how long you hold on to an investment. It's about how you plan to increase your wealth with that investment over a stated period of time.

Another word often misunderstood is *diversify*. If you listen to most financial pundits, they will always say that smart investors diversify. Yet, to quote Warren Buffett in *The Tao of Warren Buffett*, "Diversification is a protection against ignorance. It makes very little sense for those who know what they are doing."

Another reason why so many people lose so much money is because they don't know what they are doing and they are *not diversified*, even though their financial planner tells them they are. Let me give you some examples.

1. A financial planner will say you are diversified if you are invested in different sectors. For example, you may invest in a mutual fund of small cap stocks, large cap stocks, growth stocks, precious metal stocks, real estate investment trusts (REITs), exchange-traded funds (ETFs), bond funds, money

market funds, and emerging market funds. While you are technically diversified into other sectors, the reality is you are not diversified because you are in only one asset class—paper assets. When the stock market tanked in 2007, all paper assets associated with the stock market tanked. Being "diversified" was of little use to those diversified in solely paper assets.

2. A mutual fund by definition is already diversified—in paper assets. It is a fund made up of a diversified group of stocks. To make matters worse, there are more mutual funds than individual stocks. Therefore, many mutual funds contain the same stocks. A mutual fund is like a multiple vitamin. Buying three mutual funds is like taking three multiple vitamins. You may take three different pills, but in the end you are taking many of the same vitamins—and possibly even overdosing on those vitamins!

3. Most financial planners can only sell paper assets such as mutual funds, annuities, bonds, and insurance. In fact, after 1974, when ERISA was passed, many insurance salespeople suddenly changed their professional title from "insurance salesman" to "financial planner." Since most financial planners are only licensed to sell paper assets, that is what they sell you. Most do not sell tangible assets such as real estate, businesses, oil, or gold and silver. So, naturally, they will sell you what they are allowed to sell, not necessarily what you need, and that is not diversification.

As the old saying goes, "Never ask an insurance salesman if you need insurance." You know what the answer will be. Two reasons why financial planners recommend diversification are because they can sell you more paper assets, and because it spreads their risk in case they are wrong. Often, they don't have *your* best interests at heart.

A Sophisticated Investor

There are four basic investment categories. They are:

1. Businesses: The rich often own many businesses providing passive income, while an average person may have many jobs providing earned income.

2. Income-producing investment real estate: These are properties that provide passive income every month in the form of rent. Your home or your vacation home doesn't count, even if your financial planner tells you they're assets.

3. Paper assets—stocks, bonds, savings, annuities, insurance, and mutual funds: Most average investors have paper assets because they are easy to buy, require little management, and are liquid—meaning they are easy to get out of.

4. Commodities—gold, silver, oil, platinum, etc.: Most average investors do not know how or where to buy commodities. In many cases, they don't even know how or where to buy physical gold or silver.

A sophisticated investor invests in all four categories. *That* is true diversification. The average investor believes they are diversified, but most are only in category 3, paper assets. That is *not* diversification.

Same Words, Different Language

My point is that we may use the same words but speak a different language. *Long term* to a sophisticated investor means something different than to the novice investor. The same is true of *diversify* and many other words. Even the word *investing* has different meanings. To some it means *trading* in and out of the market quickly. When someone says to me, "I invest in real estate," I often wonder what he means. Does he mean he owns his home? Or is he a *flipper*, an investor who goes in and out of the real estate market? Or does he mean he buys properties that provide cash flow?

My second point about words and language is that many so-called experts want to sound intelligent so they use uncommon words like *credit default swap* or *hedge* to baffle the average person. Both the terms simply mean forms of insurance, but God forbid the "expert" uses that word. Then everyone would know what he was talking about!

In his book *Grunch of Giants*, Dr. Fuller writes, "One of my many-years-ago friends, long since deceased, was a giant, a member of the Morgan family. He said to me: 'Bucky, I am very fond of you, so I am sorry to have to tell you that you will never be a success. You go around explaining in simple terms that which people have not been comprehending, when the first law of success is, "Never make things simple when you can make them complicated."' So, despite his well-meaning advice, here I go explaining giants."

I am proud to continue in the tradition of Dr. Fuller's work. Rather than use the term *giants*, I use *conspirators*. But my goal is always to explain in simple terms what everyone else does in complex terms.

Becoming More Powerful

Dr. Fuller was adamant about the power of words. During one of his lectures I attended, he said, "Words are the most powerful tools invented by humans." In his book *Critical Path* he writes, "'In the beginning [of industrialization— i.e., technologically effective human cooperation] *was the word.*' The spoken and comprehended word greatly expedited the development of humanity's information on how to cope with life's challenges."

Before I studied under Dr. Fuller, I had never respected the power of words. In 1983, I was thirty-six years old and just finally understanding why my poor dad, a career schoolteacher, had such respect for words. I realized why I had flunked out of high school English twice. I did not respect the power of words. By not respecting the power of words, I had denied myself the power to change my life. Having a poor person's vocabulary kept me poor in actuality. Having a poor person's attitude kept me struggling financially. I finally understood why Dr. Fuller said, "Words are the most powerful tools invented by humans." I realized that words are the fuel to our brain— our greatest asset, and also our greatest liability. That is why I believe that, in 1903, financial vocabulary was taken out of the educational system. And for me, when the Bible states, "And the word became flesh," it took on a new meaning. I finally realized why my rich dad forbade his son and me from using the words, "I can't afford it." Or, "I can't do it." Rather, he disciplined us to ask, "How can I afford it?" Or to say, "How can I do it?" I finally realized my life was a sum total of my words.

I knew I would always be a pawn, victim, or slave of the conspiracy if I did not know, understand, and use the words the conspirators used. It was at that point that I forbade myself from using the words of the financially average like "Get a good job," "Save money," "Live below your means," "Investing is risky," "Debt is bad," "A house is an asset," and other popular mantras associated with money. I knew my ticket out of financial slavery was through understanding financial words and the language of money. In 1983, I became a student of financial words, of the language of the conspiracy.

Reader Comment

I have a four-year-old boy. Since he could speak, I've been teaching him simple things related to money to plant those early seeds that will hopefully stay with him as he becomes an adult. Whenever he'd receive money as a gift I would ask him, "What do we do with money?" And I taught him to say, "Save it!" I was very proud of that fact until I thought harder about it. Now I've taught him to say, "Invest it!" Of course, that was the simple part . . . now I have to teach him the four categories to invest it in.

—bgibbs

Weapons of Mass Destruction

Warren Buffett refers to *derivatives* as "financial weapons of mass destruction." Up until 2007, only a few people even knew what a derivative was. Today, billions of people have now heard of derivatives but still have no idea what the word means. As a consequence, the financially ignorant now think derivatives are bad, dangerous, or some sophisticated financial creation only the financial elite can use, create, or understand. Nothing could be further from the truth.

Repeating the advice Buckminster Fuller received from his friend in the Morgan family, "The first law of success is, 'Never make things simple when you can make them complicated.'" And that is what the financial world does. It takes the simple and makes it complex.

By making the simple complex, the financial world sounds intelligent and makes you feel stupid when it comes to money. When you feel stupid, it is easier to take your money. My wife and I founded the Rich Dad Company back in 1997 with the express goal of protecting people from financial predators and equipping them to make sound financial decisions. Our objective was to create financial education products such as games, books, web products, coaching, and advanced financial education programs that made finance simple. You can be a kid or a PhD and still understand our work.

Today, *derivative* is one of the most powerful financial words in the world. The financial establishment has worked hard to create a mystique around the word, and to make it seem like a complicated concept. That is why so few people knew the word until recently and why Warren Buffett refers to financial derivatives as weapons of mass destruction. But in reality the concept of a derivative is not complicated.

A broad definition of a derivative is *a substance that can be made from another substance.* For example, orange juice is a derivative of an orange. One definition of a financial derivative is *having a value from an underlying variable asset.* By way of example, a share of common stock is a derivative of an existing company, such as Apple Computers. Simply said, when you buy a share of Apple, you are buying a derivative of Apple, the company. And when you buy a share of a mutual fund, you are buying a derivative of that fund, which is a derivative of stocks—a derivative of a derivative.

What Warren Buffett didn't say, but should have, is that derivatives are also tools for *mass financial creation.* Derivatives are the tools that the 10 percent use to take money from the 90 percent. I believe Buffett's point was that when you begin to invest in derivatives of derivatives of derivatives, the investment becomes more volatile.

Take a grapevine, for example. Grapes come from grapevines. So grapes are a derivative of the grapevine. You can eat the grape, and it can be very beneficial to your health. You can also squeeze the grapes and make grape juice. So grape juice is then a derivative of the grape, which is a derivative of the grapevine, and it is still good for you. But when you take grape juice and create wine from the grape, the derivative, in this case the wine, becomes more potent and more volatile. If you become addicted to the derivative known as wine you become an alcoholic, and when you become an alcoholic the wine becomes a weapon of mass physical destruction. Health, families, and fortunes have been lost because of alcohol addiction. A similar chain reaction happened during this financial crisis. The irony is that many of the creators of this toxic, potent, and volatile brew of financial derivatives are still running the show—and still creating their witches' brew.

The reason the first part of this book is about financial history is because it is through history that we can better see the present and the future. Prior to 1971, the dollar was a derivative of gold. After 1971, the dollar became a derivative of debt, an IOU known as U.S. bonds and T-bills, backed by the promise of the U.S. taxpayer to pay the bills. The big questions today are: Can the U.S. taxpayer afford the trillions of dollars going to bail out the rich? And what is the future of the U.S. dollar?

Today, the real weapon of mass financial destruction is the U.S. dollar.

Print Your Own Money

Creating a derivative is as easy as squeezing juice from an orange. By simplifying and understanding the definition of a financial derivative, you can easily tap into the power of that word. You, too, can print your own money. A very simple example is an IOU with interest. Let's say you have $100, and your friend wants to borrow that money for one year. So you have your friend sign an agreement to borrow the $100 at 10 percent interest. In other words, your friend agrees to pay you back $110 in one year. You have just created a derivative. The derivative is the $10 in interest you receive in one year. You just squeezed $10 out of your $100.

Now, let's take the derivative to the next power. Let's say you do not have the $100 your friend wants to borrow. So you go to your parents and ask to borrow $100 for one year at 3 percent interest. Your parents agree, and you then turn around and give your friend the $100 at 10 percent interest. A year later, your friend pays you $110. You then take $103, pay your parents back, and all is fine. You make $7 for your efforts. You have now made money without having money, by creating a derivative of a derivative.

In Chapter 5, I wrote about the banking fractional reserve system. Banks do exactly what I just described in the last paragraph, but at a much higher level. They create a derivative to the third power—a derivative of a derivative of a derivative.

For example, let's say you place $100 in a savings account with a bank. The bank takes your savings and creates a derivative by promising to pay you 3 percent for your money. Then the banking laws allow the bank, via the fractional reserve system, to lend your $100 out in multiples at interest, let's say 10 times at 10 percent interest. So the bank pays you $3 for your $100 and lends out $1,000 ($100 × 10) at 10 percent interest. In this example, the bank earns $100 on $1,000, and pays you $3. This happens in real life every hour of every day.

One reason our current financial crisis is so large is because in 2004 the Securities and Exchange Commission (SEC) allowed the five biggest investment banks to step up their fractional reserve from about 10 to as high as 40. In other words, if you put $100 in the bank, the biggest banks could lend out $4,000, and then the hundreds of banks that borrowed that money could lend out ten times that $4,000. All that money had to be placed somewhere, and soon mortgage brokers were looking for anyone who could sign their name. The subprime mess expanded and then exploded—bringing down the entire world economy. So derivatives were not the problem; the problem was greed at the highest levels of banking and the government. To quote Buffett in *The Tao of Warren Buffett* again, "When you combine ignorance and borrowed money, the consequences can get interesting."

We Can All Create Derivatives

My point is that we can all create simple derivatives. We can all create money out of thin air—derivatives of our thoughts. We all have the power to print our own money if we train our minds to think in terms of derivatives. In other words, *money can be a derivative of financial knowledge.* This is why financial education is so important, and why I believe it is not taught in schools. The conspiracy does not want you and me getting in on their game!

Reader Comment

My wife just asked me if I remembered how empowering it was the first time we created derivatives. We created a powerful sales training program and signed up twenty-two people in one seminar. KA-BAMM! $20,000 straight into our bank account! (Plus we have twenty-two people who were happy to be selling more real estate...) Talk about a win-win situation. They say that God

> *has given everyone at least one special skill or talent. "Deriving"*
> *products or services from your knowledge or experience that other*
> *people want is very freeing, empowering, and exciting! The first*
> *time we did this we knew that we'd be financially free and attain*
> *personal sovereignty!*
>
> —davekohler

Money Is Infinite

Once you learn how to create derivatives, money becomes infinite. Let me explain in simple terms.

In order for there to be a derivative, there must be cash flow. For example, when a bank creates a mortgage, which is a derivative of a house, you agree to pay money every month to the bank. In order for a derivative to exist, there needs to be two parties. One party pays and one party receives. In the case of a mortgage, the banker sits on one side of the equation and you sit on the other. The question is, What side do you want to be on? Do you want to be on the side of the mortgagee or the mortgagor?

Once I understood the power of the word *derivative*, I knew which side I wanted to be on. I wanted to be on the receiving side, the 10 percent that receives cash flow from the other 90 percent.

The reason I do not save money is because I am a borrower, not a saver. I love debt—as long as someone else will pay for that debt. I do what the banks do. For example, I borrow $1 million at 10 percent and buy an apartment complex. I follow the first new rule of money: *Money is knowledge*, and I apply my knowledge to get my tenants to pay me at least 20 percent for the $1 million I borrowed at 10 percent interest.

In this overly simplified example, I make $200,000 a year off the $1 million I borrowed, and pay the bank $100,000 per year on that $1 million—that's a net profit of $100,000 for me. In this example, the moment I have the tenant sign a lease agreement, I have created a derivative of my apartment complex that gives the tenant the right to live there according to my rules for an agreed-upon price. If this makes your head spin, find a friend and discuss this simple example of a derivative until it sinks in, until it becomes flesh, a part of you.

Once I understood the power of the word *derivative* and put my knowledge into practice, I knew I would be a free man and would never need a job again. I did not need to buy shares of a mutual fund and hope I could retire someday.

Also, once I understood the power of the word *derivative*, I could move into areas other than real estate. For example, this book is a derivative. To increase the potency of this book, I asked my attorney to create a license for this book. A license is a derivative of this book, and the book is a derivative of me. I then sell the license to print this book to over fifty publishers throughout the world. The publishers then take the license they bought from me, and they print books, another derivative, and ship them to bookstores in their country. Once a quarter, I receive royalty payments from these fifty publishers. The royalty payments are derivatives of the books, the books are derivatives of the license, the license is a derivative of this book, and this book is a derivative of me. Most authors think in terms of books; I think in terms of derivatives. If this sounds complex, please get together with a friend and discuss this example, too, because sometimes our best learning experiences come from conversations. Speaking our ideas aloud helps us to clarify them even more.

Again, once you understand the power of the word *derivative*, you begin to gain the power imbedded in that word. As Dr. Fuller said, "Words are the most powerful tools created by humans." And the Bible said, "The word became flesh." In other words, you become your words.

I could explore more complex examples, but why? My job is to make things simple, not complex. I'd never make it in the Morgan family! However, while I may make financial concepts simple, I am not saying they are easy. I have spent many years shifting my thinking away from my poor dad's thoughts to my rich dad's way of thinking. And I still continue my education even today. If you think you know it all—you really know nothing.

I have given just two simple examples why 10 percent of the people make 90 percent of the money, and why the other 90 percent of people split the remaining 10 percent of the money. It all begins with knowing, understanding, and respecting the power of words, and then choosing your words carefully. You also have to get rid of certain words that drag you down, such as "Get out of debt," "I'll never be rich," "Investing is risky," and "Invest for the long term in a well-diversified portfolio of mutual funds." You need to know and use such words as *derivative, cash flow, cap rate,* and *mitigate,* as well as other words the conspiracy uses. If you enrich your vocabulary, you will enrich your life. I will talk about how you can accelerate this process of enriching your vocabulary in the remaining chapters. In other words, if you want to change your life, begin by changing your words, and the best news of all is that words are free.

In Conclusion

I started the chapter with an exchange between Jon Stewart, a comedian political news commentator, and Jim Cramer, a comedian financial news commentator.

During that interview, Jon Stewart said to Jim Cramer, *"I understand you want to make finance entertaining, but it's not a* [expletive deleted] *game...I can't tell you how angry that makes me, because it says to me, you all know. You all know what's going on."*

Though I can certainly sympathize with Jon Stewart's anger, I disagree with him on a part of this statement. It's possible Cramer may know how traders rip into the average person's investment savings like a shark swimming in a school of tuna, the tuna investing for the long term in mutual funds, hoping and praying the market goes up, hoping for capital gains. But I doubt if Cramer knows the real game of how the rich print their own money.

Cramer is a very smart trader and stock picker, packaged as an entertainer. But in my mind, Cramer works for the conspiracy. He needs to make stock picking entertaining and to give you tips and insights about stocks that are going up or going down. In my opinion, his job is to encourage more tuna to put their money into the stock market, to have their cash flow into derivatives known as stocks, bonds, and mutual funds—all of which are derivatives of a very big game. I believe Cramer's job is to lure the 90 percent into the game of the 10 percent. In the following chapters I will explain how you can become part of the 10 percent who print their own money. After all, if you can create an IOU, you can create a derivative—and that *is* printing your own money.

Remember the first new rule of money: *Money is knowledge.* That knowledge begins with the power of words. Words allow you to speak the language of the conspiracy, and speaking the same language allows you to tap into the power of the conspiracy without being a pawn, slave, or victim of the conspiracy. By speaking the language, you can play your own game, and the name of the game is cash flow.

Chapter 9

The Secret of Success: Sell

Question: *Why do mice have small balls?*

Answer: Because mice don't sell many tickets.

What Were You Thinking?

I can hear some of you moaning and groaning from that joke. Some of you may not get it. Some may be wondering what kind of balls I am talking about. As much as I hate to explain the joke, the balls I am talking about are charity or inaugural balls—lavish parties. I know some of you were thinking of different kinds of balls such as soccer balls, or vulgar things, which I won't get into.

My reason for talking about mice having small balls is to illustrate the power of words and how words can have multiple meanings, cause misunderstandings, deceive, and/or mislead. Many financial words of advice can actually damage a person's life. I call these words of financial deception the *financial fairy tales*.

Financial Fairy Tale #1: Live Below Your Means

To me, these words are dream killers. First of all, who enjoys living below their means? Don't most people want to live a full, rich, and abundant life? The concept "Live below your means" keeps many people financially poor, emotionally empty, and spiritually neutral. If you look into the deeper meaning of these words, you can come up with multiple meanings, such as "Don't desire the finer things of life," or, "You can't have what you want." Rather than accepting that advice as gospel, a person should ask, Will living below my means allow me to live the life I want to live? Will I live happily ever after as people do in fairy tales?

Reader Comment

I never thought of living below your means as a bad thing; to me, it just means being a good steward by spending less than you earn. If you want to spend more, then earn more first. But now I see how the wording of the saying "live below your means" is damaging. It doesn't mention expanding your means, or encourage you to do so. The way it's worded basically seems to translate to "Be happy with what you have, 'cause that's all you've got." It's death to dreams.

—Ktyspray

My poor dad believed in living below his means. Our family lived frugally, constantly trying to save money. As children of the Great Depression, my mom and dad saved everything—even used aluminum foil—and they bought everything on the cheap, including food.

My rich dad, on the other hand, did not believe in living below his means. Instead, he encouraged his son and me to go for our dreams. This does not mean he was wasteful or a spendthrift. He was not flashy, nor did he flaunt his wealth. He simply thought that advising people to live below their means was psychologically and spiritually damaging financial advice. He believed that financial education would give people more choices and more freedom to decide how they wanted to live their life.

Rich dad believed dreams were important. He often said, "Dreams are personal gifts from God, our personal stars in the sky, guiding us along our path through life." Were it not for his dreams, my rich dad would never have become a rich man. He often said, "Take away a person's dreams, and you take away their life." That's why the first step of my CASHFLOW board game begins with players selecting their dreams. In memory of my rich dad, my wife, Kim, and I intentionally designed the game's first step that way.

Rich dad often said, "You may never reach the stars, but they will guide you on your path through life." When I was ten years old, I dreamed of sailing the world as Columbus and Magellan did. I have no idea why I had that dream. I just did.

At the age of thirteen, rather than carve salad bowls in wood shop, I spent the year building an eight-foot sailboat. I was sailing on the ocean in my mind as soon as I built my little boat, dreaming of sailing it to faraway lands.

At the age of sixteen, my high school guidance counselor asked me, "What do you want to do when you graduate from high school?"

"I want to sail to Tahiti, drink beer at Quinn's Bar [an infamous Tahitian landmark], and meet beautiful Tahitian women," I replied.

With a smile, she handed me a brochure on the U.S. Merchant Marine Academy. "This is the school for you," she said, and in 1965 I became one of two students from my school selected by the U.S. Congress to attend the federal military academy that trained ships' officers for the U.S. Merchant Marine, one of the most selective schools in the United States. Without my dream of sailing to Tahiti, I would never have gotten into the academy. It was my dream that empowered me. Like Jiminy Cricket sang in "When You Wish Upon a Star," "If your heart is in your dream, no request is too extreme."

Reader Comment

In 2003, when my only daughter became engaged, our family business was about to close. Debt was piling up, and we just couldn't sell enough of our product to break even. However, I wanted a wedding to remember for my daughter; after all, she was my only child. So how does one afford a $26,000 wedding AND handle a failing business—DREAM BIG, and the answers will come.

> *We got into the tail end of the housing boom and renovated a*
> *house . . . That venture helped pay for our daughter's memorable*
> *wedding.*
>
> —synchrostl

In 1968, as a student at the academy, I sailed to Tahiti on a Standard Oil tanker. I nearly cried as the tanker's bow cut softly through the crystal-clear waters of some of the most beautiful islands in the world. And yes, I did go to Quinn's Bar—and I did meet some very beautiful Tahitian women. Four days later, as my tanker sailed back to Hawaii, I felt the satisfaction that came from fulfilling my childhood dream. It was time to move on to a new dream.

Rather than live below my means, rich dad reminded me constantly to push the boundaries of my life. Even when I was short on money, I still drove a nice car and lived in a beachfront condo on Diamond Head Beach. Rich dad's advice was never to think, look, or act like a poor person. He constantly reminded me that "the world treats you as you treat yourself."

This does not mean I was reckless with my money. My personal demand for a higher standard of living required me to always push my mind to determine how I could afford the luxuries of life, even though I had very little money. In rich dad's eyes, I was training my brain to think like a rich person by battling the poor person in me. He often said, "When you don't have money, think and use your head. Never give in to the poor person inside you."

I attained the things I wanted by using my head. I drove a Mercedes convertible by trading consulting work for the use of the car. I lived in a beautiful condo on the beach by doing marketing work for a family who lived on another Hawaiian island. In exchange for the work I did for them, they let me live in their condo located in one of most beautiful waterfront hotels at Diamond Head for about $300 a month—the price most people paid for a single night's stay. Rather than live below my means, I stretched my brain to find ways to live a life of elegance without blowing my finances to shreds. I use the same skills in business today. If I don't have money for something

I want, I use my head to figure out how to get it. I do not let the amount of money in my bank account dictate the boundaries of my life.

Whenever I hear financial advisors saying "live below your means," I cringe. What I hear is a "financial expert" saying, "I am smarter than you. Let me tell you how to live your life. The first step is to give me your money, and I'll manage it for you." Millions of people follow this advice like sheep, living below their means and turning their money over to the "financial expert," who turns it over to Wall Street.

Rather than hand our money over to "experts," rich dad encouraged his son and me to become our own experts by studying money, business, and investing. Living below your means might be good advice for some people, but not for me. Why live below your means when an abundant and full life is within your reach?

If you want to change your life, begin by changing your words. Start speaking the words of your dreams, of who you want to become, not the words of fear and failure. Look at this financial crisis as a blessing rather than a curse, an opportunity rather than a problem, a challenge rather than an obstacle, a time to win rather than a time to lose, and a time to be brave rather than to be afraid. And be glad when things are difficult because difficulty is the dividing line between winners and losers. Think of difficulty and struggle as the training ground of champions.

Rather than live below your means, dream big and start small. Start with tiny steps. Be smart, get financially educated, create a plan, find a coach, and go for your dreams. As a young man playing Monopoly, rich dad saw his dreams on the game board—the plan for his life and his plan out of poverty. He started with little green houses on the Monopoly board and dreamed of his big hotel on Waikiki Beach. It took him about twenty years, but his dream did come true. Thanks to rich dad, my mentor and my coach, once I got serious, I achieved my dream of financial freedom after ten years of perseverance. It wasn't easy. I made many mistakes. I was scolded more often than I was praised. I lost money and made money. I met many good people, a few great people, and some very, very bad people. From each person I gained wisdom not taught in school or learned from books. My journey was not so much about the money, but who I became in the process. I became a rich person who does not let money, or the lack of it, dictate the boundaries of my life.

The Game of Life

The following is a picture of the CASHFLOW game.

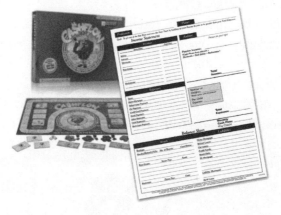

When looking at the layout of the CASHFLOW game, you see the Rat Race in the inner circle. The Rat Race is for people who "play it safe" by finding a secure job, buying a house, and investing in mutual funds. The Rat Race is for people who think it is smart to live below their means.

The outer circle on the game board is the Fast Track. This is the game of money that the rich play. The way out of the Rat Race and onto the Fast Track is by being financially smart with your use of the game's Financial Statement. In real life, your personal financial statement is your financial report card. It is a reflection of your financial IQ. The problem is that most people leave school not knowing what a financial statement is—so they are more likely to have an F on their financial report card. A person can go to great schools and get straight A's on their academic report card but be a financial failure in terms of their financial statement.

A PERSONAL TOUR OF THE CASHFLOW GAME

If you would like a more in-depth explanation of the CASHFLOW game, please go to www.richdad.com/conspiracy-of-the-rich, and through a web video presentation, I will personally explain why Kim and I created the CASHFLOW game and what lessons you can gain from playing it.

Financial Fairy Tale #2: Go to School So You Can Get a Secure Job

My poor dad valued job security. That is why he believed so strongly in school and a good academic education.

My rich dad valued financial freedom. That is why he believed so strongly in financial education. He often said, "The people with the most security are in prison. That is why it's called 'maximum security.'" He also said, "The more security you seek, the less freedom you have."

The following picture is the CASHFLOW Quadrant, which figures in the title of the second book I wrote in the Rich Dad series.

In the CASHFLOW Quadrant:

E stands for *employee*.
S stands for *small business* or *specialist*, such as a doctor or lawyer.
B stands for *big business* (over 500 employees).
I stands for *investor*.

You may notice that the school system does a very good job of producing E's and S's, the left side of the quadrant, the side where security is cherished.

The B and I quadrants, the right side of the quadrant, is where freedom is cherished. Due to a lack of financial education, the B and I quadrants remain a mystery to most people. That is why most people say starting a business or investing is risky. Anything is risky if you lack education, experience, and guidance to do it correctly and well.

CHOOSE YOUR EXPERTS CAREFULLY

I listen to many financial advisors, but follow the advice of only a few. One advisor I follow religiously is Richard Russell, an expert on the stock market. This is what Richard Russell says about investing for the long term in stocks: "[Stock] markets can be compared with gambling at Las Vegas. When you gamble at Vegas, you are bucking the house odds. Which is why if you play long enough at Vegas, you will always lose your money."

Russell also says this about people who invest in fairy tales: "Investing in the stock market is a long-term tax on people who want something [profits] without doing any real work for those imaginary profits."

The problem with most financial advisors is they are in the E and S quadrants and work for the B and I quadrants. Most financial advisors are not in the B and I quadrants, nor are they rich people. Most are called brokers—stockbrokers, real estate brokers, insurance brokers. As my rich dad often said, "The reason they are called brokers is because they are broker than you."

In *The Tao of Warren Buffett,* Warren Buffett says this about financial advisors: "Wall Street is the only place that people ride to in a Rolls-Royce to get advice from those who take the subway."

The following graphs, given to me by Rich Dad Advisor Andy Tanner, demonstrate the fallacy that using a broker to manage a diversified portfolio is generally a wise financial decision. The first shows the percentage returns of the Fidelity Magellan Fund (one of the best-known funds in the world) versus the returns of the Dow Jones Industrial and the S&P 500.

Return Performance Comparison
Fidelity Magellan Fund vs S&P 500 and Dow Jones Industrial

As you can see, the general, unmanaged Dow Jones and S&P 500 have well outperformed the Fidelity Magellan Fund for over twenty years.

But that's not the worst news. This next chart shows the relationship between the Fidelity Magellan Fund and the fees charged for the management of the fund.

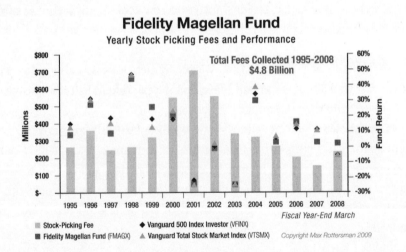

Fidelity Magellan Fund
Yearly Stock Picking Fees and Performance

As you can see, since 1995 the Fidelity Magellan Fund has generated $4.8 billion in fees while at the same time *not* outperforming the Dow Jones and the S&P 500. By investing in simple unmanaged shares of the Dow Jones and the S&P 500, not only could you have had a better return, but you could also have saved a lot of money in fees in the process.

Reader Comment

About the stock market, your advice reflects pretty accurately my experience over the last fifteen years, from the time I started working right after college and invested in the stock market, until now. I have a small variety of mutual funds and I've seen them generally lose their value, teeter, and then lose their value again. Nowhere do I see any growth or steady increase in value, like I do, say, for example, with certain businesses I've watched over that same time frame.

—obert

If your goal is to live a rich life, it is essential that you learn the difference between the right and left sides of the CASHFLOW Quadrant and that you are careful what advice and what advisors you listen to. Where you are in the CASHFLOW Quadrant has huge implications for your ability to get out of the Rat Race and onto the Fast Track.

A PERSONAL TOUR OF THE CASHFLOW QUADRANT

If you would like a more in-depth explanation of the CASHFLOW Quadrant, please go to www.richdad.com/conspiracy-of-the-rich, and I will personally explain the CASHFLOW Quadrant to you in a web video presentation.

Financial Fairy Tale #3: Social Security and the Stock Market

In December 2008, the world learned about Bernard Madoff and Ponzi schemes. Up to that time, most people had no idea who Bernie Madoff was or what a Ponzi scheme was. The term *Ponzi scheme* was named after Charles Ponzi, an Italian immigrant to America who was charged with deceiving investors in 1920. A *Ponzi scheme* means "a fraudulent investment that pays investors from their own money or pays investors from subsequent investor money. In simple terms, it means robbing Peter *and* Paul to pay Ponzi.

Bernie Madoff pleaded guilty for his Ponzi scheme on March 12, 2009, on eleven counts of criminal complaint for stealing over $65 billion in investor money.

Madoff's Ponzi scheme is considered the biggest in history, but I believe that it is not. Because few people understand what a Ponzi scheme is, they don't see that the biggest Ponzi schemes are still in operation today. In simple terms, a Ponzi scheme is a financial fairy tale. It works only if new investors keep investing money so that the manager, in this case Bernie Madoff, can pay off the old investors. In other words, a Ponzi scheme keeps working as long as there are new people willing to put money in. It does not generate enough cash flow on its own to support its operations.

If you think of the definition of a Ponzi scheme and its implications, then you might conclude that Social Security is the biggest Ponzi scheme in U.S. history. The Social Security system only works if younger workers keep putting money into the pot. Most people understand that the Social Security fund is empty, yet people keep pumping money into what I consider a government-sponsored Ponzi scheme, hoping there will at least be enough for *their* retirement.

And I don't think Social Security is the only Ponzi scheme still in operation today. I found it amusing that during George W. Bush's presidential term he pushed legislation for younger workers to put money into the stock market rather than Social Security. I think he wanted younger workers to put their money into one of the biggest Ponzi schemes of all: the stock market. In the stock market, investors only make money as long as stock prices rise—as long as new money is being pumped into the market. If money is pulled out of the market, stock prices fall and investors lose their money.

This is why knowing the difference between capital gains and cash flow is important. All Ponzi schemes are based on capital gains. For prices to go up, new money must come in. That is why I consider the stock market to be a Ponzi scheme. If no new money comes in, the market crashes. The same is true with real estate or the bond markets. As long as cash flows in, the Ponzi scheme of capital gains keeps the boats floating. But if people want their cash back, prices drop, and there is not enough to pay everyone back.

In 2009, one of the biggest problems facing mutual fund companies is outgoing cash flow. Today, many mutual fund companies are having trouble raising enough money to pay investors who are leaving. Investors are now finding out that most mutual funds are legalized Ponzi schemes.

The Importance of Financial Education

There are three different types of education required for success today. They are:

1. **Academic education:** the ability to read, write, and do math.
2. **Professional education:** learning to work for money.
3. **Financial education:** learning how to make money work for you.

Our school system does an adequate job with the first two types of education but fails miserably at providing financial education. Millions of well-educated people have lost trillions of dollars because the school system has left out financial education.

I did not do well in school. I was never good at reading, writing, or math, nor did I want to become an E or S. As a young boy, I knew the school system was not an environment in which I could be a winner. That's why I focused on my financial education. By studying for the B and I quadrants, I knew I could have more money and freedom than people preparing for the E and S quadrants.

LIFE AFTER THE DEPRESSION

As I've mentioned, the last depression had a profound effect on my poor dad. He went to school, studied hard, and achieved his fairy tale, a safe, secure job as a teacher. He felt secure in the E quadrant. The problem is that his fairy tale turned into a nightmare when he lost his job, and then lost his retirement savings when he followed bad financial advice. If not for Social Security, he would have been in serious financial trouble.

The last depression also had a profound effect on my rich dad. He knew his future was in the B and I quadrants, and though he was never a stellar academic student, he was a very astute student of financial education. When the economy recovered, his financial IQ was well prepared, and his life and business took off. His dreams came true.

In 2009, millions of people are following in my poor dad's footsteps. Many are going back to school and being retrained for the E and S quadrants, but they are not expanding their financial education. Instead, they are hoping to ride things out and just survive the downturn. Millions have found religion in frugality, making an art of living below their means and downsizing their dreams. Cheap is the new cool.

Some people, however, are following in my rich dad's footsteps and furthering their financial education. Today, most universities, even Harvard and Oxford, are offering courses in entrepreneurship. Seminars on entrepreneurship, real estate investing, and trading paper assets are filled to capacity. Millions of people know there is another type of education, financial education, which is their path to the new future, the new economy, and their dreams.

The question is, Which future are you pursuing? When the next depression or great recession ends, what will you be doing? Will you be ahead of the game or falling further behind?

A TALE OF TWO TEACHERS

One of my best friends is a young man named Greg. He is a social entrepreneur. More specifically, he runs a school for kids with severe learning disabilities, kids the California school system cannot or will not handle. Today, as President Obama hands out billions in program dollars, Greg's business is one of the businesses that will receive the extra money. In other words, his business is booming. Since his business is booming, he is buying more schools and hiring more special education teachers.

My point is this: Greg is a teacher and a social entrepreneur who operates from the B and I side of the quadrant. The teachers he hires are from the E and S side. Greg and his teachers work in the same school but live in two completely different worlds.

I have known Greg since he was nineteen years old. Today, he is a millionaire at age thirty-three, and he jokingly tells people he's successful because he has a PhD—a public high (school) degree. Many of the teachers he hires, however, *do* have real PhDs. As you can imagine, there is sometimes animosity between Greg and his teachers. Greg's dream is to own dozens of schools, hire hundreds of teachers, and be able to teach thousands of challenged kids. The teachers he hires have different dreams.

Bestselling Author—Not Best-Writing

A few years ago, a major newspaper ran an article about me, criticizing me for being a copier salesman. In effect, the journalist asked, How does a copier salesman become a bestselling author? Obviously, the journalist, probably an A student in English and a much better writer than me, misunderstood the words *bestselling author.* As I said in *Rich Dad Poor Dad,* I am not a *best-writing author;* I am a *bestselling author.* Many people can *write* well; few can *sell* well.

To many people, *sell* is a vulgar word. My poor dad thought the word *sell* was a four-letter cuss word, just as many people probably thought the word *balls* in my joke about mice was a vulgar word. As an academic and an intellectual, the idea of selling was a foul idea to my poor dad. He thought salesmen were scum. To my rich dad, however, the word *sell* was essential to an entrepreneur's financial success.

Reader Comment

I think selling is the greatest profession ever. We are all salesmen; we sell our friends on seeing a movie or trying a restaurant we loved, we sell our husbands on why they should take out the garbage, we sell our kids on why they should develop a good work ethic, and we sell ourselves on why we need that dress. Where sales gets its bad name is when money is exchanged. Then selling is bad. But stop and think . . . where would we be without selling? Just about everything we own was SOLD to us. I think we need to all grow up and realize that we can't be "sold" anything unless we really wanted it in the first place. Stop blaming the "salesman."

—synchrostl

One reason why I mentioned Greg, my social entrepreneur friend, is because of the differences between Greg and the teachers he hires. One of those differences is found in the word *sell*. For many teachers, the idea of getting rich "selling" education is a violation of their deepest-held beliefs. But Greg knows that if he doesn't sell, his teachers don't get paid.

Greg also knows that the more he sells the more money he makes, which allows him to buy more schools, hire more teachers, and teach more kids. The teachers get paid the same regardless of how many schools Greg and his wife, Rhonda, who is also a teacher, own. The difference is the mind-set of the left side of the CASHFLOW Quadrant versus the right side of the CASHFLOW Quadrant.

Another reason why I mentioned Greg is because Greg sells "tickets" to the state of California. The more schools he owns, the more tickets he can sell. His teachers sell their labor. They can only sell one ticket: themselves. My point is that people who sell many tickets (a product or service) make more money than people who only sell one ticket (their labor). In the movie industry, a movie star who can sell the most movie tickets makes the most money. The same is true for music stars. Musicians who sell the most derivatives (CDs, tickets, or downloads) make the most money. In sports, the promoters of the Super Bowl or Wimbledon make a lot of money because they can sell many tickets and media rights. In simple terms, if you can't sell "tickets" (derivatives of you), you have to sell your labor. I sell millions of "tickets" in the form of books, games, and special events, which are derivatives of me. My ability to sell "tickets" is one reason why I prosper even during this financial crisis.

In 1974, as I was leaving the Marine Corps, I knew I did not want to follow in my poor dad's footsteps. I did not want to go into the E and S quadrants. That is why I did not go back to sailing for Standard Oil or flying as a pilot for the airlines. Again, my dreams were not in the E and S quadrants. My dreams were in the B and I quadrants. I was not seeking job security, nor did I want to live below my means.

Rather, I decided to follow in my rich dad's footsteps. When I asked him for guidance to become a B and I, he simply said, "You must learn to sell." Because of his advice, I took a job working for Xerox as a sales trainee. For me, learning to sell was almost as hard as learning to fly. I am not a natural salesman, and I hate rejection. I was nearly fired many times as I struggled with knocking on doors and selling Xerox copiers against IBM copiers. After two years, my skill and confidence improved, and I began to enjoy something that initially terrified me. And for the next two years, I was consistently among the top five sales representatives in the Honolulu branch of Xerox. My income skyrocketed. While the money was good, the best part of the experience was the professional sales training I received, and my newfound confidence in selling. I left Xerox in 1978, once my part-time nylon wallet business was off the ground. But the sales training I received at Xerox has made me a rich man many times over.

Become a Student of the Word Sell

The secret to my success has been the word *sell*. In 1974, I went against my poor dad's values and became a student of the word *sell*. In the world of money, it is a very important word. For three years I struggled to learn to sell. Finally, in 1977, I became the bestselling salesman for Xerox. By 1979, my first business came out with a bestselling new product in the sporting goods industry, my nylon and Velcro surfer wallets. In 1982, my business boomed when I began working with rock bands such as Duran Duran, the Police, and Van Halen to sell rock and roll products just as MTV was taking off. In 1993, my first book, *If You Want to Be Rich and Happy, Don't Go to School*, became a bestseller in the United States, Australia, and New Zealand. In 1999, *Rich Dad Poor Dad* became a *New York Times* bestseller. In 2000, after I appeared on *Oprah*, my book *Rich Dad Poor Dad* became an international bestseller, published in over fifty languages and sold in over a hundred countries. None of this would have been possible had I not learned how to sell at Xerox in the 1970s.

Poor People Have Nothing to Sell

One big reason why so many people struggle financially is because they have little to sell, don't know how to sell, or both. So if you are struggling financially, find something to sell, learn to sell better, or both. If you are sincerely interested in improving your sales skills, one of my best friends, Blair Singer, founded a business that trains individuals and businesses in the art and science of selling. His courses are tough and demanding, but his results are phenomenal. You can contact his business at salesdogs.com. Blair is internationally recognized as a sales training genius and is the author of the Rich Dad Advisor book *Sales Dogs*. Improving your sales skills is a smart way to increase your income, regardless of what quadrant you are in.

There are many people who have great products or services. The problem is, the sale goes not to the best product or service, but to those who can sell the best. In other words, not being able to sell is very expensive. It costs you untold dollars in lost business!

This is one reason why Donald Trump and I recommend looking into a network marketing business. If you are serious about becoming an entrepreneur, I suggest investing a few years, in your spare time, in learning the skill of selling from a network marketing business. The training you receive, especially the skill of overcoming your fear of rejection, is priceless.

Sellers vs. Buyers

In 2002, I took a business public on the Toronto Stock Exchange for the first time. It was a mining venture located in China. In my opinion, building a business and taking it public, which means selling shares on a stock exchange, is the ultimate goal of an entrepreneur. Once the company went on sale to the public, I said a silent thank-you to my rich dad for encouraging me to become a student of the word *sell* rather than thinking of it as a vulgar word as my poor dad did.

Looking at the CASHFLOW game, you can clearly see why so many people have lost fortunes.

Taking my company public was a Fast Track event. In the world of the B and I quadrants, the sellers in an initial public offering (IPO) are known as *selling shareholders*. Selling shareholders sell their shares to those who are in the Rat Race for a substantial gain. The lesson is that in the world of money there are buyers and sellers. In the world of money the rich are *sellers* and the poor and middle class are *buyers*. The buyers are on the E and S side, and the sellers are on the B and I side.

For greater clarity on the game of buyers and sellers, please go to www.richdad.com/conspiracy-of-the-rich, and I will explain more in a video presentation.

In Conclusion

When you look at the world economy today, it is easy to see why we're in this financial crisis: China is selling and the United States is buying. In other words, the United States buys more than it sells. Not only that, but Americans are buying with borrowed money, using their homes as ATMs. The world often considers Americans the consumers of last resort. This causes deficits in our balance of trade, which causes the U.S. debt to grow into the trillions and our taxes to grow. China is now our biggest creditor. As a nation, we have lost our ability to sell more than we buy. It is also easy to see why many businesses are failing. When revenues go down or during hard economic times, many accountants cut the advertising budgets for a business. That is the worst thing they can do. Cutting advertising kills a business. Rather, in hard times, businesses should increase their advertising and try to capture larger market share. As the saying goes, sales solve all problems—and you can't have sales without advertising.

On a personal level, if you want to get out of the Rat Race and move onto the Fast Track to living a rich life, you have to overcome your fear of rejection and learn the valuable skill of selling. *Remember: Focus more on selling and less on buying.* The reason so many millions of people are in financial trouble is because they love to buy and hate to sell. If you want to be rich, you must sell much more than you buy. This does not mean you should live below your means. Rather than live below your means, learn to sell, and you can expand your means and go for your dreams. If you sell more than you buy, you will not have to live below your means, cling to job security, or go to small balls with the rest of the mice.

Chapter 10

Building for the Future

The Big Bad Wolf: *I'll buff… and I'll puff… and I'll blow your house down!*

Most of us have heard the fairy tale of the big bad wolf and the three pigs. It is a great fairy tale with many applicable life lessons for all ages. As the story goes, there were three little pigs. One pig built his house out of straw. The second built his house out of sticks. And the third built his house out of bricks.

The pig that built his house out of straw was finished first, so he had lots of time to play. Soon the straw pig was encouraging the second pig to hurry and finish his stick house so he could have someone to play with. When the stick pig finished, the two pigs were laughing, singing, playing, and making fun of the third pig, the brick pig, for working so hard and taking so long to build his house. Finally, the brick house was finished, and all three pigs could enjoy life.

Then one day, the big bad wolf stumbled across the happy little subdivision and saw three tasty meals. Spotting the approaching wolf, the three pigs ran into their respective homes. Stopping first in front of the house of straw, the wolf demanded the little pig come out. When the pig refused, the wolf simply huffed, puffed, and blew the house of straw away. The straw pig escaped to the house of sticks. Again, the wolf demanded that the pigs come out, and they refused. With a huff and a puff, the wolf blew away the house of sticks, and two pigs ran to the house of bricks.

Now confident that he had three meals in one house, the wolf boldly approached the house of bricks and demanded that the three pigs come out, and once again the three pigs refused. As the story goes, the wolf huffed, puffed, and blew as hard as he could, but the brick house did not come down. Again and again, the big bad wolf huffed and puffed, but he failed to blow the house down. Exhausted, the wolf finally left, and the three little pigs celebrated.

In the fairy tale, the first two pigs learned their lesson and soon built their own houses of brick, and they all lived happily ever after. But as you know, "The Three Little Pigs" is just a fairy tale. In real life, people ask the government to rescue them with taxpayer money, and then they rebuild their straw and stick houses all over again. The fairy tale continues, lessons are not learned—and the wolf lurks in the darkness.

Houses of Straw and Sticks

In 2007, a big bad wolf—subprime debt—came out of the woods. When the wolf huffed, puffed, and blew, the giant house of straw, our biggest banks, came down. As the banking house of straw crumbled, it took other houses of straw and sticks with it. Today, corporate giants such as AIG, Lehman Brothers, Merrill Lynch, Citibank, Bank of America, GM, and Chrysler are crashing to the ground. The world is finding out that the corporate giants we thought were made of bricks were really made of straw and sticks. As these giant houses crumble, the shock wave is taking smaller businesses and individuals with them.

Today, businesses are closing, unemployment is soaring all over the world, housing values are dropping, and savings are being depleted. Even an entire country, Iceland, has gone into default, and many others, including the United States, and states like California (the eighth largest economy in the world) are on the brink. Unfortunately, rather than learn the lessons as the little pigs did and rebuild with brick, we expect the Federal Reserve, Wall Street, and government leaders to solve our problems for us.

All over the world, people are asking, "What are our leaders going to do?" I believe a more important question is, What are you and I going to do? More specifically, How can you and I build our own house of bricks?

Building a House of Bricks

Building my house of bricks began with rebuilding and educating myself. As you'll remember, New Rule of Money #4 is: *Prepare for bad times and you will only know good times.* In 1984, I began talking to Kim about what I saw as the future of the economy and why we had to prepare for it. Rather than being frightened, she simply took my hand, and we began our life journey together—and together we've built a strong house of bricks. At the start of our journey, we were in debt. I still owed about $400,000 out of a $790,000 loss from the failure of a past business, and I had no money, job, home, or car. All we had were the clothes on our backs, two small suitcases, our love, and a dream for our future.

In 1986, we broke out a bottle of champagne and celebrated "zero." Working together, we had paid off the $400,000 in bad debt. By 1994, we were financially free. Together we had built our life's brick house. We prepared for the bad times and have since only known good times—even in this terrible financial crisis. This does not mean we have not had our setbacks, struggles, failures, losses, and some tough lessons to learn. But it *does* mean that we saw our setbacks, struggles, and tough lessons as part of the building process for our house of bricks.

Reader Comment

My biggest setbacks have been "easy credit." I've fallen into that pit several times. I've learned that compounding interest is more than just an interesting math problem. Now I'm working on ways to get the compounding effect working for me instead of against me.

—Robertpo

PLANS FOR A HOUSE OF BRICK

The diagram below was the plan for our house of brick. It is known as the *B-I Triangle.*

The B-I Triangle is a derivative of the CASHFLOW Quadrant that was covered in Chapter 9 and more extensively in my book *Rich Dad's CASHFLOW Quadrant.* The following is a picture of the CASHFLOW Quadrant:

Simply said, Kim and I designed our lives together on the B and I side of the CASHFLOW Quadrant. You can, too, even if it is best for you to remain on the E and S side. Let me explain.

1. Technically, a B-I Triangle is applicable to every part of the quadrant.

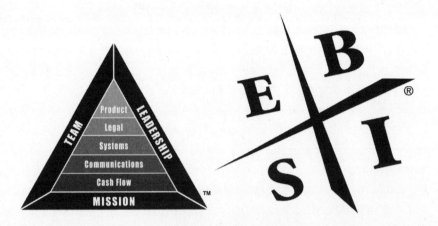

2. Every person's life is made up of and affected by the eight integrities of the B-I Triangle—no matter what quadrant they are in. The problem is, most people do not know what the B-I Triangle is.

If one or more of the eight integrities is missing from a person's life, he lacks financial integrity, even though he may be an honest, hardworking person. I say this based on the definition of the word *integrity* as "whole or complete," not based on the more common meaning that has moral implications. *Integrity* can also mean "operating in harmony." It is impossible for someone to be in harmony if he is missing one or more of the eight integrities in his life. The following are brief explanations of the eight integrities.

Integrity #1: Mission. I believe everyone has a personal mission in life. It is important for you to figure out what your mission is and to write it down and revisit it often. Personal missions can occur at different levels. For example, when I entered the Merchant Marine Academy in 1965, the first thing we did was memorize the academy's mission. My mission for four years was to support the mission of the academy. As a Marine pilot in Vietnam, I was very clear on my mission, which was to bring my men home alive. To me, it was spiritual.

Today, my mission is to elevate the financial well-being of humanity and to bring financial education to the world. In the late 1970s, when I was a manufacturer working only to make money, I felt terrible, off-purpose, and lifeless. Life was fun, but I knew something was missing. In 1981, I met Dr. Fuller, and he reminded me about the importance of mission. After our meeting, I knew I could no longer be a manufacturer and prepared to take a leap of faith to become a teacher of what my rich dad had taught me. In 1984, just as I was about to take my leap of faith, I met Kim, and together we set out on that mission to be teachers of financial literacy. We started with nothing but a sense of mission.

Kim and I believe that if a person's life lacks integrity and is out of alignment with his mission in life, problems will occur. The foundation of life, a personal mission and a spiritual reason for living, is crucial to all eight integrities.

Integrity #2: Team. There is an old saying that goes, "No man is an island." When it comes to business and investing, there is nothing more important than assembling a team of experts—lawyers, accountants, etc.—to help you achieve your goals. A team makes you stronger by complementing your weaknesses and enhancing your strengths. A team also keeps you accountable and pushes you forward.

One of the problems I had with school was that it trained us to take tests alone. If I were to collaborate or ask for help from my classmates on a test, that was called cheating. I believe that this line of thinking causes millions of people to operate as islands, afraid of cooperating with others because they are trained that cooperation is somehow akin to cheating.

In life, our success depends upon the quality of our team. For example, Kim and I have a great team of doctors for our health. We have a great team of mechanics, plumbers, contractors, suppliers, and others whom we know and trust to call on for help with problems we cannot handle. In our businesses, we have a fantastic group of employees and specialists who help us solve our business problems. And spiritually, we have spiritual team members who keep our hearts, minds, and emotions tuned in to the power of a higher authority. We could not be successful without our team.

Integrity #3: Leader. At the military academy, we were trained to be leaders. Most people think being a leader is akin to knowing it all and having others do whatever you say. Nothing is further from the truth. True leaders understand that their team has valuable insights and is the key component to their success.

The way to become a leader is to first learn to be a team member. When I later joined the Marine Corps after the military academy, my leadership and teamwork development continued. Today, as a leader of my businesses, my leadership development continues. One way to be a great leader is to keep learning and keep accepting feedback from your team—even if it's not feedback you like. Some of the best training in leadership I have ever received was through blunt, in-your-face feedback.

You may have seen pictures of a Marine drill instructor screaming in a young recruit's face. That recruit is learning to accept feedback. The real world is a feedback mechanism. When you climb on the bathroom scale and find you are twenty pounds overweight, that is feedback. If you are fired, broke, or divorced, that, too, is feedback. Accepting feedback is essential to being a leader. Unfortunately, many of our business, labor, political, and educational leaders don't accept or learn from the feedback they receive in the form of messages from the world economy. They don't seem to get it.

If a person, family, business, or economy is hurting, it is due to poor leadership. As the saying goes, "The fish rots from the head." An important question to ask is, How good a leader am I relative to my own life? You may want to ask about the quality of your leadership in your family, the business you own or work for, and the city and country in which you live. Don't be afraid to ask for honest feedback from your family, clients, boss, and friends. Only by accepting feedback, and making positive changes based on that feedback, can you become a better leader.

Integrity #4: Product. Product is whatever we bring to market. It could be a commodity such as an apple or a service such as a legal consultation, web design, or lawn mowing. Product is what we exchange for money in the world economy. Product is our vehicle for incoming cash flow.

If a person's product is bad, poor in quality, slow, or obsolete, that person suffers financially. Let's say I own a restaurant and the food is slow in coming, tastes bad, and is overpriced. Odds are that my income will go down. Slow, horrible, and overpriced products cause families, businesses, and governments to suffer.

When I meet a person who is struggling, one of the first things I look into is his product or service. If the person does not work to improve or update his product, the person's financial struggle will probably continue. Also, if a product is not in line with a person's mission, that person may suffer. For example, when my product was nylon wallets, my business suffered because I was not spiritually aligned to my product—my real mission was to be a financial educator, not a manufacturer. I believe one reason why my books, games, and businesses do well is because they are derivatives of my spirit and my mission for life.

Integrity #5: Legal. Like it or not we live in a world of rules. Success comes with understanding the rules and working as efficiently as possible in accordance with those rules—which is why it's smart to have a good lawyer on your team! Without rules, civilization crumbles. For example, as an American, if I decide to follow American driving rules in England, a country where they drive on the other side of the road, chances are I will wind up in jail or in the hospital.

Problems occur in a person's life when he or she does not follow the rules. For example, if a person smokes, eats, drinks, and does not exercise, violating the rules of his body, the person will have health problems. The same is true with money. If a person robs a store, the chances are that the person will wind up in jail. If a person cheats on his or her spouse, that person will have severe personal problems. Breaking the rules is not good for life, families, businesses, or nations.

Integrity #6: Systems. A key to success in business and life is to understand the importance of efficient systems. The human body has many systems working in conjunction with one another. For example, we have a respiratory system, skeletal system, digestive system, blood system, and others. If one system is not functioning, the entire body is in trouble.

In businesses, there are accounting, legal, and communication systems, among others. And in government, there are judicial, highway, welfare, tax, education, and other systems to manage. If one system is damaged, the entire government suffers or struggles. Many individuals have broken or damaged financial systems, which cause them to struggle, no matter how much money they make or how hard they work.

Integrity #7: Communications. "What we've got here is a failure to communicate" is a famous line from the movie *Cool Hand Luke* and a popular sentiment in any organization. The same sentiment is true with individuals and families. In Vietnam, I witnessed many defeats and deaths simply because there was a failure to communicate. Many times we bombed or shelled our own troops due to poor communication. We often do the same to ourselves.

Most of this book has been about communication, learning to use the words and speak the language of money. For most people, the language of money is a foreign language. If you want to improve your communications with money, begin by learning the words of money.

Integrity #8: Cash flow. Cash flow is often called the "bottom line." If a banker wants to evaluate your financial IQ, he will ask for your financial statement. Since most people do not know what financial statements are, they ask you for a credit application. This subprime mess was triggered by the biggest banks in the world giving credit to the poorest people, businesses, and countries in the world.

New Rule of Money #3 is: *Learn to control cash flow.* This is an important rule because by controlling cash flow, you control all eight integrities. If you can control cash flow, you can control your life, regardless of how much money you make. That is one reason I created my CASHFLOW games, and why there are CASHFLOW Clubs all over the world—to teach people about the importance of controlling cash flow.

If you would like a more in-depth explanation of the eight integrities of the B-I Triangle, go to www.richdad.com/conspiracy-of-the-rich, and I will personally explain their importance for you or your business in a video presentation.

Reader Comment

I thought I was in financial integrity. I kept telling people how I lived a life of integrity. My idea of integrity was keeping out of trouble, not cheating on my spouse, and those sorts of things. Little did I realize that integrity was financial, too. After reflecting and examining my life, I am not in financial integrity. Thankfully, we have the opportunity to change the direction of our journey.

—msrpsilver

The B-I Triangle is explained in greater depth for entrepreneurs and investors, those interested in the B and I quadrants, in my books *Rich Dad's Before You Quit Your Job* and *Rich Dad's Guide to Investing.* Both books are available at your local bookstore, online, and in audiobook format.

Self-Analysis

Take a moment to look at the integrities of the B-I Triangle and ask where you are strong and where you are weak in terms of each. Ask questions like, Who is on my legal team? or, Who advises me on taxes and accounting? or, Who do I turn to when I need to analyze a financial decision or make an investment?

My point is that when you look at your life and your business through the prism of the eight integrities of the B-I Triangle, you can see your life and your world through the eyes of the B and I quadrants. The way to build a house of brick is to organize your life according to the eight integrities.

When I see a person or business struggling, I find that the reason for that struggle is often due to one or more of the eight integrities being weak or nonexistent in that person or business. So you may want to stop and take time to go through the eight integrities and do a little self-analysis. If you are brave and want to build a stronger house of brick, get together with a group of friends and discuss the eight integrities with truth and compassion. Be willing to give *and* receive honest feedback. This is important because sometimes our friends and loved ones can see things about us that we cannot see for ourselves. I promise you that if you go through this process honestly, on a regular basis, once every six months, for example, you will automatically find yourself building a castle of bricks.

Business and Investing Are Team Sports

Millions of people go through life repeating what they learned in school, taking the test of life on their own, not asking for help, and being bullied or told what to do by big and powerful organizations. They take on their problems with the mantra, "If you want it done right, do it yourself." On the other hand, my rich dad often said, "Business and investing are team sports." The reason most people are at a disadvantage in life is because they go onto the financial playing field of money as individuals, not as a team, and are pounded by the massive corporate teams that dominate the world—or giants, as Dr. Fuller called these mega-corporations.

When a young couple talks to their financial planner, odds are the financial planner is a player for the other team, the mega-corporations. Every credit card in your wallet is attached to a major B and I quadrant business. When you buy a house, your mortgage is attached to one of the biggest financial markets in the world, the bond market. Your house, car, and life are insured by some of the biggest corporations in the world. In other words, millions of people are playing life's game of money as E's and S's against the biggest B's and I's in the world. That's why so many people feel powerless and look to the government to take care of them. But as you know, our laws are dictated by the same B and I corporations that contribute billions of dollars to political elections. You have one vote, but they have millions of dollars to influence votes.

The same is true in medicine. One of the reasons why the medical field is broken and expensive is because the mega-insurance companies make the rules. The doctors in the E and S quadrants have very little power over the B's and I's of the world of pharmaceuticals and insurance. The same is true in education. It is the powerful teachers unions that dominate the world of education. Unions are about money and benefits for teachers, not for the education of the kids.

My message is simply this: If you want to protect your life, home, and family from the big bad wolves of the B and I quadrant, you need to build your own B-I Triangle. Put your own team of eight integrities together.

Now, I know that many people do not have all eight integrities. In fact, few people do. That's why so many corporate people cling to job security, terrified of being fired, setting aside their personal, God-given mission in life for the mission of the corporation. These people live in fear because their personal lives are built of straw and sticks.

Start Building Your Own B-I Triangle

One of the first things Kim and I did in building our house of brick was to hire a bookkeeper to get our finances in good order. I wrote about this in my book *Rich Dad's Increase Your Financial IQ*. It was an important step in putting our team together. Even if you have very little extra money, *Rich Dad's Increase Your Financial IQ* will assist you in building your own B-I Triangle. Another good book to help you build a solid B-I Triangle is *Own Your Own Corporation*, written by attorney Garrett Sutton, a Rich Dad Advisor. This book will assist you on integrity #5, legal. The book *Sales Dogs*, written by Rich Dad Advisor Blair Singer, will assist you with integrity #7, communication, because increasing your sales skills will increase your ability to sell your product, service, or résumé through effective communication techniques. In this world of over-communication, your ability to sell can make the difference between success and failure, job or no job, and money or bankruptcy.

Building your team is not an easy project, or one that can be quickly completed. It takes time to build a good team. Team members can come and go. Over the years I have had some great team members and some very poor team members, but that is part of the process. And as your knowledge and wealth increase, you may need to upgrade your team. Turning your house of bricks into a castle of bricks is a constant work in progress. As the saying goes, "The road to success is always under construction."

Storm Clouds Ahead

By preparing for bad times you have a better chance of seeing the silver lining when storm clouds gather, and a better chance of finding a pot of gold at the end of the rainbow. For those in houses made of straw and sticks, the coming years could be bad ones; for people in brick houses, a silver lining can be seen in those approaching storm clouds and a pot of gold can be found at the end of the rainbow.

The following graphs depict why I think the coming years could be bad for those in houses of straw and stick. Few people have ever seen them. I thank Michael Maloney, my advisor on gold and silver, for them. Michael is the author of the Rich Dad Advisor book *Guide to Investing in Gold and Silver*. If you love charts and graphs, you will love Michael's book.

A. GRAPH OF A FEDERAL RESERVE BANK PRINTING MONEY

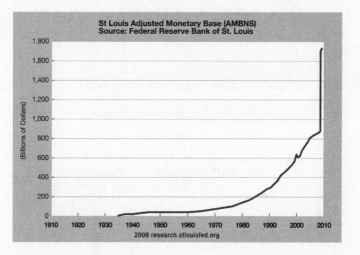

This graph shows all the base money (coins, paper money, and bank reserves) in circulation since 1913, the year the Federal Reserve was created. It took eighty-four years, from 1913 to 2007, to put $825 billion in circulation. Look at what happened to the dollar supply after 1971, the year President Nixon, without permission of Congress, took the world off the gold standard. It began to climb at an accelerated rate. You may also notice that since 2007, the year the subprime mess rocked the world, the Fed has essentially doubled the previous eighty-four years' worth of currency supply, increasing the base money in circulation to roughly $1,700 billion.

What do you think this graph means to you and your family? Some possibilities I see are:

1. Hyperinflation: This means prices of essential items such as food and energy will increase at unheard-of rates. This will be devastating to lower- and middle-income families.

2. All countries will probably be forced to print money: Because the United States is printing money, all other countries will probably have to print money. If other countries do not print, then their countries' currency will become too strong against the dollar and exports to the United States will slow down, causing a slowdown in the exporting country's economy. This probably means inflation in every country that trades with the United States.

3. Increased cost of living: People living in straw and stick houses will find it harder to survive because higher prices will eat up more of their paychecks.

B. GRAPH OF PRESIDENT OBAMA'S PROPOSED BUDGET

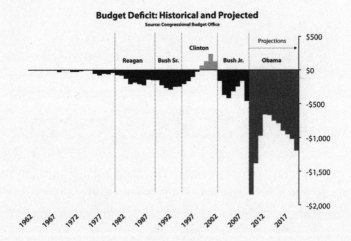

This graph begins with the budgets of Presidents Reagan, George H. W. Bush, Clinton, and George W. Bush . . . and then President Obama's proposed budgets.

What does this graph mean to you? To me it means more government, more taxes, and more debt. It means we are expecting the government to rebuild our houses of straw and sticks for us.

C. GRAPH OF MORTGAGE RESETS

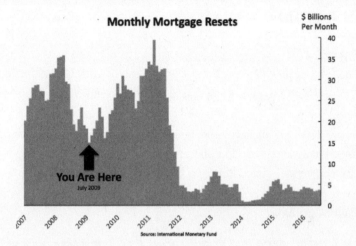

This graph illustrates the dollar amount of mortgage resets throughout the world. A mortgage reset occurs when a mortgage comes due and the banker resets the interest rate to the prevailing market rate, which often results in a higher interest rate for the buyer and means a higher loan payment.

For example, let's say a subprime couple buys a $300,000 house they cannot afford. To lure the couple in, the bank offers them a $330,000 loan, financing for 110 percent of the home's value, at a ridiculous teaser rate of 2 percent. Sometime later, the loan resets to a higher interest rate of 5 percent, and then still later at 7 percent. With each reset, the monthly mortgage payment becomes more expensive, and soon the couple defaults, the mortgage is foreclosed, and the couple loses their house. In recent cases, the house has probably fallen in value, as much as 50 percent of the mortgage amount. So, in this example, the house might now be worth only $150,000, but still have a loan of $330,000. The bank has to write down losses of $180,000, causing havoc in the banking sector and major losses for shareholders as more and more foreclosures stack up.

Notice the left-hand side of this graph. The subprime credit mess began in mid-2007, when mortgage resets hit $20 billion a month. I talked about this in the timeline in Chapter 1 of this book:

August 6, 2007

American Home Mortgage, one of America's largest mortgage providers, filed for bankruptcy.

August 9, 2007

French bank BNP Paribas, because of problems with U.S. subprime mortgages, announced it couldn't value assets worth over 1.6 billion euros.

Once again, looking at the mortgage reset graph, you can see that by late 2008 mortgage resets hit $35 billion a month, the peak of the storm. Everything looked bleak in late 2008.

Reader Comment

In reading the charts and thinking about the future, I personally see a lot of opportunities around the corner. Now is the time to start preparing to take advantage of them...I was glad to see you mention that you think we are in the eye of the storm. I was beginning to feel I was the only one thinking this way. I have a feeling there is more trouble to come from the banks and the consequences that go with that.

                                      —newydd105

The Eye of the Storm

Now, in Graph C, look at the "you are here" arrow pointing to summer 2009. As I write, mortgage resets are at a low, approximately $15 billion a month. Financial news commentators are now saying the storm is over; "green shoots" are appearing in the economy. With that happy news, the little pigs in the straw and stick houses are coming out to play—the big bad wolf is gone. People are back to spending on sales at the shopping malls and some restaurants are beginning to require reservations again. Yet, if you look at November 2011, the graph shows nearly $38 billion in mortgage resets coming due. It seems the big bad wolf has only been catching his breath.

What does this mean for you?

As I write this in June 2009, I believe we are merely in the eye of the storm, and the worst is yet to come. Back in August 2007, it took just a $20 billion a month mortgage reset to blow down the financial straw houses of Lehman Brothers and Bear Stearns. The economy of Iceland collapsed with the first huff from the big bad wolf. Bank of America, Royal Bank of Scotland, and AIG, financial houses of sticks, are weak and wobbly today. California, the eighth largest economy in the world, is on the brink of a financial meltdown, as is the Japanese economy. My question is: What will a nearly $40 billion a month mortgage reset from October to November 2011 bring? What does this mean to you, your family, your business, the country, and the world?

Remember New Rule of Money #4: *Prepare for bad times and you will only know good times.* Looking at the mortgage reset graph, preparing for the bad times means putting my financial house in order by strengthening my B-I Triangle. There is still time to prepare. And even if the storm does not hit, there is nothing wrong with building a house of brick, a solid B-I Triangle.

The Combined Meaning of the Graphs

When you look at all three graphs together, you get a sobering picture of the future.

1. Graph A: The amount of base money in circulation. It took eighty-four years to go from a small amount of dollars in circulation to $825 billion in circulation; it took just two years to double that amount to over $1,700 billion in circulation—and we're still printing. To me this means there will be inflation in essential items such as food and energy, because the more dollars there are in circulation chasing the same amount of goods, the more the price of those goods will be. This also means inflation all over the world because all central banks will be forced to print their own currency to weaken its purchasing power. If a country does not weaken its currency, the currency will be too strong, which means the country's products and services will be too expensive on the world market, exports will slow, and the country's economy will stagnate. In simple terms, life is about to become more expensive all over the world.

2. Graph B: President Obama's proposed budget. I see an increase in government controls and taxes to cover the increase in debt. While prices for food and energy will go up, housing prices will not rise as rapidly for two reasons, one being that debt or credit will be harder to come by, and tougher credit keeps home prices down, and the other being that with higher taxes, business growth will be slower, which means fewer jobs—and real estate prices are directly linked to jobs.

This is bad news for homeowners hoping for appreciation (capital gains) because they will not be able to sell their houses to get more money. But it is good news for real estate investors who profit from cash flow because they can purchase homes at very low prices and the rent will cover the cost of mortgage payments and maintaining the asset.

3. Graph C: Mortgage resets. I see mortgage resets causing more increases in Graphs A and B—that is, if and only if the world economy does not simply collapse under the weight of all this debt, taxes, and toxic money.

The Silver Lining and the Pot of Gold

In fairy tales, there is always a silver lining in all storm clouds and a pot of gold at the end of the rainbow. And while it is certainly not a fairy tale, the same is true with this global crisis.

The following chart compares the quantities and prices of gold between 1990 and 2007. As I write in June 2009, gold is priced at around $900 an ounce and silver is around $15 an ounce.

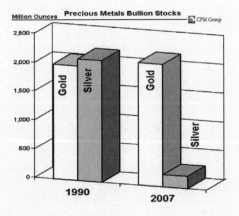

Printed with permission from the CPM Group, a leading commodities research firm. Visit www.cpmgroup.com for more information.

Notice that the supply of silver is going down compared to gold. This is because the supply of silver is lower than gold because silver is a consumable, industrial precious metal used in cell phones, computers, light switches, and as a reflector in mirrors. While gold is being hoarded, silver is being used up. To me, gold and silver are the best and brightest opportunities for most people during this crisis.

Looking at Graphs A, B, and C, I predict the public will soon lose faith in the government manipulation of our money and awaken to the reasons to hold gold and silver as a hedge against inflation. When the public wakes up, the next bubble of greed and fear will be on. Gold may go above $3,000 an ounce, and silver may someday be the same price as gold because it is an industrial precious metal in short supply—but those are only my predictions and may be wishful thinking in a world of financial insanity.

As in any bubble, the crooks and con men of gold and silver are already out in droves, running ads on television, online, and in print. Once again, the little pigs who did not prepare for the crisis will have their hard-earned money taken away with the sweet reassuring words of the smooth-talking, silver-tongued, big bad wolf. As with all investments, you need to be educated about gold and silver before you invest in them.

If you would like to learn more about investing in gold and silver, I suggest reading Rich Dad Advisor Michael Maloney's book *Guide to Investing in Gold and Silver.*

New Rule of Money #7: Life Is a Team Sport. Choose Your Team Carefully.

The big bad wolf has not gone away. He's just catching his breath. To protect yourself, start putting your financial team together and begin building or reinforcing your financial house of bricks using the B-I Triangle as your blueprint. The conspiracy plays the game of money with a very strong team. So should you.

Reader Comment

I am finally beginning to realize the value of having a team and am working on building one through the people I already know. I get references and talk to the different members of the team, asking questions that will help me to know whether or not we will have the ability to work well together. It helps to be honest about what my mission is and how I want to go about accomplishing my goals.

—mgbabe

If you are committed to building a strong financial house of bricks, I suggest you sit down with friends and financial advisors and discuss your personal B-I Triangle, taking their feedback gratefully, even if you do not like what you hear.

The reason I created the Rich Dad Advisor series of books is to give you access to my team. For example, my partner for real estate is Ken McElroy. You can get into his head by reading his Rich Dad Advisor book series on real estate. Mike Maloney is my advisor on gold and silver. Donald Trump and Steve Forbes are my advisors on financial intelligence. You can read their comments on this important subject by reading my book *Rich Dad's Increase Your Financial IQ*. In the near future, there will be more books from my team on subjects such as entrepreneurship and investing in paper assets like stocks and options. By seeing the world through my advisors' eyes, you will be better able to choose your own team of advisors and build your own solid B-I Triangle and house of bricks.

Even if you do not plan on building a financial house of bricks, at least buy a few silver coins. Today, as I write, silver coins are less than $15 each at your local coin shop. As Einstein said, "Nothing happens until something moves." Fifteen dollars may not be much, but it is a start, and almost everyone can afford a silver coin.

Financial Education: An Unfair Advantage

Bankruptcy

It is ironic that I write this chapter on June 1, 2009, the day General Motors declared bankruptcy, another form of Chapter 11. Again, the old saying goes, "As goes General Motors, so goes America." Even if America and GM survive, the fact is that millions of people all over the world are following General Motors into their own personal form of bankruptcy.

Life Will Become More Expensive

No one has a crystal ball. Yet by studying history, as we did in the first part of this book, and by observing what our leaders are doing today, a probable future can become clear. As our leaders print more money to save the rich in the name of saving the economy, life will become more expensive due to increases in taxes, debt, inflation, and retirement.

The Increase in Taxes: In the United States, President Obama is already talking about raising taxes on people earning more than $250,000 a year. He has already hired more IRS agents to enforce tax collection. There is a proposal to tax employer-sponsored health benefits to provide for those who do not have health benefits. This means that more businesses will be closing due to rising operational expenses and that there will be more unemployment. And there is another proposal to reduce the tax deductions for interest on mortgages for families making over $250,000 a year. If this happens the second-home real estate market will collapse, and housing prices will fall further.

As I write, states like California, the eighth-largest economy in the world, teeter on the edge of bankruptcy. Sacramento, the capital of California, has a growing tent city filled with people who were once employed and once had homes but are now living in tents and shanties like the ones in Cape Town, South Africa, that I wrote about earlier in the book. As the economy shrinks, the demand for government services from people who have no way to provide for themselves will increase, which will mean an increase in taxes.

The Increase in Debt: Raising taxes forces people to live with more debt, since more and more of people's money goes to the government to fund programs. Credit cards will become more essential for daily survival. People without access to credit will slip below the poverty line.

The Increase in Inflation: The primary cause of inflation is the government printing money, which increases the money supply. Inflation is caused by the purchasing power of your money going down as more and more dollars flood the existing pool of money, which means prices of many essential products, such as food, fuel, and services, go up as more dollars chase the same amount of goods. Inflation is often called "the invisible tax," which is hardest on the poor, elderly, savers, low-income workers, and fixed-income retirees.

The Cost of Retirement: One of the primary reasons GM is in financial trouble is because it did not control the cost of retirement and medical expenses for its workers. America and many other Western nations face the same predicament. They face a financial and moral dilemma: How do you take care of an aging population that cannot provide for themselves? The answer to that question may well be more expensive than this present financial crisis. Today, many families are entering into financial bankruptcy due to retirement and medical costs.

The Unfair Advantage

Today, those who have a strong financial education have an unfair advantage over those who do not. With a sound financial education, a person can use taxes, debt, inflation, and retirement to become rich rather than poor. Conversely, the forces of taxes, debt, inflation, and retirement rule those who do not have a strong financial education.

Albert Einstein once said, "We can't solve problems by using the same kind of thinking we used when we created them." Today, this is the real tragedy. Our leaders are trying to solve our financial crisis by using the same thinking that caused the problem in the first place. For example, our leaders are printing more money to solve the problem caused by too much printed money.

Using the same thinking to solve their financial problems is also causing many people to make their personal financial situation worse, not better. Today, most people are trying to solve the problems of taxes, debt, inflation, and retirement by working harder, getting out of debt, saving money, living below their means, and investing for the long term in the stock market. Life will become more expensive for those who insist on following this line of thinking.

Reader Comment

I see a tremendous parallel in healthcare in general. Although I would not trade what we have here for any other country's healthcare system, I do believe the treatment of chronic problems (a major portion of healthcare expenses) is misguided and ridiculously expensive.

—MicMac09

Explaining with Pictures

The following diagram is a snapshot that shows why I believe that life will become more expensive.

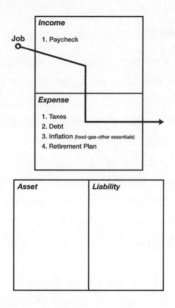

In America, the average person with a job has taxes, debt, inflation, and savings for a retirement plan taken from their paycheck *before* they get paid. In other words, everyone else gets paid before the employee gets paid. A good chunk of a worker's paycheck is taken before he receives a penny to live on.

You may have noticed that most of a person's money is spent to cover living expenses such as taxes, debt, inflation, and savings for a retirement plan, and thus goes into the pockets of the conspiracy. I believe this is why there is no financial education in our schools. If people knew where their paycheck was going, they would revolt. With a sound financial education, people can minimize those expenses or even use those expenses to put that money into their own pockets.

For example, there are two reasons I do not have a traditional retirement plan filled with mutual funds. One reason is that the stock market is too risky. The average person has very little control over the market, and odds are a market crash will take most of their money eventually. And the second reason is that I would rather put that retirement money into my own pocket, not the pockets of those who control Wall Street. With a financial education, a person does not need to pay a mutual fund company to lose their money.

Two Different Lifestyles

To better illustrate my point that a financial education is an unfair advantage, I will use the example of some friends of mine. Don and Karen (not their real names) are married and run their own business together, much like Kim and I do. We are all about the same age, and we all have college degrees. The problem is that Don and Karen have very little financial education or investing experience.

While Don and Karen technically own their own business, in reality they are self-employed business owners in the S quadrant, which means that if they stopped working, they would have no income. Kim and I own our businesses in the B quadrant, which means the income comes in regardless of whether we work or not.

Over dinner a few months ago, Don and Karen confided in us that they were concerned about their future because business was down, expenses were up, and their retirement portfolio had lost 40 percent of its value. They let four employees go, cut back on their lifestyle, and were wondering if they could afford to retire. They wondered how we were doing and whether we were concerned about the future and our ability to eventually retire.

Our reply was that we are always concerned and never take things for granted, but that we were not cutting back. Instead, our income was increasing, primarily because we were using taxes, debt, inflation, and retirement money to our advantage.

The difference is that Don and Karen see the world through the E and S eyes, and Kim and I see the world through the B and I eyes.

I will share a simple diagram of our financial statements to help explain what I mean. If you are not familiar with these diagrams, a more in-depth explanation can be found in my book *Rich Dad Poor Dad*.

When you look at our respective financial statements, you can see that Don and Karen have a different focus than Kim and I do. Don and Karen focus on working harder to earn more money. Kim and I focus on our investments and increasing our business and personal assets to earn more money.

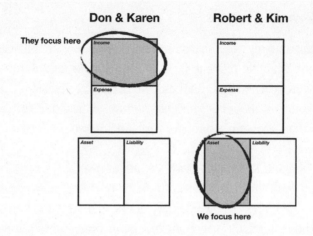

As two self-employed business owners, Don and Karen have to work harder to earn more money. As business owners from the B quadrant, Kim and I do not focus on working harder. We focus on increasing our assets, which in turn increase our income. By focusing on increasing our assets, we pay less in taxes, use debt to acquire more assets, and watch inflation increase our cash flow, which means that rather than sending our retirement savings to Wall Street, we put our money into our pockets via cash flow from businesses and personal assets.

The telling difference is seen when you compare Don and Karen's income statements with ours.

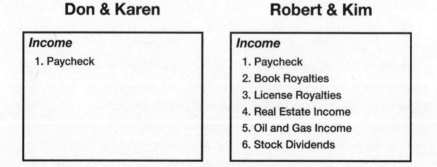

Don and Karen's only income comes from their business and, again, if they stop working, they have no income. That is why they worry. For

Kim and me, most of our income comes from our business and personal assets such as book royalties, invention royalties, licensing rights to use the Rich Dad trademarks, real estate income, oil and gas income, and stock dividends. Every month we receive a check for our assets—cash flow. And if you have read *Rich Dad Poor Dad* you will recall that income produced from assets like real estate and businesses is taxed at lower tax rates than income from personal labor (wages)—if it is taxed at all.

Three Types of Income Taxes

There are three basic types of taxable income in the United States: earned, portfolio, and passive. Earned income is derived from labor and is taxed highest of all incomes. Portfolio income is general income from capital gains earned by buying an asset low and selling it high. It is the second-highest taxed income. Passive income is generally income from cash flow and is the lowest taxed of the three incomes.

The irony is that when a person invests in mutual funds through his retirement savings plan, in most cases, when that person retires and begins to withdraw money from his retirement plan, the income is taxed as earned income, the highest of all taxes. Don and Karen are saving for the future, and without knowing it, they are going to be taxed at the highest levels when they retire. This is another unfair advantage a person with a financial education has over those that do not—the advantage of paying less in taxes, our single greatest expense.

When I listen to schoolteachers proudly tell me that they have financial education in their classes, that they bring in bankers and financial planners to teach their kids about saving for the future, I simply shake my head. How can anyone understand the world of money by looking through the eyes of a person educated for work in the E and S quadrants?

Different Financial Report Cards

I had horrible grades all through school. My poor dad, a schoolteacher, was a great dad, because with his encouragement I stayed in school and graduated. My rich dad also encouraged me to improve my grades, but he had this to say about academic grades and report cards: "When you leave school, your banker does not ask you for your report card. Your banker does not care if you had good grades or bad grades. All the banker wants to see is your financial statement, because your financial statement is your report card when you leave school."

When you compare Don and Karen's balance sheet, where assets and liabilities are tallied, to our balance sheet, you will see who has the better financial grades after twenty years of work.

Don & Karen

Asset	Liability
Savings	1 House
	2 Cars
	Unfunded Retirement

Cash flow from assets: Zero

Robert & Kim

Asset	Liability
Businesses Royalties	2 Houses
1,400 Rental Properties	6 Cars
Oil and Gas Wells	
Gold and Silver	

Cash flow from assets: Millions

As couples, we both receive paychecks from our businesses, but for Kim and me, most of our income comes from our business assets like books, games, and trademark licenses, and from personal investments in real estate, stocks, and oil and gas wells. Kim and I do not count gold and silver as cashflow assets since they do not put money in our pockets. Rather, we hold gold and silver much like a person would keep money in a savings account. Gold and silver are liquid, and when politicians are printing more and more money, gold and silver have a better chance of retaining their purchasing power.

Another big difference can be found in our expense columns.

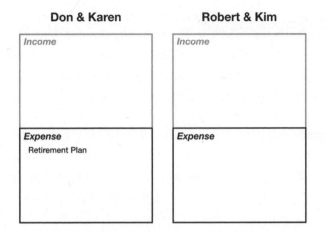

Ironically, because we do not need nor do we have a retirement plan, Kim and I have an unfair advantage when it comes to taxes, debt, inflation, and retirement. Since most of our income comes from our business assets and investments, we pay much less in taxes. For example, the taxes on my income from my books, games, and trademark royalties are less than the taxes on income from my paycheck. By investing in real estate, we use debt to increase our monthly cash flow, and again the taxes on real estate income are much less than the income taxes on my paycheck. By investing in oil and gas, inflation increases our cash flow, and again taxes on oil and gas income are much less than the taxes on my paycheck income.

Since we do not have a retirement plan, that is one big expense, via fees and commissions, that we do not have, and we increase our income with our assets every year, so we don't worry about the future. Rather than send a part of our income to Wall Street every month, Kim and I invest our own money, and that money puts more money in our pockets. Why risk investing for the long term in the stock market and lose control of your investment when you can invest with less risk and receive more income every month, as well as pay less in taxes, use debt to become richer, and have inflation increase your cash flow?

I trust this simple comparison of couples helps explain why Don and Karen worry more than Kim and I do during this financial crisis, and how financial education can give a person a long-term unfair financial advantage in life.

Other Unfair Advantages

As life becomes more expensive due to increases in taxes, debt, inflation, and retirement plans, a financial education can offer other unfair advantages not available to most people. Some of these advantages are:

1. Expanding your means rather than living below your means. Every year, Kim and I take a few days and focus on our financial goals. Rather than focus on living below our means, we focus on expanding our means by increasing cash flow from our assets. The following diagram illustrates this concept.

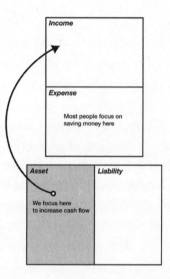

In 2009, Kim and I plan to publish three new books, purchase 200 to 500 new rental units, drill two more oil wells, and increase our business by creating more franchises. We focus on increasing cash flow through our assets rather than cutting back and counting on capital gains via the stock market or our homes appreciating in value.

2. Printing our own money. The title of Chapter 6 of *Rich Dad Poor Dad* is "The Rich Invent Money." To me, being able to print your own money is one of the better advantages of investing in your financial education. Since the government is printing more money, doesn't it make sense to print your own money…legally? Doesn't printing your own money make more financial sense than working harder and paying higher percentages in taxes, saving money in the bank and losing purchasing power to inflation and taxes, or risking your money for the long term in the stock market? The way you can print your own money is via a financial term known as *return on investment*, or ROI.

When you talk to most bankers, financial planners, or real estate brokers, they will tell you that a 5 percent to 12 percent ROI is a good return on your money. Those are returns for a person without much of a financial education. Another fairy tale or fear tactic they will say is, "The higher the return, the higher the risks." That is absolutely not true—if you have a solid financial education. I always look to achieve infinite returns with my investments.

Money for Nothing

The way you print your own money is by achieving an infinite return on your money. The definition I use for an infinite return is "money for nothing." More specifically, I print my own money when I get back all the money I used to acquire an asset, still own the asset, and enjoy the benefits of the cash flow from the asset. I write about this process in my books *Rich Dad Poor Dad*, the bestselling personal financial book of all time; *Rich Dad's Who Took My Money*, a book on how the stock market and financial planners take your money via the retirement system; and *Rich Dad's Increase Your Financial IQ*, a book endorsed by Donald Trump and Steve Forbes.

With a strong financial education, I can print my own money via a business, real estate, stocks, and even commodities such as gold, silver, and oil. Again, the key is going for an infinite return—going for money for nothing.

Print Your Own Money in Business

Kim and I started the Rich Dad Company at our kitchen table. Rather than use our own money, we raised $250,000 from investors. Again, that is a benefit of investing time in learning how to sell. In this case, we sold our business idea to our investors. In less than three years, thanks to the growth of our business and the profits it provided, we returned 100 percent of our investors' money, plus interest, and an additional 100 percent on their money to buy their shares back. Today, the Rich Dad Company puts millions of dollars in our pockets, even though we have none of our own money invested in the business. By definition, that is an infinite return. In other words, our business prints our own money.

The key to the success of the Rich Dad Company is that the business designs and creates assets rather than products. For example, we will not produce this book. Rather, we will create a derivative of the book, a literary license, and sell the rights to the license to publishers for different languages. We also sell licenses for the rights to produce our games, brand trademarks, and franchise rights. Our financial statement looks like this:

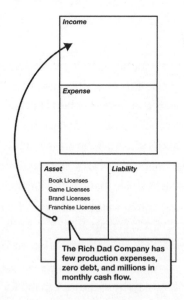

The Rich Dad Company has few production expenses, zero debt, and millions in monthly cash flow.

Again, I reiterate the importance of knowing the word *derivative*, since licenses are derivatives. Used properly, derivatives can be incredible tools for mass financial creation. I also remind you to *focus more on selling and less on buying*. You may notice that the Rich Dad Company creates assets to sell for the long term.

For a more in-depth explanation on printing your own money via a business, go to www.richdad.com/conspiracy-of-the-rich, and in a video my friend Kelly Ritchie and I will explain how infinite returns work via a franchise model.

PRINTING YOUR OWN MONEY IN REAL ESTATE

With real estate, our business plan is to use debt, other people's money, to achieve an infinite return and print our own money. The following is an overly simplified real-life example.

Purchase: We buy a two-bedroom, one-bath house in a great neighborhood for $100,000.

Financing: We pay $20,000 as a down payment and borrow $100,000 for the house and extra money for improvements from a bank and/or investors.

Improve property: We improve the property by adding on an extra bedroom and a bathroom.

Increase rents reflecting increased property value: We raise the rent from $600 a month (what two-bedroom, one-bath houses rent for in the market) to $1,200 a month (the market rent for three-bedroom, two-bathroom houses).

Refinance property at new appraised value of $150,000: When we refinance the house, the banker gives us a loan of $120,000 (80 percent of new value). We get back $20,000, plus get an extra $20,000 to invest in a new property.

Costs: The loan interest at 6 percent costs approximately $600 a month. Expenses are another $300 a month, which puts a net $300 a month in our pocket in the form of cash flow.

Key: The new loan and expenses are financed by rent from the tenant.

The net final transaction looks like this:

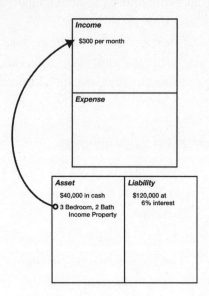

The keys to this investment working are:

1. Improvements to the property
2. A good location—real estate is only valuable if there are jobs nearby
3. Good financing and/or investors
4. Good property management

If any one of these four elements is missing, the investment will struggle.

I started my real estate investing with a one-bedroom, one-bathroom condo on the island of Maui, purchased for $18,000 in 1973. Kim started with a two-bedroom, one-bathroom house in Portland, Oregon, purchased for $45,000 in 1989.

Today, we own over 1,400 units of residential property and a number of commercial properties using the same 100 percent financed formula. We have none of our own money in any of our properties. The difference today is that we invest in bigger projects using millions of dollars rather than thousands of dollars—but the principles are the same. Even in this economic climate, we do well simply because we choose our tenants carefully and have professional management teams making sure our tenants are happy.

If you would like more information on how we invest for infinite returns, watch our video at www.richdad.com/conspiracy-of-the-rich. With our real estate partner and author of the Rich Dad Advisor book *The ABC's of Real Estate Investing,* Ken McElroy, we will go into more detail on how we buy multimillion dollar properties, get all of our money back, keep the property, and pocket the cash flow for an infinite return. The point to remember is that we do not buy to flip our properties. Our formula is to buy assets for years and then sell rental time by the month.

PRINTING YOUR OWN MONEY WITH PAPER ASSETS

There are many ways you can print your own money with paper assets such as stocks. One way is to use option strategies. For example, let's say I buy a thousand shares of a stock for $2 a share. I then go to the options market and sell an option to buy my thousand shares for a $1 premium per share ($1,000) for thirty days. If the stock hits $3 per share or higher, the person who purchased the option can buy the stock at $3. If the stock does not hit $3 in thirty days, I keep his option money of $1,000. Again, notice that I buy for the long term and sell time by the month.

In this overly simplified example, selling a thirty-day option puts $1,000 immediately in my pocket. If I sell another thirty-day option with the same stock on the same terms and the stock does not go above $3, I make another $1,000 off my original $2,000 investment while still owning my stock. I will have made 100 percent of my initial $2,000 back, and have printed my own money via my financial knowledge. To me, this makes more sense than leaving your money in mutual funds for the long term and having your money stolen legally by short-term stock and option traders.

If you would like to see a video with more information on using paper assets and options to create infinite returns and print your own money, visit www.richdad.com/conspiracy-of-the-rich. In one segment, my friend and advisor Andy Tanner will explain how to use options as a way of legally printing your own money.

PRINTING YOUR OWN MONEY WITH GOLD AND SILVER

I have printed my own money by building gold and silver mines and sell-ing shares (derivatives) of the company in the stock market. I am currently working on a copper mining company, which will go public when copper prices improve. I realize that taking a business public is not realistic for most people's current situations, yet it is one of the best ways to take an idea and create a personal fortune.

Taking a company public is what Colonel Harland Sanders did, at the age of sixty-five. As legend has it, after a highway bypassed his chicken restaurant and significantly reduced his customer flow, and after he realized his Social Security check was not going to keep him alive financially, he hit the road selling his recipe (a derivative) and was turned down over a thousand times. Finally, after many rejections, someone bought his recipe, built a business, franchised it, and sold shares (another derivative) of his company to the public. By evolving from the S quadrant to the B quadrant, the Colonel took bad luck and turned it into a fortune. He changed his thinking and changed his life. Whenever someone says to me, "I'm too old to change," I simply tell them the story of the Colonel and his chicken recipe.

The reason I mentioned gold and silver is because I would rather hold gold and silver than cash. Since I am able to print my own money, I do not need to worry about saving money for a rainy day. With governments printing so much money, I feel safer saving gold and silver.

If you would like to learn more about gold and silver, visit www.richdad.com/conspiracy-of-the-rich for a video presentation. In one segment, friend and author of Rich Dad Advisor book *Guide to Investing in Gold and Silver*, Mike Maloney, tells why gold and silver are vital investments for today's economy.

New Rule of Money #8: Since Money Is Becoming Worth-less and Less, Learn to Print Your Own

Starting at the age of nine, my rich dad gave me one of the best of gifts, the gift of a financial education. New Rule of Money #8 links all the way back to

New Rule of Money #1: *Money is knowledge.* Given the financial crisis we are in today, and with money becoming worth-less and less, a person with a financial education has an unfair advantage over those with a traditional education.

In 1903, when I believe the conspiracy took over the educational system, the true power of the conspiracy took control of our minds and left millions financially incompetent and dependent upon the government to take care of them. Today, the world is in a crisis of financial ignorance and incompetence. The biggest cash heist in history is taking place. Our wealth is being legally stolen via taxes, debt, inflation, and retirement accounts. Since it is the lack of financial education that got us into this crisis, it is financial education that can lead us out. As you know, our leaders are using the same thinking that created our financial problems to solve them. Rather than expect them to change, I think it is best that you and I change, just as Colonel Sanders changed. We can change ourselves by changing the way we think and what we study.

Reader Comment

While I am very well educated financially—MA in international economics and finance from Georgetown University, two years in investment banking writing private placement memorandums, five years in business as a CFO, and fifteen years founding, running, and selling my own businesses...I was missing a very important element in my financial education. That element is overcoming my fears in investing in my own projects and in real estate. It only became worse as I accumulated more money because there was more to lose...One of the things I did was to hire a Rich Dad coach, who just kept reminding me calmly and gently every Wednesday during our noon conference call, "Remember, your goal is to invest in real estate." I am now in escrow on my second apartment building—I still wake up in the morning with anxiety, but I'm pushing through it.

—*cwylie*

Education's Biggest Mistake

The primary reason most people are afraid of changing is because they are afraid of making mistakes, especially financial mistakes. Most people cling to job security because they are afraid of failing financially. The reason most people turn their money over to financial planners is because they hope the financial planner will not make mistakes, which, ironically, is a mistake.

To me, our education system's biggest problem is that it teaches kids not to make mistakes. If children do make mistakes, the system punishes them rather than teaching them to learn from their mistakes. An intelligent person knows that we learn by making mistakes. We learn to ride a bicycle by falling off the bike and climbing back on. We learn to swim by jumping in the water. How can people learn about money if they are afraid of making mistakes?

Why Most Kids Fail to Learn in School

The following diagram is called the Cone of Learning, developed by Bruce Hyland based on Edgar Dale's Cone of Experience, created in 1946. It explains why so many kids dislike school, find school boring, and fail to retain much information after years of sitting in a classroom.

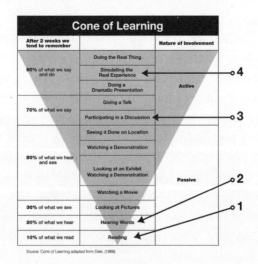

From Dale. *Audio-Visual Methods in Teaching*, 1E. © 1969 Wadsworth, a part of Cengage Learning, Inc. Reproduced by permission. www.cengage.com/permissions

Arrow #1: Reading. According to the Cone of Learning, the worst way to learn and retain knowledge is by reading, because long-term retention is less than 10 percent.

Arrow #2: Lecture. The second worst way to learn is via lecture.

You may notice that the primary methods for conveying knowledge in schools are reading and lecture.

Arrow #3: Participating in group discussion increases retention. In school I always wanted to participate in group discussions, especially at test time. The problem is that the schools call that cheating. In the real world, I take my real-life financial tests with my team because we all know two minds are better than one.

Arrow #4: Learning via simulation or games. The reason simulations or games are effective teaching tools is because we learn by making mistakes in the simulation or game. Even in flight school, I spent many hours flying simulators before flying a real plane. Today, the airlines spend billions training their pilots to fly on simulators. Not only is it cost effective, but the pilot can also try different maneuvers without risking crashing a real plane.

I learned to think like a person on the B and I side of the quadrant playing the game of Monopoly for hours with my rich dad. In other words, I made my mistakes on a board game first, and then practiced by making small investments and making small mistakes in order to gain real-life experience. I am a rich man today not because I was smart in school, but because I figured out how to make mistakes and learn from them.

Retiring Early

In 1994, Kim and I retired. Kim was 37, and I was 47. We retired early because we had more assets than liabilities. Today, in spite of this financial crisis, we do even better because we continue to acquire or create more assets. Millions of people are in financial trouble today because they found out the things they thought were assets were really liabilities when the markets crashed.

In 1996, Kim and I created our CASHFLOW board game to allow people to make mistakes with play money before using real money for investing. Today, there are three versions of the game, CASHFLOW for Kids; CASHFLOW 101, which teaches fundamentals of business and investing; and CASHFLOW 202, which teaches technical investing and managing the ups and downs of markets. All three games are available in electronic versions. If you would like to learn more from the games, there are CASHFLOW Clubs around the world, some of which have a ten-step curriculum that I created to maximize the lessons of the game. If you want to increase your financial IQ and possibly retire early without living below your means, then CASHFLOW games are an excellent opportunity to make mistakes and learn from them with play money, before trying the real thing.

In 1997, I self-published *Rich Dad Poor Dad*, which stated that your house is not an asset, that the rich pay less in taxes, that the rich don't work for money, and that the rich know how to print their own money. In 2007, when the subprime mortgage mess hit, millions of people found out their homes were not assets but liabilities.

In 2002, I wrote *Rich Dad's Prophecy*, stating that the retirement plans millions of people were counting on would soon come tumbling down. Today, in 2009, my message has not changed.

Reader Comment

Knowledge may be the new money, but it is only useful if all the other B-I Triangle components are fully understood and implemented by the serious investor. This book is a good start to providing direction for those of us looking for clarity on investments during these uncertain times. Thank you for sharing your experiences to help us through all the market chaos.

—Ray Wilson

Chapter 12

If I Ran the School System

For many people, life is a struggle due to a lack of financial education. As we've discussed throughout this book, much of this financial crisis was caused by a lack of financial education. Though people often don't think so, I am an advocate for education. I believe education is more important today than it ever was. Without financial education as part of the core curriculum, schools do a huge disservice to our children, our country, and the world, failing to prepare them for the real world.

Much of the following has been covered in this and in other Rich Dad books. As a bonus, I thought I would place some of my ideas on financial education in one place. While this chapter cannot possibly include everything a financial education program should include, I believe it covers many of the points that are different from conventional financial thinking. If I ran the school system, I would create a financial education program that included the following fifteen financial lessons.

1. The History of Money

Just as humans have evolved, money has evolved. "Money" was originally in the form of barter, such as chickens or milk, then shells and beads, then gold, silver, and copper coins. They were physical objects that were deemed to have tangible value, and thus were traded for other items of a similar value. Today, most money is paper money, an IOU from a government, also known as a fiat currency. Paper money is worthless in and of itself. It is simply a derivative of the value of something else. In the past, the dollar was a derivative of gold; now it is a derivative of debt, an IOU from taxpayers of a country.

Today, money is no longer a tangible object like chickens, gold, or silver. Today, modern money is simply an idea backed by the faith and trust of a government. The more trustworthy the country, the more valuable the money, and vice versa. This evolution of money from a tangible object into an idea is one reason why the subject of money is so confusing. It is difficult to understand something we can no longer see, touch, or feel.

A FEW IMPORTANT DATES IN THE HISTORY OF MONEY

The following is a brief summary of the key dates we've explored in this book.

1903: I believe the U.S. education system was taken over when the General Education Board, founded by John D. Rockefeller, decided what kids should learn. This put the influence of education in the hands of the ultra-rich, and the subject of money was not taught in school. Today, people go to school to learn to work for money, but they learn nothing about how to have money work for them.

The following is the CASHFLOW Quadrant.

E stands for *employee.*

S stands for *self-employed, specialist* such as doctor or lawyer, or *small business owner.*

B stands for *big business owner,* with the business having 500-plus employees.

I stands for *investor.*

Schools do a good job training people to be E's and S's, but do almost nothing to train them to be B's or I's. Even MBA students are trained to be highly paid E's working for the businesses of the rich. Some of the most famous B's are Bill Gates, founder of Microsoft; Michael Dell, founder of Dell Computers; Henry Ford, founder of Ford Motor Company; and Thomas Edison, founder of General Electric—all of whom never finished school.

1913: The Federal Reserve is formed. The Federal Reserve is not American, not federal, has no reserves, and is not a bank. It is controlled by some of the richest and politically influential families in the world. It has the power to create money out of thin air.

Institutions like the Federal Reserve have been staunchly opposed by designers of the Constitution, and by presidents such as George Washington and Thomas Jefferson.

1929: The Great Depression. Following the crisis of the Great Depression, the U.S. government created many government agencies such as the Federal Deposit Insurance Corporation (FDIC), the Federal Housing Administration (FHA), and Social Security; and the government took more control over our financial lives via taxes. This led to an acceptance of increased government intervention via social programs and agencies. Many of these government programs and agencies, such as the FHA, Fannie Mae, and Freddie Mac, are at the eye of today's subprime crisis. Today, unfunded government liabilities such as Social Security and Medicare are estimated to be $50 to $60 trillion time bombs that will eventually blow up and dwarf our current sub-prime crisis. In other words, government efforts created to solve the Great Depression will probably cause a bigger depression in the future.

1944: The Bretton Woods Agreement was made. This international currency agreement created the World Bank and the International Monetary Fund (IMF). The agreement replicated the Federal Reserve System globally and, in effect, installed the U.S. dollar as the reserve currency of the world. Basically, while the world was involved in a world war, the world's bankers were hard at work changing the world. This meant that all currencies worldwide were now essentially backed by the U.S. dollar, which was pegged to gold. As long as the U.S. dollar was backed by gold, the world economy would be stable.

1971: President Nixon, without permission from Congress, took the U.S. dollar off the gold standard. When this happened, the U.S. dollar became a derivative of debt—not of gold. After 1971, the U.S. economy could only increase by increasing debt, and that's when the bailouts started. In the 1980s, the bailouts were in the millions; in the 1990s, they were in the billions; and today they are in the trillions and growing. This change in the rules of money, one of the biggest financial events in world history, allowed the United States to print money at will by creating more and more debt, known as U.S. bonds. Never in the history of the world had all the world's money been backed by one nation's debt, an IOU from U.S. taxpayers.

In 1971, the dollar stopped being money and became a *currency*. The word *currency* comes from the word *current*, like an electrical current or an ocean current. In other words, a currency must keep moving or it loses value. To retain value, a monetary currency must move from one asset to another. After 1971, people who parked their money in a savings bank or in the stock market lost money because their currency stopped moving. Savers became losers and debtors became winners as the U.S. government printed more and more money, increasing debt and inflation.

After 1971, the economy expanded by creating more debt. In theory, if everyone paid off his or her debt, modern money would disappear. In 2007, when subprime borrowers couldn't pay their mortgages any longer, the expansion of debt stopped and the debt market collapsed, which led to our massive financial crisis today.

The United States has financed its excessive spending by selling its debt to Europe, Japan, and China. If these countries lose confidence in our government and stop buying our debt, another financial crisis will occur. If you and I stop buying homes and stop using our credit cards, this crisis will last longer.

Financial education is important because we need to learn there is good debt and bad debt. Bad debt makes us poorer. Good debt makes us richer. Since modern money is debt, a strong financial education would teach people to use debt to get richer rather than become poorer.

1974: The U.S. Congress passed the Employee Retirement Income Security Act (ERISA), which is now known in the United States as a 401(k). Prior to 1974, most employees had what is known as a *defined benefit (DB) pension plan*. A company's DB pension plan provided employees a paycheck for life. After 1974, employees were moved into *defined contribution (DC) pension plans*. This meant they had to save money for their retirement. The amount an employee received at retirement depended upon how much was contributed to his or her pension. If the pension ran out of money or was wiped out due to a stock market crash, the retiree was out of luck and on his own.

This change from DB to DC pension plans forced millions of workers into the uncertainty of the stock market. The problem is that most employees lacked, and still do lack, the financial education needed to invest their money for retirement wisely.

Today, millions of workers throughout the world are faced with insufficient funds to retire on. Without a financial education, millions go back to the same institutions—the savings banks and stock market, the very institutions that caused much of today's financial crisis—and attempt to save enough money to enjoy a secure retirement. These people are most affected and worried by our financial crisis.

Now that you've reviewed a little bit of the history of modern money, you may begin to appreciate why a financial education is important. And the first step in beginning your financial education is to understand a financial statement.

2. Understanding Your Financial Statement

My rich dad often said, "Your banker never asks to see your report card. A banker does not care what your grades were. A banker wants to see your financial statement. Your financial statement is your report card once you leave school."

A financial education begins with understanding that there are three parts to a financial statement.

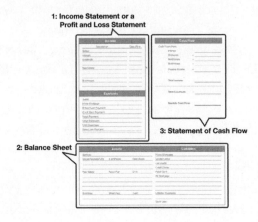

To better explain the full financial statement, we move on to financial lesson #3, the difference between assets and liabilities.

3. The Difference Between an Asset and a Liability

My poor dad often said, "Our house is an asset." My rich dad said, "If your father had a sound financial education, he would know his house is not an asset. His house is a liability."

One of the main reasons so many people are in financial trouble is because they refer to their liabilities as assets. In today's financial crisis, millions of people are finding out their homes are not assets. Even our political leaders refer to liabilities as assets. For example, the Troubled Asset Relief Program (TARP) is not a program for troubled assets. It is a program for troubled liabilities. If they were really assets, there would not be a problem, and the banks would not need rescuing.

One important aspect of a financial education is to understand the vocabulary of money. To increase your power over money, begin by using the words of money like *assets* and *liabilities*.

My rich dad had very simple definitions for *assets* and *liabilities*. He said, "Assets put money in your pocket without you working, and liabilities take money from your pocket, even when you're working."

Looking at the financial statement in picture format makes explaining assets and liabilities easier.

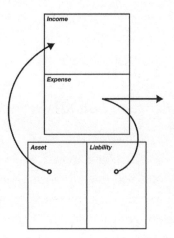

The arrows represent the Statement of Cash Flow. One arrow shows cash flowing from an asset such as a rental property or a dividend from a stock into your pocket, the *Income Column*. The other arrow shows cash flowing out of the *Expense Column* and to a liability such as a car payment or a mortgage on your personal residence.

One reason why the rich get richer is because they work to acquire assets and everyone else acquires liabilities that they think are assets. Millions of people struggle financially because they work hard and buy liabilities, such as homes and cars. When they get a pay raise, they buy a bigger house and nicer cars, hoping to look rich but really becoming poorer, more deeply in debt.

I have a friend, a minor star in Hollywood, who told me his retirement plan was to invest in personal residences. His main home is in Hollywood, and he has expensive vacation homes in Aspen, Maui, and Paris. I saw him recently as we both were about to appear on a television show, and I asked him how he was doing. With a sour look he said, "I'm not working much, and I'm losing everything. My homes have gone down in value, and I can't afford the mortgage payments." That's one problem with referring to liabilities as assets and not understanding the importance of *cash flow*.

During this last real estate boom, many people entered the real estate market thinking they were investors, when in reality they were speculators and gamblers. A popular name for them was "flippers." There were even TV programs featuring real estate flippers, people hoping to make a killing by fixing up homes. The problem is that when the housing bubble burst, many flippers were decimated and wound up in foreclosure.

This leads to financial education lesson #4.

4. The Difference Between Capital Gains and Cash Flow

Most people invest for *capital gains*. That is why they get excited when the stock market goes up or their home appreciates in value. That is how my Hollywood friend and most real estate flippers invest. It is also what most workers do when they invest for their retirement in the stock market. People who invest for capital gains are gambling. As Warren Buffett has said, "The dumbest reason in the world to buy a stock is because it is going up."

Investing for capital gains is also why most investors get depressed when the stock market drops or their home declines in value. Investing for capital gains is much like gambling because the investor has very little control over the ups and downs of a market.

A person with a financial education invests for both cash flow and capital gains. There are two main reasons why.

Reason #1: A currency must flow from an asset that produces cash flow, or it loses value. In other words, if your money is just parked waiting for appreciation or an increase in the share price, your currency is not productive and not working for you.

Reason #2: Investing for cash flow takes most of the risk out of investing. It's hard to feel like a loser as long as cash is flowing into your pockets—even if your asset price has depreciated. On the other hand, if your asset appreciates, it's an added bonus since you are already collecting cash flow.

The following is a diagram showing the difference between capital gains and cash flow.

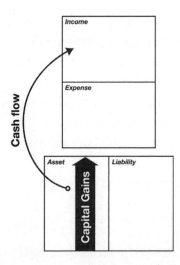

My wife and I are partners in an oil company. We invest in oil for both cash flow and capital gains. When we first drilled for oil, it was about $25 a barrel. We were happy with the cash flow every month. When oil hit $140 a barrel, our wells increased in value due to capital gains, and we were even happier. Today, with oil at $65 a barrel, we are still happy because cash continues to flow into our pockets regardless of the oil well's value.

If you like stocks, it is still best to first invest in a stock that pays a steady dividend, which is a form of cash flow. In a down economy, when stock prices are low, it is a great time to buy stocks that pay dividends at bargain prices.

A stock investor also understands the power of cash flow, or *dividend yields*, as cash flow is called in the stock market. The higher the dividend yield, the better the value of a stock. For example, a dividend yield of 5 percent of the stock's price signals a great stock at a great price. A dividend yield of less than 3 percent of the stock price means the stock is priced too high and will probably fall in value.

In October 2007, the stock market hit an all-time high of 14,164. Suckers jumped into the market, betting on stocks going higher (capital gains). The problem was that the Dow had a dividend yield of only 1.8 percent of its total value, which means that stocks were too expensive, and professional investors began to sell.

In March 2009, the Dow hit a low of 6,547, and many people jumped back into the market, thinking the worst was over. The problem was that the dividend yield was still only 1.9 percent, which to a professional investor meant the price of stocks was still too high and the stock market would probably go lower and long-term investors would probably lose even more of their money as cash flowed out of the market.

To me, investing for both cash flow and capital gains makes more sense than worrying about the ups and downs of any market. This is why I created CASHFLOW 101 and 202 as educational board games to help educate people on the merits of such investing.

Since every market goes up and down, this leads to financial education lesson #5.

5. The Difference Between Fundamental and Technical Investing

Fundamental investing is the process of analyzing a company's financial performance, and that begins with understanding its financial statement.

Income
Expense

Asset	Liability

A financially educated person wants to know how intelligently a business or property is managed, and that can only be determined by analyzing the financial statement of a business. When a banker asks you for your financial statement, he or she wants to know how well you manage your own financial life. The banker wants to know your income as compared to your expenses, the number of cash-flowing assets and cash-draining liabilities you own, both in the short and long term. When investing in a company, you want to know the same things.

My board game CASHFLOW 101 teaches the basics of fundamental investing.

Technical investing is measuring the emotions or moods of the markets by using technical indicators. Technical investors may not care about the fundamentals of a business. They look at charts that measure prices, like the one pictured below.

Charts are important because they are based on facts, primarily the buy/sell price of something, for example, the price of a stock or commodities such as gold or oil. Charts with lines going up indicate rising prices, which means cash is flowing into the market. A market that has money flowing into it is often called a bull market. Charts with lines pointing down indicate cash flowing out of the market. A market that has money flowing out of it is often called a bear market. A technical investor looks for historical patterns in markets based on cash flow and makes investments based on past patterns and future predictions of market behavior.

A financially educated investor also wants to know where cash is flowing from and which market it is flowing into. For example, when the stock market was crashing and people were afraid, a lot of money was flowing into the gold market. A technical investor may have been able to predict that gold was going to rise and that the stock market was going to fall based on technical indicators and would then have moved his money to gold before everyone else.

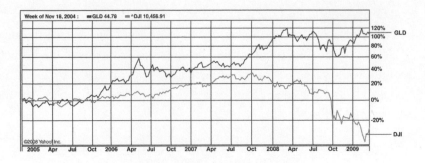

Reproduced with permission of Yahoo! Inc. ©2009 Yahoo! Inc. YAHOO! and the YAHOO! logo are registered trademarks of Yahoo! Inc.

Again, notice the importance of cash flow upon price, or capital gains. One reason why financially educated people want to keep their money moving is because if they park their money in one asset class, as many amateur investors do, they may lose their money when cash flows out of that asset class.

Since all markets go up and down, and all markets boom and bust, this leads to financial education lesson #6, how strong is the asset.

6. Measuring an Asset's Strength

Many times a person will come up to me and say, "I have an idea for a great new product," "I've found a great investment property," or "I want to invest in the stock of this company. What do you think?"

For these questions I refer to the following B-I Triangle.

The B-I Triangle gets its name from the CASHFLOW Quadrant mentioned earlier and pictured here.

Again:

E stands for *employee*.
S stands for *self-employed*, *specialist*, or *small business owner*.
B stands for *big business owner*, with the business having 500 employees or more.
I stands for *investor*.

You may notice that the product is the smallest or least important part of the B-I Triangle. The reason so many people fail when starting a business is because they focus on the product, not the entire B-I Triangle. The same is true in real estate. Many investors look only at the property rather than the entire B-I Triangle.

Rich dad said, "When a person, business, or investment is struggling, one or more of the eight integrities of the B-I Triangle are missing or not functioning." In other words, before investing in anything or starting your own business, evaluate the entire B-I Triangle and ask yourself whether that investment or business has a strong B-I Triangle.

If you are planning on starting your own business, or want to learn more about the B-I Triangle, you may want to read my book *Rich Dad's Before You Quit Your Job.*

Today's world needs more entrepreneurs who know how to build strong B-I Triangles. And by creating strong entrepreneurs, we create more jobs for people who are E's and S's.

Rather than the government creating more jobs, the government should create more entrepreneurs.

This leads to financial education lesson #7.

7. *Know How to Choose Good People*

Rich dad often said, "The way to find a good partner is to know a bad partner."

In my business career, I have had great partners and horrible partners. As rich dad said, the way to know a good partner is to experience the pain of a bad partner, and I have known some deep pain when it comes to partners.

The problem with life is that you do not know how good or bad a partner is until things get bad. The good news is that for every bad deal or partner I have had, I have *always* met a great partner as a result. For example, I met my real estate partner, Ken McElroy, out of a horrible investment with a bad partner. Since that broken deal, Ken and I have gone on to make millions, and he is one of the best partners Kim and I have.

One of the lessons I learned from Ken is that there are three parts to a great deal. They are:

1. Partners
2. Financing
3. Management

This is true for any investment or business. When you invest your money you are becoming a partner in that investment enterprise, even if you may not personally know anyone else involved. For example, when a person invests in a mutual fund, he or she becomes an equity partner of that mutual fund.

So the first component of an investment is to choose your partner carefully, before you give him or her your money.

As my rich dad said, "You can't do a good deal with a bad partner." Ken's second component, financing, focuses on how well structured an investment is and, as a partner, what your chances are of winning financially.

There are four reasons why I do not want to be a partner with a mutual fund.

1. A mutual fund's financial structure is weighted to the benefit of the mutual fund company, not you, the equity partner.
2. A mutual fund's expenses are too high and not fully disclosed. I put up 100 percent of the money, take 100 percent of the risk, and the mutual fund takes 80 percent of the rewards. That is not a good partner when it comes to finance.
3. When I invest in real estate, I use as much of the bank's money as possible, which means I get more leverage investing in real estate than I do with mutual funds.
4. I can lose money in mutual funds and still be charged capital gains taxes on money I did not make. That is definitely not fair.

Ken's third component to a great deal is management. A good partner must be a great manager. A poorly managed business or real estate property is an investment that is not maximizing investor returns and may fail. The main reason so many small businesses fail and real estate properties do not perform is mismanagement of the enterprise.

Today, I can quickly analyze most investments by simply asking myself, Who are the partners, and do I want to be a partner with them? What is the financing structure and is it favorable? And, How competent is the management? If those questions are satisfied, I may look further into the investment.

This leads to financial education lesson #8.

8. Know What Asset Is Best for You

There are four basic types of assets to invest in.

Balance Sheet

Assets	Liabilities
Business	
Real Estate	
Paper Assets	
Commodities	

BUSINESSES

Advantages: A business is one of the most powerful assets to own because you can benefit from tax advantages, leverage people to increase your cash flow, and have control of your operations. The richest people in the world build businesses. Examples are Steve Jobs, founder of Apple; Thomas Edison, founder of General Electric; and Sergey Brin, founder of Google.

Disadvantages: Businesses are "people intense." By that I mean that you have to manage employees, clients, and customers. People skills and leadership skills, as well as talented people who can work as a team, are essential for a business to be a success. In my opinion, of all four asset classes, a business takes the most financial intelligence and experience to be successful.

REAL ESTATE

Advantages: Real estate can have high returns due to using a bank's money for leverage via financing and other people's money (OPM) via investors, capitalizing from tax advantages like depreciation, and collecting steady cash flow if the asset is managed well.

Disadvantages: Real estate is a management-intensive asset, is illiquid, and if mismanaged can cost you a lot of money. After a business, real estate requires the second highest level of financial intelligence. Many people lack the proper financial IQ to invest well in real estate. That is why most people who invest in real estate invest in real estate mutual funds called REITs.

PAPER ASSETS: STOCKS, BONDS, SAVINGS, AND MUTUAL FUNDS

Advantages: Paper assets have the advantage of being easy to invest in. Additionally, they are liquidity-scalable, which means investors can start small by buying only a few shares, and thus it takes less money to get into paper investments than some of the other asset types.

Disadvantages: A major disadvantage of paper assets is that they are very liquid, meaning they are easy to sell. The problem with liquid investments is that once cash starts flowing out of a market, it is very easy to lose money quickly if you do not sell soon enough. Paper assets require continual monitoring.

Since most investors have little financial education, most people invest in paper assets.

COMMODITIES: GOLD, SILVER, OIL, ETC.

Advantages: Commodities are a good hedge or protection against inflation—which is important when governments are printing a lot of money, as they are today. The reason they buffer against inflation is because they are tangible assets that are purchased with currency. So when the currency supply increases there are more dollars chasing the same amount of goods. This causes the price of the commodities to rise, or inflate. Good examples of this are oil, gold, and silver, all of which are worth much more than they were a few years ago thanks to the Fed's printing presses.

Disadvantages: Because commodities are physical assets, you have to make sure they are stored properly and that they have proper security.

Once you decide which asset class is best for you, and which asset class you are most interested in, then I suggest studying that asset class and investing your time *before* investing your money. The reason I say this is because it is not the asset itself that makes you rich. You can lose money in any of the asset classes. Rather, it is your knowledge of each asset class that makes you rich. Never forget that your greatest asset is your mind.

Each asset class uses different words. For example, real estate investors often use the words *cap rate* or *NOI*, while a stock investor will use *P/E* or *EBITA*. Each asset class speaks its own language. For example, oil investors do not use the same words as gold investors. The good news is that the more words you understand, the higher your returns and the lower your risk, simply because you speak the same language.

I created my CASHFLOW games to teach some of the language of accounting and investing in different assets. We have advanced education classes as well as coaching programs available for when a person decides what asset class they are most interested in.

This leads to financial lesson #9, which is about focusing or diversifying.

9. Know When to Focus and When to Diversify

Most people recommend diversification as a protection against market uncertainties. Yet Warren Buffett says in *The Tao of Warren Buffett* that "diversification is a protection against ignorance. It makes very little sense for those who know what they're doing."

You may notice that most people diversify into mutual funds. The problem with a diversified portfolio of mutual funds is that you are not really diversified, since all mutual funds are in the stock market—paper assets.

True diversification includes investing in all four asset classes, not just different types of one asset class. My asset column contains all four assets: businesses, real estate, paper assets, and commodities. In many ways I am diversified, but in many ways I am not, since I focus on only great investments in each asset class.

The acronym FOCUS stands for Follow One Course Until Successful. If you want to be successful on the B and I side of the quadrant, it is important to focus. Choose the asset class you want to be good in and follow one course until you are successful. For example, if you are interested in real estate, study, practice, start small, and focus until you have cash flowing into your bank account consistently. Once you are certain you can produce cash flow in your small deals then cautiously go after bigger deals, staying focused on making sure the investment cash flows.

I do not live below my means. Rather than try to save money, I prefer to focus on increasing my assets. Every year, my wife and I set our investment goals for the coming year. By focusing on increasing cash flow from our assets, our income from assets goes up. In 1989, Kim started with a two-bedroom, one-bath house in Portland, Oregon. Today, she owns over 1,400 investment properties. Next year she plans to add 500 more. I plan on adding three more oil wells to the asset column. We also will increase our assets by expanding our business through selling Rich Dad Franchises to people who want to own their own businesses. A Rich Dad Franchise costs a person approximately $35,000, and in about two years, if they follow our business training programs, they have the potential to earn $100,000 to $200,000 a year. That is a great return on investment.

In 1966, I started studying commodities, specifically oil, as a student sailing for Standard Oil of California. In 1972, I started studying gold as a pilot in Vietnam. In 1973, I began my focus on real estate once I returned from the war. Before investing, I invested in a real estate program and went on to make millions. But, more important than money, that course gave me freedom and financial stability even in this economy. In 1974, I began my focus on business when I left the Marine Corps and started with Xerox, learning the skill of selling. In 1982, I began studying the stock market and options market. Today, I own all four asset classes, so I am diversified, but I never lose my focus.

This leads to lesson #10.

10. Minimize Risk

Building a business and investing is not necessarily risky. Being financially uneducated is risky. Therefore, the first and best step to minimize risk is education. For example, when I wanted to learn to fly, I took flying lessons. If I had just climbed into a plane and taken off, I would have probably crashed and died.

The second step is to hedge your investments. Professional investors invest with insurance. Most of us would not drive a car or own a home without insurance. Yet most people invest without insurance. That is very risky.

For example, when I invest in the stock market, I can buy insurance, such as a put option. Let's say I purchase a stock for $10. I can also buy a put option for $1 to pay me $9 if the stock price falls. If the stock drops to $5, the put option acts as insurance and pays me $9 for a stock worth $5. That is just one of many ways that professional investors use different forms of insurance in the stock market.

For my real estate investments, I have insurance against losses to fire, floods, and other natural disasters. Another bonus of owning real estate is that the rent my tenants pay me covers the cost of the insurance. If my property burns down, I do not lose money, because I have insurance to cover my losses.

Diversification in the stock market did not protect investors from the market crash of 2007. The reason diversification did not protect most investors is because they had no insurance, and because being 100 percent in the stock market is not really being diversified.

If you look at the B-I Triangle pictured below you will see other ways I minimize my risk.

Notice that one of the eight integrities is "Legal." Having an attorney on your team is essential to minimize risk. First of all, good legal advice is always priceless. Legal advice that prevents you from getting in trouble with the law is always less expensive than legal advice once you are in trouble.

Second, when designing a product, I want to protect my product and business from thieves and pirates. My products and businesses utilize the services of an attorney to patent, trademark, and copyright my work. And third, by having a patent, trademark, or copyright, I turn these derivatives of my products into assets. For example, when I write a book, I protect it legally and sell the license for a publishing company to print my book. Today, when I write one book, I may sell forty to fifty licenses to different publishers for different languages. My products would have no value if they were not protected and legally turned into an asset.

My point is that only the financially uneducated would invest without insurance and count on diversification to protect them. This leads to the biggest risk of all, the risk of losing money through taxes.

11. Know How to Minimize Taxes

When you say to a child, "Go to school and get a job," you are sentencing that child to a life in the land of maximum taxes. It is also true when you say to a child, "Become a doctor or lawyer because you will make a lot of money." Those jobs are in the E and S quadrant.

Take a look at the CASHFLOW Quadrant pictured below.

People working in the E and S quadrants pay the most in taxes.

Those working in the B and I quadrants pay the least in taxes, and sometimes pay zero taxes, even while making millions of dollars. One reason for this is because those in the B-I quadrants produce much of the wealth a nation needs and hence are rewarded for creating jobs and building homes or offices for people and businesses to rent.

There are three basic types of incomes. They are:

Earned income—most taxed
Portfolio income—mildly taxed
Passive income—least taxed

Earned income: People who work for a living as employees or who are self-employed work for earned income, the highest-taxed income. And the more they earn, the higher percentage in taxes they pay. Ironically, people who save money have their interest earnings taxed at earned income levels as well. When a person invests in a retirement plan, that plan is also taxed at earned income levels. Those on the E and S side of the CASHFLOW Quadrant have the cards stacked against them in every respect.

The reason most financial planners say, "When you retire your income will go down," is because most people are planning to be poor when they retire. So if you are poor, then the taxes on your savings and your retirement will not be that much of a factor. But if you plan on being rich when you retire, the money from your savings and your retirement plan will be taxed at the highest levels—and that is not financially intelligent.

Portfolio income: Most people invest for portfolio income. Portfolio income is generally income from capital gains, buying low and selling high. It is almost certain that President Obama will raise the tax rates on capital gains. Right now the maximum capital gains rate is 28 percent. Who knows how much higher taxes will go for investors who invest for capital gains?

As a side note, people who buy and sell stocks or who flip houses may appear to invest for capital gains, but they are often taxed at earned or ordinary income levels since they often do not hold the assets for a year or more. That's because they are really working in the S quadrant, not the I quadrant. Taking all the risk of an investment, buying low and hoping to sell high, and then paying the highest percentage in tax is not financially intelligent. Check with a tax accountant to determine in which quadrant you are investing.

Passive income: Cash flow from assets such as my apartment houses is taxed at passive income tax rates, the lowest tax rates.

On top of plain passive income, real estate investors have other forms of cash flow that can offset their tax exposure: appreciation, amortization, and depreciation, which can be tax-free income (aka phantom cash flow). I love phantom cash flow.

Again, it is best to talk to a tax accountant before investing for these cash flows.

12. The Difference Between Debt and Credibility

As many of you know, there is good debt and bad debt. Owning your own home is bad debt because it takes money out of your pocket. Owning a rental property that pays you money every month by covering your expenses, including your mortgage payment, is good debt because it puts money in your pocket.

Good debt is tax-free money. Since it is borrowed money, you don't pay taxes for it or to use it. For example, if I put $20,000 as a down payment on a rental property and borrow $80,000, in most cases the $20,000 is my money after taxes and $80,000 is tax-free money.

The key to using debt is to know how to borrow wisely and how to pay the money back. Knowing how to borrow money wisely, and getting someone else, such as your tenants or your business, to pay the money back is your credit-ability, or credibility. The higher your credibility, the more debt you can use to become rich—tax-free. But again, the key is your financial education and real-life experience.

Even in today's financial crisis, there are banks still lending millions of dollars to investors who have credibility. There are five reasons why banks are still lending to investors with high credibility like me.

1. ***We invest in B-class apartment buildings.*** In the apartment business, there are A-, B-, and C-class buildings. A-class is the high-end apartment houses, which are hurting because people cannot afford them and are moving out. C-class apartment houses rent to low-income people. B-class apartment houses rent to working-class people. My company provides safe, clean apartments at affordable prices. Even in this financial crisis, our buildings are still full and rent continues to roll in. Banks lend to us because we have steady cash flow.

2. ***We buy in areas where there are jobs.*** The real value of real estate is related to jobs. We own apartment houses in Texas and Oklahoma, where there are jobs in the oil industry. We do not own anything in Detroit, where jobs are leaving and real estate values are dropping.

3. ***We own property where there are natural or government***

constraints. For example, we own apartments where there is a no-growth boundary around the city. In other words, the city cannot spread out any farther, which makes properties more valuable because it limits supply. We also own properties that are bordered by a river, a constraint of nature, prohibiting further growth.

4. **We have been in the same business for years and have a solid reputation.** This gives us credibility as good operators, even in a bad market. Great deals come to us because the banks trust us and send us deals that other investors can't get financing for.

5. **We *stay with what we know.*** As you know, there are many different types of real estate. We do not invest in office buildings or shopping centers. That is not the business we are in—although if prices keep crashing, we might be tempted to start looking at these businesses.

If you have read *Rich Dad Poor Dad*, you may recall the story of Ray Kroc, founder of McDonald's. In the book, I tell a story about Ray Kroc asking, "What business is McDonald's in?" After most people answered, "Hamburgers," Ray Kroc replied, "My business is real estate." McDonald's uses the fast food business to buy real estate. I use the apartment business to buy real estate. Knowing what business we are in, and being good at it, gives us credibility. And credibility gets us access to good, tax-free debt—even in this tight credit economy.

13. Know How to Use Derivatives

Warren Buffett referred to financial derivatives as weapons of mass financial destruction. Much of this financial crisis is due to financial derivatives such as collateralized debt obligations (CDOs) and mortgage-backed securities (MBSs). In simple terms, these are derivatives of debt, packaged and rated as AAA by Moody's and S&P, and then sold as assets. Everything was fine until subprime homeowners could not afford to pay the debt on their real estate bubble–induced overpriced homes. The house of debt came tumbling down, wiping out the wealth of millions of people all over the world.

But financial derivatives are also tools for massive financial creation. In 1996, Kim and I created the Rich Dad business, a derivative of our minds.

We also created the CASHFLOW games and books, such as *Rich Dad Poor Dad* and this book—again, derivatives of our minds. When we create and sell those games and books, we are acting like the Federal Reserve and creating money out of thin air. Presently, we are working on franchising the Rich Dad business, another derivative of our minds. In real estate, we often pull out tax-free money by refinancing a mortgage, another derivative, and having our tenants' rent pay the mortgage payments. In the stock market, I often sell a derivative of my stocks—for example, a call option—and make money out of nothing but a derivative of my stock and my mind.

Always remember: Your greatest asset is your mind. With the proper financial education, you, too, can invent your own derivatives of mass financial creation.

14. Know How Your Wealth Is Stolen

When you look at a person's financial statement, you can see why people on the E and S side of the CASHFLOW Quadrant struggle financially.

Income	
Expense	
1. Taxes	
2. Debt	
3. Inflation	
4. Retirement plan	

Asset	Liability

These expenses go straight to those that operate on the B and I side of the quadrant.

For those on the right side—the B and I side—it is possible to legally earn millions of dollars without paying anything in taxes, to use debt to increase wealth, to profit from inflation, and to not need a retirement plan filled with risky paper assets such as stocks, bonds, mutual funds, and savings.

The big difference between the two quadrants is that the E's and S's work for money and the B's and I's work to create assets that produce cash flow.

For a more detailed explanation of how your wealth is stolen and why people struggle financially, visit www.richdad.com/conspiracy-of-the-rich and watch my video called "The Everyday Cash Heist."

15. Know How to Make Mistakes

We all know that it is impossible to learn without doing, and doing often means making mistakes. A child cannot learn to walk if he is punished for falling. You cannot learn to swim unless you get into the water. You cannot learn to fly a plane by reading a book or listening to lectures. Yet our school system teaches by reading, lectures, and punishing people who make mistakes.

The following picture is the Cone of Learning. It explains the best ways that we learn. At the bottom of the Cone of Learning is reading, with a 10 percent retention rate. Next is hearing words, or listening to a lecture, with a 20 percent retention rate.

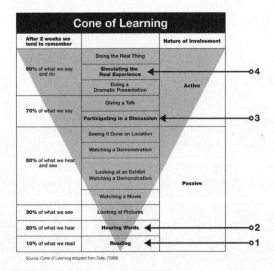

From Dale. *Audio-Visual Methods in Teaching*, 1E. © 1969 Wadsworth, a part of Cengage Learning, Inc. Reproduced by permission. www.cengage.com/permissions.

When you look at simulating the real experience, you can see it has a 90 percent retention rate and is considered the next best thing to doing the real thing.

The main reason simulations or games are such powerful teaching tools is because they allow students to make mistakes and learn from their mistakes. When I was in flight school, I spent many hours in flight simulators. Not only was it a less expensive way to learn, it was safer. I made many mistakes during flight training and became a better pilot by learning from my mistakes.

One of the reasons I was not afraid of operating in the B and I side of the quadrant as an adult was because I played Monopoly for hours as a kid, and I understood the power of cash flow from assets such as green houses and red hotels. Kim and I created our game CASHFLOW, often called Monopoly on steroids, to be a simulation of investing in real life. It's a great way to make mistakes, learn from those mistakes, and prepare for the real world. We all know people who are afraid of investing because they are afraid of making mistakes and losing money. Play CASHFLOW, and even if you make mistakes and lose money, it's only paper money. But more important, you become smarter and smarter, the more mistakes you make.

A Big Mistake in Financial Education

The biggest mistake in financial education today is that schools bring in bankers and financial planners to teach young kids about money. How can we expect the financial crisis to end when the employees of the very organizations that caused this crisis teach our children?

That is not financial education. That is financial exploitation. This is where the cash heist begins.

If we educated people to see the world through the prism of the B and I sides of the CASHFLOW Quadrant, their world would be changed forever. People would discover a whole new world of financial abundance and opportunity.

Just recently, I met a gentleman who spent much of his life in the E quadrant as a truck driver. He worked long hours for a decent wage but never really felt financially secure. When times got tough as fuel prices rose, his company had to make cuts, and he was let go. At that point he committed to his financial education and to increasing his financial IQ. Eventually, he bought a franchise business in the trucking industry, an industry he already knew a lot about, and became an entrepreneur. Today, he is financially free.

As I talked with him, he told me that before he became an entrepreneur, he saw the world as a place of limited possibilities where he was stuck with long hours, low income, high taxes, and increasing expenses such as food, gasoline, and heath costs cutting into his wages. Today, he sees a world of infinite possibilities. His life is changed forever because he changed his mind-set and viewed the world through the B and I side of the CASHFLOW Quadrant. He could have easily applied for unemployment and looked for another job, but instead he elevated his financial intelligence.

To me this is a perfect example of my belief that giving people money won't solve their problems. I believe it is time to stop giving people fish. It is time to teach people to fish and give them the power to solve their own financial problems. Financial education has the power to change the world. I predict the first country that adopts a comprehensive financial education program for all students, rich or poor, will emerge as a financial world power.

The End and the Beginning

We have now reached the end of our journey exploring the conspiracy of the rich. While this is the end of this book, it should not be the end of the story—your story. My fifteen financial lessons may never be taught in schools, but those who are willing to put in the time and effort to increase their financial IQ can learn them. And they can be passed on from parents to their children, just as my rich dad passed them on to his son and me. Live them, and teach your children to live them. You hold in your hand the power to opt out of the conspiracy of the rich, and to make a rich life for you and your loved ones.

The Rich Dad mission is to elevate the financial well-being of humanity through our books, games, products, seminars, as well as advanced education and coaching programs for those who want to go further. Just as this book spread like wildfire over the Internet through conversations and blogs, so, too, can the message of Rich Dad, a message of a rich life and financial freedom, spread throughout the world. Together, one person and one child at a time, we can elevate the financial well-being of humanity. Together, we can spread the message that *knowledge is the new money*, and our minds are our greatest God-given asset.

Thank you for being a part of history and making this book such a success.

In Conclusion

How We Steal From Ourselves

Have we been financially brainwashed? I believe we have. The primary reason why most people cannot see the daily cash heist happening all around them is because we have been financially programmed, turned into Pavlov's dogs, to steal from ourselves via our words. We mindlessly repeat mantras that cost us our wealth.

As I've said, words have the power to make us rich—or keep us poor.

Our school system does a good job training people for the E and S quadrants. During our formative years, our families and our schools teach us to repeat what they believe to be words of financial wisdom, but in reality they are words that train us to steal from ourselves. These words are mantras drilled into our consciousness, conditioning us to submissively surrender our hard-earned money to those on the B and I side of the quadrant. Without a solid financial education you remain a prisoner of the E and S quadrants.

Our leaders don't encourage us to change or to seek ways to move from the E and S side of the quadrant to the B and I side. Rather, our leaders teach us to live below our means instead of expanding our means. In my opinion, living below your means kills your spirit. That's no way to live.

The Heist: Words We Use to Steal from Ourselves

As you already know, those in the E and S quadrants lose their wealth via taxes, debt, inflation, and retirement. The following are examples of how our words relate to those forces and cause us to steal from ourselves.

Taxes: "Go to school to get a good job." These words program a child to be an employee who pays the highest percentage of his income in taxes. When you advise a child to work hard to make more money, you inadvertently push that child into a higher tax bracket and sentence him or her to work for the highest taxed income: *earned income.*

Those educated in the mind-set of the B and I quadrants operate by a different set of tax rules and can earn a lot more money and pay much less taxes, if any. As stated in the book, a person in the B and I quadrants can earn millions of dollars and pay no taxes—legally.

Debt: "Buy a house. Your house is an asset and your biggest investment." Advising most people to invest in a home is training them to go to the bank and get into bad debt. A house is a liability because it only takes money out of your pocket. Often, your house is not your biggest investment; it is your biggest liability. It does not put money into your pocket. That truth is no more apparent than in today's economic crisis.

Those in the B and I side of the quadrant use debt to purchase cash-flowing assets like apartment buildings—assets that put money into their pockets, not take money out of them. People on the B and I side of the quadrant know the difference between good debt and bad debt.

Inflation: "Save money." When people save money in a bank, they unwittingly increase inflation, which ironically devalues their savings. Due to the fractional reserve system of banking, a bank can take a person's savings and lend it out multiple times, charging much more interest on the loans than the saver receives for his or her savings. In other words, savers cause their own erosion of the purchasing power. The more they save, the more inflation increases.

Some inflation is better than deflation, which is very destructive and hard to stop. The problem is that if the bailouts and stimulus packages do not stop deflation, the government may print so much money that we go into hyper-inflation, and then savers will truly be the biggest losers.

For every dollar you save, you give the bank license to print more money. When you understand that concept, you can see why those with financial education have an unfair advantage.

Retirement: "Invest for the long term in a well-diversified portfolio of stocks, bonds, and mutual funds." This bit of wisdom makes people on Wall Street very rich for the long term. Who would *not* want millions of E and S quadrant people sending them a check every month? I ask myself: Why would I want to give my money to Wall Street when I know I can legally "print" my own money by using my financial knowledge and intelligence?

In Summary

By removing financial education from our schools, the conspiracy has done an excellent job of having the cash heist take place in our own minds. If you want to change your life, change your words. Adopt the vocabulary of a rich person. Your unfair advantage is your financial education.

And this is why today...*knowledge is the new money.* Thank you for reading this book.

Afterword

July 1, 2009

One Last Note

When I first conceived of *Rich Dad's Conspiracy of the Rich*, I truly didn't know what to expect. For me, the process of writing a book interactively on the Internet was a completely new idea, but at the same time, it was one that excited me. Because the economic crisis was happening in real time to all of us all over the world, I also wanted my book to happen in real time.

I knew that if I wrote *Rich Dad's Conspiracy of the Rich* in a traditional publishing format that we would be too deep into the economic crisis—or even past it—for my book to help, since it can often take a year or more to bring a book from an idea to a words-on-paper reality. As the economy worsened every month and I began to see the feedback from online readers, I knew I had made the right decision in publishing the book on the Internet and in making it interactive.

Every time I sat down to write a chapter, at the same time major world-changing events were happening everywhere...In a sense, I felt like I was back in my old Vietnam days, riding in a helicopter over battlefields, bullets buzzing all around and explosions rocking as I focused on my task. Just as I had a clear mission in Vietnam, I had a clear mission in writing this book.

My experiences over the years have taught me that people are hungry for relevant financial education that is simply explained and easy to understand. I also knew that there were many people who were scared, frustrated, and let down by our politicians and the economy. This book was designed to address those two realities by giving plain and straightforward financial education that was relevant to our current economy and beyond—and by giving a voice to you, the reader, to express your thoughts, fears, and triumphs.

And that is what surprised me the most. The quality of the feedback I received from you, the readers, blew my mind. I expected intelligent and well-thought-out insights, questions, and comments—but your feedback was exceptional and contributed immensely to the book and its formation. Not only that, but the breadth of experience and perspective was incredibly vast, as readers from all over the globe engaged in the book and contributed to the conversation.

In the end, *Rich Dad's Conspiracy of the Rich* is a much bigger success than I imagined it would ever be. Here are a few highlights of the incredible reception you gave the project:

- Over 35 million hits from 167 countries
- Over 1.2 million visits to the website
- 90,000 registered readers
- Over 10,000 comments, questions, and insights from readers
- 2,000 bloggers from all over the world helping expose the conspiracy

And the reason for this success is you.

So let me take this opportunity to personally thank you for being a part of the *Rich Dad's Conspiracy of the Rich* community, and for making this project such a huge triumph. The book you are holding in your hand is truly as much yours as it is mine. Your thoughts, comments, and questions helped influence the content of this book as it was being written. Indeed, many of your comments are now even part of the book.

Together we have made publishing history.

Together we have exposed the conspiracy of the rich.

Thank you.
Robert T. Kiyosaki

Conspiracy of the Rich Special Bonus Q&A

The following nine questions were hand-selected by me out of hundreds of questions asked in the discussion forums on the *Rich Dad's Conspiracy of the Rich* website. I wish I could have answered all of your great questions, but that would have been a whole book in itself. I believe that these questions represent the majority of inquiries from the readers. Thank you to everyone for your insights, comments, and questions. Remember: *Knowledge is the new money!*

Q: *Do you have any comments on what the outcome would be if somehow we see a new "international super-currency" like the one that Russia keeps going on about?*

—isbarratt

A: I don't have any comments on an international super-currency. Whether we are on the dollar or some other form of reserve currency, the basic problem still remains: Those currencies will be fiat currencies that can be printed out of thin air. They have no value. They are just government-manipulated frauds designed to steal money from your pocket via inflation. In my opinion, gold and silver are still better assets to hold than any currency.

Q: *My question is how does investing in gold and/or silver fall into the plan of cash flow rather than capital gains? Rich Dad's Conspiracy of the Rich has shown me that I am getting off the cash-flow track and need to reassess my direction. I am* *having trouble expanding my context and seeing how gold and silver are not just safety nets to protect wealth. Can they be used to generate cash flow as well?*

—Foresight2Freedom

A: In my case, when I have excess amounts of cash flow, rather than hold the excess cash in a savings account, I choose to hold it in gold and silver. The reason I do this is because gold and silver can be used as a hedge against uncertain monetary policy like the Fed's printing of trillions of dollars and pumping them into the economy. Rather than hold my excess money in dollars and watching those dollars fall in value as inflation rages, I hold my excess money in gold and silver and watch their prices rise with inflation. So while gold and silver do not create cash flow in and of themselves, they do protect me from losing money to inflation. Again, as with any asset, you can lose money in gold and silver if your financial IQ is low. It's not gold and silver that make you rich, but rather what you know about gold and silver.

Q: *Do you think that during a hyperinflation scenario rental properties will be beneficial to an investment portfolio?*

—colbycl

A: There are other factors than just hyperinflation that come into play. As with any deal, you will have to do your homework and make sure that the numbers are good. For instance, is there enough cash flow from the rent to cover your expenses and pay for your debt? Are there jobs and people flowing into the area where you are looking to buy? Real estate is only good if the answers to these and other questions like them are positive. Remember, there are always good and bad real estate deals no matter what the state of the economy. It always comes down to cash flow.

Q: *I would like to ask you about the conspiracy against our health and what can you tell me about it.*

—ovortron

A: I am not a doctor, nor is my expertise in the healthcare industry, but I do suspect that the pharmaceutical and health insurance industries and their players have tremendous power over the healthcare system and the healthcare we receive. Personally, I utilize alternative medicine techniques such as acupuncture, naturopathy, and chiropractic treatments, in addition to traditional medical treatments. I also try to minimize my intake of medicine. As with anything, the more you know, the better equipped you will be to make sound decisions for your health and money. I encourage you to begin a personal course of study on the subject.

Q: *My question is about starting out. You stated in the book that you made some considerable capital gains before your rich dad reminded you about investing for cash flow. Most people that I know who have made some good amounts for investment have done so using capital gains as opposed to cash-flow gains. While cash flow is for the long term, what are some suggestions as to how someone can begin intelligent investments with little to no capital in the short term?*

—*Miguel41a*

A: My answer to questions like this is always the same. Get financially educated. As I've stated throughout *Rich Dad's Conspiracy of the Rich*, knowledge is the new money. The best way to learn is through practice or simulation. You are going to make mistakes, but the key is to learn from those mistakes. If you are hesitant to use real money at first, my CASHFLOW game is an excellent way to learn how to analyze and put together deals in a simulated environment where you can learn from your mistakes. This will prepare you for the real world of investing. I would say that it is more important to know how to find, analyze, and present a good deal than to have money—money does not make you rich; your knowledge does. There is always money available from investors and banks for good deals.

Q: *I have a young daughter of fourteen years. She is brilliant in her studies. What can I recommend that she do when she is an adult so she will not be a victim of the conspiracy? She has already read your books for teenagers.*

—*Madelugi*

A: A child's best teachers are his or her parents. So the question is really not what the child is doing, but rather what you are doing to teach her. Even if you give your children good knowledge, they need to see you putting it into practice. You have a huge influence on your child's financial education just by your example.

Also, I have heard of children as young as seven or eight years old reading my books and playing the CASHFLOW game. These children will undoubtedly have the best chance at a bright financial future because they are receiving a financial education—something their peers do not receive. I developed my board game CASHFLOW for Kids so that children as young as six years old can begin learning about money and investing.

Q: *What are your thoughts on whole life insurance policies? I have two financial planners who push these.*

—rzele

A: I do not like investing in life insurance. Personally, I think it is a rip-off, especially with the Fed printing so much money. Inflation makes your policy worth less and less every year. Also, financial planners push these investments because they make money off of them, not because they are necessarily good for you. That being said, whole life insurance policies are good for people who are not able to save and for those who have very little financial education and do not know how to invest successfully. Term life insurance is another option for those who are uncomfortable investing, and it is a cheaper option than whole life insurance. I leave that choice up to you.

Q: *As a new entrepreneur who has read most of your books and has seen for the first time the slippery path our kids will follow, is there hope for our education system?*

—jack47

A: Unfortunately, I am not hopeful for the education system—at least not in the short term. Every industry moves at a different rate of change. For instance, technology changes rapidly and can change every ten years or less. The construction and education industries take much longer to change as institutions. It can sometimes take more than fifty years to see effective and meaningful change become institutionalized in these industries. That is why

I am an advocate of you taking charge of your own financial education and the financial education of your children.

Q: *The current economy got the best of me, so I am just "trying to get by." What's the best single piece of advice you would give anyone who is getting back on his or her feet and wants to make things happen?*

—msrpsilver

A: As I've said, knowledge is the new money. Continue to educate yourself in money and investing. Increase your financial IQ. Also, study the CASHFLOW Quadrant and understand what makes you poor: taxes, debt, inflation, and retirement accounts. Train yourself to think on the B and I side of the quadrant, and learn how to minimize your losses in taxes, debt, inflation, and retirement accounts. By shifting your knowledge to the B and I side of the CASHFLOW Quadrant you can learn to make millions without paying taxes, make your money with other people's money, and find assets that increase in value with inflation and provide passive income for your retirement. There is no magic bullet, just hard work and education.

About the Author

Robert T. Kiyosaki
Investor, Entrepreneur, Educator

Robert T. Kiyosaki is best known as the author of *Rich Dad Poor Dad*—the #1 personal finance book of all time—which has challenged and changed the way tens of millions of people around the world think about money. Rich Dad titles hold four of the top ten spots on Nielsen Bookscan List's Life-to-Date Sales from 2001–2008 alone, and Robert has been featured regularly on shows such as *Larry King Live, Oprah*, and countless other shows and publications.

With perspectives on money and investing that often contradict conventional wisdom, Robert has earned a reputation for straight talk, irreverence, and courage. His point of view that "old" advice—get a good job, save money, get out of debt, invest for the long term, and diversify—is "bad" (both obsolete and flawed) advice challenges the status quo. His assertion that "your house is not an asset" has stirred controversy but has been proven to be accurate for many homeowners with the popping of the real estate bubble.

Rich Dad Poor Dad ranks as the longest-running bestseller on all four of the lists that report to *Publishers Weekly—The New York Times, Business Week, The Wall Street Journal,* and *USA Today*—and was named USA Today's #1 Money Book two years in a row. It is the third-longest-running how-to bestseller of all time.

Translated into 51 languages and available in 109 countries, the Rich Dad series has sold over 28 million copies worldwide and has dominated bestseller lists across Asia, Australia, South America, Mexico, and Europe. In

2005, Robert was inducted into the Amazon.com Hall of Fame as one of that bookseller's Top 25 Authors. There are currently 27 books in the Rich Dad series.

In 2006, Robert teamed up with Donald Trump to coauthor *Why We Want You to Be Rich—Two Men, One Message.* It debuted at #1 on the *New York Times* bestseller list.

Robert writes a biweekly column, "Why the Rich Are Getting Richer," for *Yahoo! Finance* and a monthly column titled "Rich Returns" for *Entrepreneur* magazine.

Robert's most recent books include *Rich Brother Rich Sister,* a biographical book coauthored with his sister Emi Kiyosaki, and *Rich Dad's Conspiracy of the Rich: The 8 New Rules of Money.*